Entrepreneurship

Music
Entrepreneurship

*Allan Dumbreck and
Gayle McPherson*

Bloomsbury Methuen Drama
An imprint of Bloomsbury Publishing Plc

B L O O M S B U R Y
LONDON · OXFORD · NEW YORK · NEW DELHI · SYDNEY

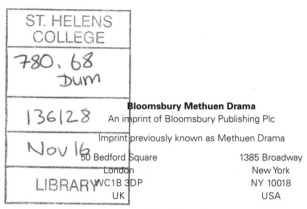

Bloomsbury Methuen Drama
An imprint of Bloomsbury Publishing Plc

Imprint previously known as Methuen Drama

50 Bedford Square
London
WC1B 3DP
UK

1385 Broadway
New York
NY 10018
USA

www.bloomsbury.com

BLOOMSBURY, METHUEN DRAMA and the Diana logo are trademarks of
Bloomsbury Publishing Plc

First published 2016

British Library Cataloguing-in-Publication Data
A catalogue record for this book is available from the British Library

ISBN: PB: 978-1-4725-2540-6
        ePDF: 978-1-4725-3110-0
        ePub: 978-1-4725-3097-4

Library of Congress Cataloging-in-Publication Data
A catalog record for this book is available from the Library of Congress

Typeset by RefineCatch Limited, Bungay, Suffolk
Printed and bound in Great Britain

Being a music entrepreneur . . . is definitely one of the best things about my life. It's the most action packed existence you can have, I feel very privileged to earn a living out of doing something I love.

HENRY VILLAGE, STACKHOUSE MANAGEMENT
(LILY ALLEN, RUDIMENTAL)

CONTENTS

ACKNOWLEDGEMENTS

The editors would specifically like to acknowledge and thank: all contributors and interviewees for their time and engagement; Amanda Charleson, Sarah Killick, Holly Tessler, for help with transcription and editing; Hannah Neaves at Atlantic Records and Sharon Matheson at INgrooves for industry contacts; Sean Ban Beaton for technical support; Anna Brewer at Bloomsbury for unfaltering support and understanding, and finally, Allan and Gayle wish to thank their families for their understanding and support throughout the editing process.

In memory of Steve Broadfoot – a true music entrepreneur.

LIST OF
CONTRIBUTORS

Clare K. Duffin has a Masters degree in Music Innovation and Entrepreneurship and currently lectures at the University of the West of Scotland, specializing in digital music platforms. Clare has a portfolio career spanning a multitude of work including community music practice, social media consultancy for music artists, record label management and as a drummer in Scottish rock band, Suspire.

Allan Dumbreck is a musician and educator with over thirty years' experience of the music industries. As a keyboard player with a number of Scottish acts, including the Big Dish, he has performed and recorded internationally, supporting, amongst others, BB King. As a music educator he has developed a series of university and college music programmes, teaching across the UK and Europe, and is behind a group of initiatives that include the international music exchanges at the University of West of Scotland where he leads the BA (Hons) Commercial Music.

Matt Flynn has an MA in Music Industries Studies from the University of Liverpool. Since 2004 he has lectured music undergraduates in professional development at the Liverpool Institute for Performing Arts (LIPA). Between 1996 and 2009 he worked in the UK as a self-employed independent music practitioner, setting up and running rehearsal studios and an independent record label.

Dr Kenny Forbes is a Lecturer in Commercial Music, in the School of Media, Culture and Society at the University of the West of Scotland. Kenny has recently completed his PhD at the University of Glasgow: his thesis concerned the 'legendary' reputation held by the Glasgow Apollo theatre (1973–85). His research interests cover locality, live music/liveness and collective memory.

Dr Matt Frew is a Senior Lecturer in Business and Enterprise at the University of the West of Scotland. His academic interests are really driven by a rather eclectic range of experiences from arts, music, dance, events and festivity. A lover of philosophy, socio-cultural theory and all things techno he enjoys the challenges of applying theoretical and technological insights to challenge the creative process and develop new innovations. In this age of acceleration and techno-culture he is fascinated by how the impact of ubiquitous, convergent, augmented and virtual technologies are challenging the structuring relations of space, time and our embodied condition. As current developments see the integration of technologies that enable us to place shift, create and relive immersive multi-sensory experiences we are witnessing the re-shaping, if not re-booting, of life, culture and creativity.

George Howard is an Associate Professor of Management at Berklee College of Music, where he teaches courses in entrepreneurship, marketing, copyright law and leadership. He is the former president of Rykodisc, manager of Carly Simon, original co-founder of TuneCore, and COO of Wolfgang's Vault. Via his consulting firm, he advises a wide range of clients on how to integrate technology with strategy to increase awareness and revenue. He is a columnist for *Forbes*, and a frequent contributor to the *New York Times* and numerous other publications. He holds an MA, MBA, and JD.

Dr Jeffrey Izzo is an experienced entertainment lawyer, an accomplished composer and lyricist, and a full-time university instructor. He holds degrees in Composition from Berklee School of Music and the University of Edinburgh, and a Juris Doctor from Seattle University School of Law. In addition to over twenty years representing musicians, filmmakers, authors, and media companies, Jeffrey composes in an array of genres, but especially enjoys writing for musical theatre. He is currently Assistant Professor of Recording Industry at Middle Tennessee State University near Nashville, Tennessee, where he teaches legal and business aspects of music such as copyright, contracts and publishing.

Dr Gayle McPherson is a Professor in Events and Cultural Policy. She leads and works on a wide range of research, knowledge exchange and consultancy projects within the School of Media, Culture and Society at the University of the West of Scotland. Her research interests focus on the use of events and festivals to leverage social change and impact, and include cultural, sporting and music events. She is a member of the European Cultural Parliament and a visiting Professor at the Institute of Cultural Diplomacy. She has published widely in the events, culture and festivals area and conducted evaluation and consultancy work on events and music festivals.

Dr Helen Reddington is Senior Lecturer in Music Production at the University of East London, where she lectures in songwriting and production, and employability and entrepreneurship. Her research focuses on music production and women in popular music; her book *The Lost Women of Rock Music: Female Musicians of the Punk Era* was published in 2012 and at the time of writing she is researching British female audio professionals. She performs and records under the name Helen McCookerybook; her bands The Chefs and Helen and the Horns were favourites of the late John Peel.

Dr Holly Tessler is a Senior Lecturer in Commercial Music at the University of the West of Scotland. Previously, she held the position of Assistant Professor of Music Industry at Northeastern University in Boston. Holly completed both her MBA (Music Industries) and PhD at the Institute of Popular Music, School of Music, University of Liverpool. Her PhD is titled Beatles for Sale: The Role and Significance of Storytelling in the Commercialisation and Cultural Branding of the Beatles since 1970. Holly also has nearly ten years of commercial radio experience, having worked with several commercial and public radio stations in her native Philadelphia, as well as serving as Music Manager for Radio Computing Services (RCS) in New York.

Dr John Williamson is a Research Associate in Music at the University of Glasgow and has recently completed a history of the British Musicians' Union. As well as teaching on the University's M.Litt in Popular Music Studies since its inception, he has previously worked as a journalist, concert promoter and band manager.

LIST OF CASE STUDIES

Abovitz, M. (Tom Tom Magazine)
Atkinson, H. (producer/engineer at RAK Studios)
Bothra, S. (ATC artist management)
Broadfoot, S. (LugPlugs hearing protection)
Carmody, J. (PledgeMusic – crowdfunding platform)
Coachella Festival (branding)
Epp, C. (SynergySounds – music production)
Frank, J. (DigSin – digital record label)
Gorman, C. (Rage Music – music composition/publishing)
Gray, A. (EmuBands – digital distribution)
McFarlane, R. (professional musician)
Muirhead, R. (Scottish Alternative Music Awards)
Nyah, P. (independent artist)
O'Callaghan, G. (ArcTanGent – festival)
Orr, M. (Lab Records)
Riley, D. (Signature Brew – branding)
Smillie, J. (The Glad Café – venue)

LIST OF
INTERVIEWS

Abovitz, M. Interviewed 4 September 2014, London
Atkinson, H. Interviewed (email) 19 August 2014
Bain, V. (BASCA). Interviewed 20 March 2014, London
Barnes, J. Interviewed 18 September 2014, Glasgow
Bothra, S. Interviewed 17 January 2014, London
Broadfoot, S. Interviewed 6 March 2014, Glasgow
Buckland, M. (PPL/Fairwood Music). Interviewed 20
    November 2014, London
Carmody, J. Interviewed 6 October 2014, Glasgow
Crowe, M. (BPI). Interviewed 15 January 2014, London
Denny, L. Interviewed 17 January 2014, London
Epp, C. Interviewed (email) 19 August 2014
Frank, J. Interviewed (email) 19 September 2014
Glossop, M. (MPG). Interviewed 20 March 2014, London
Gorman, C. Interviewed 28 February 2014, Glasgow
Gray, A. Interviewed (email) 13 February 2014
Izzo, J. Interviewed (email) 1 August 2014
Marot, M. (Crown Talent Management). Interviewed 9 April
2014, London
McFarlane, R. Interviewed 1 April 2015, Glasgow
Muirhead, R. Interviewed 30 September 2014, Glasgow
Nyah, P. Interviewed 21 February 2014, London
O'Callaghan, G. Interviewed 17 January 2014, London
Orr, M. Interviewed (phone) 22 May 2014
Riley, D. Interviewed 19 November 2014, London
Smillie, J. Interviewed 18 September 2014, Glasgow
Village, H. Interviewed (phone) 7 November 2014
Webster, J. (MMF). Interviewed 20 March 2014, London
Wenham, A. (AIM). Interviewed 15 January 2014, London

PART ONE

Overview

1

Introduction:

Valuing Music

Gayle McPherson and Allan Dumbreck

The idea that everyone who works in the music industries is an entrepreneur is the core debate of this book. They may not own a business. They may not have employees, or even an office. They may work from a spare room in their parents' house. They may actually work for someone else or be part of a multi-national company, but they need certain key skills to be part of professional music. Throughout this book we will examine and consider entrepreneurship as the cornerstone within those key skills.

A number of themes became clear as our research progressed. One area, for example, in which nearly all of our interviewees were in agreement is that emerging music professionals need an entrepreneurial spirit. They need to think like an entrepreneur (even if some don't like the term) to sustain a career in the diverse fields of the music industries. Another factor that arose is that there is an obvious divide between the

US and the UK (the two key music markets on which we focused) regarding what constitutes an entrepreneur and whether those who are successful in music see themselves in this light. These elements (and others) will be considered in greater detail as the narrative of this book progresses.

The British Phonographic Industry (BPI) is one of the organizations representing the UK recorded music industry, one of the most thriving music sales territories in the world. It is a trade body that represents more than 300 independent music companies and the UK's major record labels, including Universal Music, Sony Music, and Warner Music. Their members account for up to 85 per cent of all music sold in the UK (www.bpi.co.uk). Maggie Crowe, Director of Events and Charities at the BPI told us that, 'BPI supports entrepreneurship as a key element of development and growth in recorded music'; she discussed the work of key players including M People (Mike Pickering et al.) and the work they did in establishing the Deconstruction label; highlighting this as a good example of how entrepreneurship in the recording sector is fundamental to its progression. Vick Bain, CEO of the British Academy of Songwriters, Composers and Authors (BASCA) echoes the sentiment of Crowe above suggesting that she 'feels like we represent two thousand entrepreneurs, all of our members have to be entrepreneurs, whether it is Elton John, Paul McCartney (or) our student members; it is of primary importance' (Bain, March 2014). The general response from the people involved in writing this book and those we interviewed was that overwhelmingly most of those involved in the music business are employed in companies comprising fewer that ten employees and all need entrepreneurial skills. But they also need to understand the sectors and how they function. The business mechanisms are changing but a new model is slowly emerging. That model includes more than just the product, it includes understanding the consumer; knowing the sectors and engaging with the digitally literate who are convergent 'prosumers' in co-creating the image, lifestyle and brand of the artists and direction of the music.

The debate surrounding what a music entrepreneur is was central to the premise that we set out to explore in the research for this book. One line of questioning we adopted looked at the way emerging music industries professionals think about themselves. We purposely chose a provocative statement to gain more active responses. The more passive 'do you think you need to be an entrepreneur to work in the music industries?' generally met with indecision and deflection. Interviewees withdrew and answered a different question. The more pointed approach 'everyone who works in music is in some way an entrepreneur, do you agree?' gained a more definitive reaction and the responses we gathered gave us a clearer picture of the nature of employment in the digitally altered landscape of the music industries.

We explored what was specifically entrepreneurial for them; either in their approach, their personality, skillset or a more fundamental ideological position that underpinned their work. If some didn't see themselves as an entrepreneur, they still believed they were working for an entrepreneur or were inspired by entrepreneurs and their drive, enthusiasm and passion. As the book unfolds you will see how this differs from some of those working in growing sectors such as music branding, who engage with this more comfortably than those in live music or digital distribution, for example, and illuminates clear divisions between US and UK music industry personnel. To establish the scale and value of global music this chapter now presents a snapshot of the growth of the music industries and their inherent value.

Valuing music: Production and consumption

Music is an economic and cultural growth area. Taking the UK as one example, the core music industries generated £3.5bn in gross value added in 2012, £1.4bn of which was in export value. Collectively they employ over 100,000 individuals excluding retail and education (UK Music, 2013). The UK is a world leader in these industries, the fourth largest global consumer of recorded music (IFPI, 2013) and the birthplace of a series of internationally successful performers and songwriters.

Another example is the digital music industry. In 2012, the global recorded music sector saw 'its best year on year performance since 1998' (IFPI, 2013) and digital music is responsible for most of that growth. The global network of music providers, service providers, aggregators and subscription services has seen unprecedented growth across the world, including Mexico, China, Brazil and other developing nations. In the US, the global digital revenues have increased year-on-year since 2008; music streaming was up 32 per cent in the US and 33.7 per cent in the UK in 2013 (Nielson, 2013). In 2014, the US market stabilized and with growing demand for streaming services, a similar picture emerged in Europe. This is not a universally positive message, however. In the same period, Japan (the world's number two music market) witnessed a significant fall in revenues (16.7 per cent); but overall the trend is towards growth (IFPI, 2014). Moore highlights that, 'It is now clear that music streaming and subscription is a mainstream model for business; in 2011, there were 8 million paying subscribers to subscription services – today there are 28 million' (IFPI, 2014). That said, the issue of piracy is still the main threat to the industry. Globally, the industry's digital revenues were US$5.9bn, a growth of 4.3 per cent. This takes digital music sales to 39 per cent of the recorded music industry's global revenue and it is clear that this is an area that will need further engagement; especially with increasing use from hand-held devices by young people. A challenge for the sector will be how to reach parts of Africa, South America, etc., where payment methods are not as secure or well established, but where demand is already growing exponentially. Latin America had the fastest digital growth in recent years with revenues up 7.3 per cent in 2014 (IFPI, 2015).

Overall, in the UK, the gross value added by the creative industries (which includes music) was £74.4bn in 2012 and accounted for 5.2 per cent of the UK economy (this has risen 15.6 per cent since 2008). Employment in the creative industries in the UK was 1.68m in 2012 and accounted for one out of every eighteen jobs. The number of jobs also increased by 8.6 per cent between 2011 and 2012 (see Table 1.1). It is worth taking a look back to see just how significant the growth is in the creative industries. Latest figures from the DCMS (Department of Culture, Media and Sport) show that there has been a significant overall growth in the creative industries in the UK between 1997 and 2013 of 83.5 per cent, surpassing the UK as a whole, which saw a 10.6 per cent growth over the same period (DCMS, 2015). The evidence shows that the millennials are more entrepreneurial, seek high salaries and are more often self-employed now than ever before (Mitchell, 2015).

As a comparison to other Blue Book industries, Table 1.2 details the significance of the increase in the gross value added for the creative industries as a whole, showing the second largest increase between 2008 and 2012, only superseded by real estate.

The nature and function of the sectors that comprise the business of music are in a somewhat unpredictable, on-going state of evolution. It is unlikely that anybody who works in music carries out the same tasks, the same way for a complete working life (as we have to regularly clarify with our students). Five years is normally considered a successful career span for a recording/performing artist and, for example, while record companies saw their sector diminish in the years following the emergence of filesharing (14 per cent reduction in global value between 2007–10) (IFPI, 2013), the live events sector has recently seen significant growth, bearing in mind that the economic crash hit both the UK and the USA in 2008. Live music festivals in particular are seeing unprecedented growth in the USA following European success, with the two largest music companies Live Nation and AEG promoting

Table 1.1 *Employment in the creative industries*

Creative industries group	Creative industries employment 2011	Creative industries employment 2012	Percentage change
Advertising and marketing	147,000	143,000	–2.8
Architecture	93,000	89,000	–4.2
Crafts	9,000	7,000	–19.5
Design: product, graphic and fashion design	100,000	116,000	**16.2**
Film, TV, video, radio and photography	209,000	238,000	**13.6**
IT, software and computer services	482,000	558,000	**15.6**
Publishing	207,000	223,000	7.5
Museums, galleries and libraries	90,000	85,000	–5.4
Music, performing and visual arts	212,000	224,000	5.6
Creative industries total	1,551,000	1,684,000	8.6
UK total employment	29,935,000	30,150,000	0.7
Percentage share of UK total	5.2%	5.6%	–

** Figures in **bold** represent statistically significant changes*

Notes:
1. Source, ONS Annual Population Survey (2011 and 2012)
2. Figures have been rounded to the nearest thousand, and therefore totals may not sum

Source: DCMS, Creative Industries Economic Estimates, January 2014

Table 1.2 *Gross value added of the creative industries and Blue Book sectors*

Blue Book sector or creative industries	Percentage change in GVA between 2008 and 2012
Real estate activities	29.3
Creative industries	*15.6*
Other services	13.3
Government, health and education	12.9
Total professional and support	8.6
Information and communication	5.8
Distribution, transport, hotels and restaurants	3.9
Agriculture, forestry and fishing	–0.4
Production	–3.4
Construction	–5.4
Financial and insurance activities	–12.6
Wider UK economy total	*5.4*

Notes:
1. Source – ONS Blue Book Dataset (2012)
2. Current prices (i.e. not accounting for inflation)

Source: DCMS, Creative Industries Economic Estimates, January 2014

more festivals. Bob Roux (co-chairman for Live Nation in North America) has stated that 'the growth in live festivals is just the beginning of what it will look like for the next decade' (IFPI, 2014). Social media skills and social media analytic skills are increasingly prevalent as skills wanted in the sector both in producing and in understanding consumers. Even those agencies bidding for music events, e.g. MTV music awards, are using online analytics that tell them which part of their bid the evaluation team looked at, so when it comes to the presentation to win the right to host an event they know what to focus on. We look at this area in more depth in key chapters in the book (see Duffin and Dumbreck [Chapter 8], and Frew and McPherson [Chapter 10] below).

Just as digital media has already changed (seemingly irreversibly) the way we consume recorded music, so social networking is redefining the way we promote and distribute it. Fresh social, cultural and technological developments occur regularly and their impact on the music industries is usually significant and often permanent. The music industries already change at a considerable pace in comparison to other fields (including the weekly sales charts) suggesting there is an inherent need for creativity and entrepreneurship. Each of these elements causes change. Collectively they generate an arguably unstable environment in which the business of music is conducted. However, this in turn may equally be viewed as a fertile landscape offering opportunity to an imaginative entrepreneur.

Who is the young music entrepreneur?

In this book we interview almost twenty entrepreneurs from different cultural backgrounds, different territories and operating across a range of music sectors. You may not have heard of them but you will be familiar with some of the projects that they have developed. Some are very successful (in terms of the profile, income or scale of the projects they are developing). Most, as we discovered, are simply, and sometimes quietly, working on an 'idea' or a project that has become a wage-earner for them. Many are happy to have achieved a level of comfortable sustainability, which they do not intend to raise any further. Some even intend to leave music in the near future to seek opportunities in other fields. All of them, however, started with an idea, a perceived window of opportunity, a spark. What we are witnessing is the continued rise of self-employment with the DCMS predicting that self-employment will overtake public sector employment by 2020 (DCMS, 2015). This is not necessarily met with unqualified enthusiasm. Many of the young people we interviewed said this was out of necessity rather than choice. The days of career progression in one area are seen as long gone. The 'post-fordist' or 'portfolio worker' is how many in the sector are seen. It is no longer enough to be a good musician, or a great project manager, or technician; you need more than one skillset and more than one job. This is often seen as negative but necessary as one job tends to subsidize the creative job but for some this is the future. This was a consistent finding in the USA, UK and beyond. Many young people were playing in a band, running their own record label or working at events and festivals (if they were lucky, others in a bar) at key times throughout the year. They were building networks, making contacts and developing their own personal brand of identity.

Many of the individuals we met and interviewed are developing their own projects within their existing job specification. Some of these projects will grow to become their next job. Then they imagine and create their next idea. Their interview responses often detail this activity. These responses have then been categorized within this book into chapters by the sector of the music industries within which they operate and analysed by academics (most of whom continue as active practitioners at some level in the same sector) working in music departments in universities across the UK and North America.

Outline of the book

The book is split into two parts: the first part gives an overview of the music industries, presenting some of the debates and the conceptual background currently circulating within the sectors along with an introduction to what we mean by the music industry entrepreneur and the importance of music in a global marketplace. It examines the impact digitalization has had on entrepreneurship in the music industries and raises the question of what title can be given to music project developers if not 'entrepreneur'.

Part two goes on to present case study chapters, each one designed to give an insight into a specific sector. Each of these chapters has the same format, to make it easier for the reader to follow. An introduction to the area, followed by a review of the current literature and key issues for the sector, then case study examples (normally two) are examined. These are intended to highlight sector developments in a practical setting drawing upon interviews with young entrepreneurs in the field, the skills they require, the difficulties they have encountered and the success they have experienced. We will now give you a brief summary of the individual chapters in the book, hopefully giving you a flavour of the interesting and diverse material yet to unfold.

The second chapter by Allan Dumbreck starts the debate by questioning the need for entrepreneurship in music and who the music entrepreneur might be. He examines key skills, the evolving music landscape and the role of entrepreneurship in music education. He questions and argues for a more coherent understanding of the role of entrepreneurship in university courses and suggests that the US approach of celebrating success aligns more closely to the entrepreneurial model than the traditional British model of modesty verging on embarrassment that you might actually have achieved something valuable. This is followed by an in-depth discussion from Holly Tessler and Matthew Flynn, taking an historical look at entrepreneurship in music to the present day with an exploration of the term 'musicpreneur'. They assert that the rise of the digital landscape has led to young people entering this field requiring the business acumen of a business graduate but still needing creativity and community at the core. The chapter essentially gives us a reflective journey from Punk to post-Punk, analogue to digital, and seeks to contextualize the evolving and often-contested nature of music entrepreneurship from the 1970s to the present. It finishes by stating that creating new cultural and economic constructs does not easily fit one model. This is followed by a short chapter presenting a sample case study to examine the professional musician (representing two-thirds of the employment opportunities) (UK Music, 2013), and which introduces some of the key debates and theorists, which will be developed throughout the second part of the book.

In part two, the book moves forward to look at specific areas of the music industries and presents case study examples. Each of the case studies draws on interviews that were conducted with those working in music in both the UK and USA. This section starts with Chapter 4, an examination of artist management. John Williamson attempts both to address the neglect of managers in historic accounts of the music industries and argue their contemporary importance. In doing so, he acknowledges the entrepreneurial aspects of management, and questions the role of the artist manager when at times it is to provide a safe pair of hands (for example, in managing U2 now) and at other times it needs the manager to take risks (for example, in managing U2 before they became successful). This, of course, comes with experience and therein lies the age old problem of requiring to know that when you are young. In Chapter 5, Kenny Forbes takes us into the live music sector and the milieu of key parts of this industry, albeit dominated in part by global conglomerates, which does still allow for a range of entrepreneurial initiatives. The uniqueness of the live music sector encourages the development of the relationship between the artist and the audience; one that doesn't exist in the digital download market. It is the epitome of symbolic consumption; it plays into the temporal nature of the event and allows for diversification into small-to-medium sized festivals as well as the more established large hallmark events. Forbes suggests that the ability of live music enterprises and entrepreneurs to tap into this smaller-sized market has added to the growth in this sector due to the ability to build significant and meaningful relationships with audiences and stakeholders.

The book then moves on to the issue of music production and this is covered by Helen Reddington in Chapter 6, where she examines changes in the practice of record production, and the role of entrepreneurship as part of the skillset of the successful recording professional. She highlights that an understanding of the close relationship between creativity and future developments in audio technology is vital to a studio professional. Her case studies illustrate different perspectives on the ways that entrepreneurship skills can be used in music production: one from a sole practitioner approach that demonstrates the integration of business and music-technology skills, and the other from the supply of an adaptable and practical music engineering 'toolkit' to a mainstream commercial organization. This leads us appropriately into Jeff Izzo's Chapter 7, which suggests that as downloading and streaming music overtake physical sales, new technologies and delivery systems influence customers' buying preferences. The chapter explores, within an historical context, how such factors are heralding significant changes in traditional record company business models. The issue of downloading and streaming as key tenets of the music industries is also referred to by Frew and McPherson, Duffin and Dumbreck, and George Howard showing how these areas are permeating many of the sectors within the industry. Izzo's chapter finishes by looking at two entrepreneurs discussing how they are creatively and successfully facing these new challenges.

Claire Duffin and Allan Dumbreck offer the other side of the spectrum to Izzo in that they embrace the debate surrounding digital music distribution (Chapter 8). They suggest that the apparent paradigm shift of music artists becoming more in control of their audio repertoire from a rights holder perspective (PPL UK, 2014) has arguably presented new opportunities for digital distributors in the facilitation of artists' seemingly entrepreneurial activity. The artists who are using increasingly more accessible digital platforms are now in control of their data. They can see from their online dashboards who their fans are, what their geographical location is, watch spending patterns and more if they have the skills. Essentially, they assert we have arrived at a point where digital distribution is not just mirroring that of the traditional-physical, but it is now counterpart to social media platforms aiming to provide new business opportunities to independent (and increasingly, also major label) music artists. The focus of the book then shifts towards music publishing in Chapter 9. George Howard explains music publishing, and some of the copyright issues that songwriters and publishers face, and are continuing to face in the myriad of possibilities of new usage. It illuminates this process and helps new music entrepreneurs to make better decisions about whether and how to enter this particular space.

The book then embraces an issue that has been gathering momentum throughout the text; how artists, artists' managers, agencies and corporate businesses are creating branded images, sponsorship opportunities and retail buying possibilities tied to the music industry. We are on the verge of a cultural turn of what a music artist is and who owns them. The discussion embraces the competitive environment of brand management but turns full circle to demonstrate that the artist is now fully aware of the need to engage on a more personal level with their fans and audiences, dealing with D2F (direct to fan) issues raised by Duffin and Dumbreck. Fans and audiences are now doing more than consuming the music and artists, and their management are now able to access the data that is widely available on consumer spending patterns, streaming, geography and demographics. Frew and McPherson (Chapter 10) dissect the concept of brand, and how the branded music celebrity has become synonymous with the music industries, before turning to consider the birth of the connected or convergent consumer. Here the emergence of ubiquitous digital and social media technologies is highlighted, and the impact of a networked fan/consumer base driven by the visibility, immediacy and engagement of this age of acceleration are considered (Dijck, 2013). Framed in this way, the chapter turns to practically locate music, brand and the artist through two case studies. The last case study chapter by Allan Dumbreck (Chapter 11) reviews additional and alternative opportunities in music that are not easily encompassed in other parts of the book. Examples such as music print media, and health and safety products that are inherently part of professional music are examined here, where individual entrepreneurs have identified a gap in the market. The case is made to extend the scope of what is categorized as the music or creative industries in order to gain a clearer perspective of their value to the economy. We finish with our conclusion outlining the key issues facing the music industries and the future trends that present both opportunities and challenges for the sector.

Conclusion

This book is intended as a guide to the theoretical and conceptual discussions taking place in both academia and industry, and to act as a roadmap to aid progress and avoid pitfalls for both academics and students alike. It is also intended for those wishing to develop their own music project professionally, whether it represents entrepreneurship in performance, production or business. It has been written with the intention of being interpretable to anyone who has an interest in this field without necessarily already having achieved college or university qualifications, but it is hoped that it would be particularly useful for those in degree level education. Its primary purpose is to focus on the drivers and activities of the music entrepreneur. Additional study into other areas of the creative industries, and surrounding fields and concepts, are highlighted throughout the book and reference is made to further reading.

The case studies and supporting analysis will de-mystify the process of taking an idea from concept to reality and encourage those who read it to see the value in their own project and to have the passion and spirit to take the opportunity to develop their initial spark into what product, service or output they dream of creating. It is hoped that this work will continue, and add to, the debate on the driving forces behind the music industries helping others thrive in this continuously evolving environment. The authors anticipate that this offers a greater understanding to the reader and encouragement to emerging music entrepreneurs.

References

DCMS (2014), *Focus on Employment*, London: DCMS.

DCMS (2015), *Creative Industries Economic Estimates*, London: DCMS.

Dijck, J.V. (2013), *The Culture of Connectivity: A Critical History of Social Media*, Oxford: Oxford University Press.

IFPI (2013), 'Digital Music Report: Engine of a digital world', available at: https://www.bpi.co.uk/assets/files/BPI_Digital_Music_Nation_2013.pdf

IFPI (2014), 'IFPI Digital Music Report: Lighting up new markets', available at: http://www.ifpi.org/downloads/Digital-Music-Report-2014.pdf

Knopper, S. (2012), 'Music Festivals Enjoy Record Expansion in 2012: Events are "a rite of passage" for new generation', *Rolling Stone Music Magazine*, 28 September.

Mitchell. S. (2015), *Building a Creative Nation: The Next Decade, Creative and Cultural Skills*, The National Skills Academy.

Nielson. (2014). *Nielson Music Report 2014*. Available: http://www.nielsen.com/. Last accessed 23rd April 2014.

OECD (2012), *Entrepreneurship Skills for Growth-Orientated Businesses*.

O'Leary, D. (2014), *Going it Alone*, London: Demos.

Shoup, B. (2013), 'Deconstructing: Coachella and the Music Festival Industry', Stereogum, 28 January.

UK Music (2013), *The Economic Contribution of the Core UK Music Industry*, London, UK Music.

2

The Need for the Music Entrepreneur

Allan Dumbreck

In nearly thirty years of teaching music (performance, production, business and cultural theory) at college and university level, I have rarely experienced a shortage of talent, of ideas, or of enthusiasm amongst student cohorts beginning their final years of education. Almost all of the young people I have taught have been very passionate about their music or their business ideas, about their career aspirations, about the specific sector in which they wish to work. They are passionate about music. They can talk at length about who, or what, inspired them; how they believe in what they are doing and their potential future success.

Where they are generally less convincing is when they are asked about how they intend to achieve that success; how they intend to make it happen. They often appear to lack the practical business skills to take their ideas forward. Whether they see themselves as artistically driven rather than business orientated or whether their belief and enthusiasm diverts them from the need for a realistic business development plan, many of them simply don't want to engage with the business aspects of the music industries.[1] This can make progress difficult when they first encounter the individuals Caves describes as 'gatekeepers', the key business agents who may assist or stall their career (Caves, 2002).

In every class, a small percentage is focused and organized. Whether performance, production or business orientated they plan their career development and activate projects well. Many more struggle to create a genuine business plan from their original concept in practical project classes. The final group has difficulty in motivating themselves in business terms or even starting a project at all. In other words, in my experience, a significant percentage of every class group nearing the end of their professional education either feel they can't or won't take entrepreneurial control of their career development. Lecturers wishing to deliver their charges into gainful employment in professional music therefore often face significant initial difficulties, perhaps even resistance to business thinking from many of the young people they teach. This, of course, may or may not be a problem. We are often asked by those wishing to enter the music industries how much they need to understand about how business functions. Do they need entrepreneurial skills? The community aspect of music education, particularly where you have a critical mass of budding musicians, producers and managers working in the same catalytic environment, would surely allow the business-orientated students to take the entrepreneurial lead (effectively to manage the performers and producers). Would that be enough? Do *all* music students need to be entrepreneurs, regardless of which direction they wish to follow?

To better understand this question, and ultimately to try to answer it, we must first investigate how the music industries function and how emerging professionals progress. In the first part of this chapter, I will examine the music industries as a functioning environment and assess the potential value of an entrepreneurial approach. In the second part of the chapter, I will investigate what being a music entrepreneur might mean and which skills might be required. Finally, in the conclusions, these elements will be drawn together to make the case (and assertion) for entrepreneurial skills (particularly within music education) as a necessary pre-requisite for the music professional.

The nature of the music industries

The music industries are part of the broader creative industries,[2] which in the UK are defined by the DCMS[3] as, 'those industries which have their origin in individual creativity, skill and talent and which have a potential for wealth and job creation through the generation and exploitation of intellectual property' (DCMS, 2001). These industries, then, depend on the creation of products and services derived from an individual's intellectual property (IP). Relevant examples would include a song, a play, a work of art or a recording of a performance. Howkins, for example, quite reasonably defines a creative product as 'an economic good or service that results from creativity and has economic value' (Howkins, 2007).

The music industries (including but not limited to the fields of recorded music, live performance, music publishing and artist management) as one example can arguably be seen to continuously re-invent themselves in terms of new songs, new artists and new genres, but this does not necessarily prove that entrepreneurship is at work. Could it simply be the harvesting of random experimentation?

Our research began by speaking with some key music professionals working in representative organizations. Jon Webster (Chief Executive of Music Managers Forum) stated, 'the MMF obviously think that [entrepreneurship is] a requisite for the modern manager'. Considering the work which his members have to undertake with the acts they represent he further extended this to the artists: 'performers need to know more about business than they have in the past' (interview, 2014). Malcolm Buckland (formerly of UK royalty collection agency, the Performing Right Society, now with Fairwood Music[4]) stated, 'being an entrepreneur is a fundamental characteristic of anybody working in the music industry' (interview, 2014). Alison Wenham (CEO, Association of Independent Music) referring to the difficulties in locating full-time employment in music observed that 'most of those working in independent music have a portfolio career' (interview, 2014). Might this suggest that a more entrepreneurial mindset is required to negotiate and sustain a series of part-time positions and projects?

The increasing need to operate as your own manager appears to run across a series of music sectors. Mick Glossop (veteran music producer[5] and Director of the Music Producers Guild) asked, 'how important is entrepreneurship to the role of producers? It is incredibly important, much more so now than before. Budgets are down so ... we're all building our own studios so we can work on lower budget projects. This immediately means you've got to take on the idea of negotiating, as you've got to think, what's their budget? What can they afford? What can I negotiate in the way of back end royalties?' (interview, 2014).

Alison Wenham did, however, also identify activity which was distinctly anti-entrepreneurial: 'One example of that within the recorded music sector would be the reaction amongst record company personnel to the advent of digital music. The (initial) resistance to digital formats and digital distribution was significant and ultimately quite destructive. I think this shows that while entrepreneurial abilities are important in setting a business up an individual can become quite conservative and significantly un-entrepreneurial when faced with something that looks like a threat.'

So are music professionals entrepreneurs? We might begin by examining the progress of the performing artist in music. They do, after all, work with every other sector of the music industries. In the UK, until the emergence of, and universal public access to the web, a recognized artist development process had been in place for several decades (many parts are still active). In this model, events promoters, music journalists and record company scouts try to stay ahead of the fashion curve, supporting emerging acts, artists, songwriters, DJs and music producers who they believe to be part of the latest vanguard. Recorded songs supported by the media (web, radio, social media and TV) help some of these artists become successful. The public then hear the song regularly and are more inclined to buy a physical copy, download or stream it. New charts are compiled every week, listing the top-selling tracks and albums whether digital products such as downloads, or physical products such as CDs. Hence an artist becomes successful (or not). All these activities have been examined and well documented by music professionals, usually lawyers such as Passman (2013) and Harrison (2008), and by academics (Caves, 2002).

The emergence of the model featuring the artist as a singular self-contained web-orientated business, often referred to as music 2.0 (Young and Collins, 2010) presents an alternative, parallel development process. Here the act or artist has direct access to financially affordable recording processes, online marketing and sales and crucially, via the web, their own fanbase. Hence, they can effectively be their own manager, record company and events promoter and their audience has a more personal link to the performer. This new model is still evolving. Currently it appears to be most successful for those artists who have already been commercially developed by the previous model of record company support (Radiohead and Trent Reznor are often cited as particularly good examples). However, increasingly, the long tail of many more but smaller marketplaces described by Chris Anderson (2008) is beginning to create opportunities for the emerging artist. This model may become the prevalent mechanism in due course. Revolutionary as this may be, it still appears to share the need for entrepreneurial activity with its predecessor. In fact, if anything, it appears to require greater entrepreneurial input on the part of the artist.

Taking a longer time frame, we have seen that performers who can sustain success over a period of years have often done so by diversifying into bordering industries to extend their careers and/or broaden their income streams. Victoria Beckham (formerly a performer with the Spice Girls), for instance, has developed a clothing line, Beyonce Knowles (Destiny's Child/ solo performer) has a perfume brand, Lauren Laverne (Kenicke) and Cerys Matthews (Catatonia) have branched out into radio presenting (BBC 6 Music) and writing (authors and *Guardian* columnists). Hence, the artists themselves are required to be creative, not only in their music but in the overall management and direction of their careers across the broader creative industries.

In the live music sector also (as we shall see in Chapter 5), festivals are becoming more numerous, partly by new events becoming more niche, catering to discrete groups of fans by marketing to a smaller regional audience or by hosting narrower definitions of genre. Examples in the UK include ArcTanGent (math-rock, post-rock, noise rock) and Celtic Connections (traditional, acoustic and more modern Celtic genres). Again, it could be argued that the individuals behind these initiatives are taking a creative, entrepreneurial approach which is driving change and progress in music.

As one of our live events interviewees, Goc O'Callaghan (ArcTanGent) noted, 'What does being a music entrepreneur mean to me? Finding a niche in the market, and fulfilling the requirements of that niche, working tirelessly to achieve your goal, it's about exploring new opportunities and challenging yourself every single day. I'm learning something new every day, and I need to' (O'Callaghan, 2014). Therefore, as this comment suggests, there is potentially an inherent need for creativity, innovation and new business development skills to keep the music industries running. In other words, perhaps the successful music professional *needs* to be an entrepreneur.

In 2013, UK Music reported that of the 101,860 full time equivalent positions in the UK music industries, around 68,000 were musicians or composers (66.7 per cent) (UK Music, 2013). This statistic implies that artists and songwriters make up the significant majority of those employed in music in the UK. However, to ensure that all sectors are properly represented and give the reader the broadest perspective of possible directions, we have interviewed emerging project developers from a range of music industries giving each sector equal weighting. Our intention has always been to examine the value of entrepreneurship in as diverse a group of music sectors as possible, not only, or particularly, performance and composition. As we hope to demonstrate, we believe our research has identified evidence of entrepreneurial activity in all of those sectors which we investigated.

To progress this train of thought, we will now consider a series of environmental aspects of the music industries (which are indicative but by no means exhaustive) to examine more closely the changing environment and whether or not individuals and companies are behaving entrepreneurially.

Record labels: Fluctuating economy/ new business models

The arrival of peer-to-peer filesharing in the final years of the twentieth century meant that consumers for the first time had unparalleled access to free music simply by downloading it from each other's computer hard drives. As Alison Wenham has already identified, the recording industry initially reacted punitively and often unpopularly, taking individuals to court (*Billboard*, 2001; *Music Week*, 2005), before developing their own legal digital distribution systems and slowing the rate of illegal downloading. While digital sales were trying to catch up with the drop in physical revenues (only achieved globally in 2012) (Pfanner, 2013), the world economy fell into well-documented recession.

In March 2011 *The Guardian* reported, 'Global recorded music sales fall almost $1.5bn amid increased piracy' (Sweney, 2011). Tracking global sales figures in April the same year, the IFPI (International Federation of the Phonographic Industry) recorded a fall in total global recorded music sales for the twelfth successive year (IFPI, 2011). The causes were again generally felt to be the global recession that had begun in 2008, which compounded losses from the deterioration of physical sales (CD, audio cassette, vinyl) affected by the public illegally downloading digital music. Both these factors, it appeared, had detrimentally affected recorded music sales.

In this changing environment, record companies in particular were required to take action to protect their businesses. One mechanism devised was the '360-degree model' that allowed record companies to take a percentage of the artists' income from sources outside the direct sales of CDs, DVDs and digital downloads in order to give the companies additional income streams. 'The 360 model has been gaining momentum since it emerged as a solution to the "crisis" in the industry in the early 2000s' (Karubian, 2009). For example, part of artist income gained from live performance revenue, merchandise and other sources could be requested by the record company within the record contract. In this way, the record company takes a '360-degree view' of the income of an artist. This model has contributed positively to record company profits as reported in UK trade journal *Music Week*, which identified that '360 deals brought in extra revenue worth £76m to UK record companies last year' (Ingham, 2012) but these agreements have not been without controversy: '360 deals are "immoral", says Neil Warnock' (Jones, 2013). The model, however, still exists – as such does it evidence record companies operating entrepreneurially in a falling market or does it demonstrate a risk-averse (and therefore arguably non-entrepreneurial) reaction?

Emerging territories

In 2005, the IFPI listed South Korea as the twenty-ninth most significant territory for recorded music consumption. By 2012, only seven years later, it had risen to eleventh place (IFPI, 2013), increasing its music consumption from $89.2m to $187.5m. This put South Korea ahead of Spain, Switzerland,

Belgium and South Africa in terms of recorded music sales. This development is partially attributable to government intervention in introducing anti-piracy legislation (Lindvall, 2011) but perhaps more so to the high energy pop-dance genre unique to South Korea known as K-pop (Korean pop music). Importantly, unlike other East Asian countries, the South Korean artists appearing in their country's charts often sing at least partially in English. Their websites are also in English so they are therefore accessible to an English-speaking audience. This offers a greater possibility of a South Korean artist crossover success into Western markets.

In March 2012, *Time* magazine recognized K-pop as 'South Korea's greatest export' (Mahr, 2012), identifying three artist management companies which made around 40 per cent of their income from record sales and 60 per cent from other sources (product endorsement and TV). At the same time, the most notable Korean hit song was self-released by South Korean-born Psy who achieved global notoriety with his hit 'Gangnam Style', largely through the uploading of a video featuring a dance replicating the actions of horse-riding which became, at one point, the most watched video on YouTube (over 2bn views as of December 2014). In November 2012, *Billboard* stated that, 'The Korean music industry grossed nearly $3.4 billion in the first half of 2012, according to *Billboard* estimates, a 27.8% increase from the same period last year' (Billboard, 2012). This growth is happening at a time when western music markets are struggling to recover.

There may be some value in music professionals taking notice of the growth of new music markets like South Korea, where recorded music sales increased over a seven year period while traditional markets (Europe, Japan, North America) shrunk significantly within the same timescale. Can business be done in these countries by incomers? What can be learned from the national successes within these territories? Again, the proposition of thinking entrepreneurially (in this case in geographical terms) becomes important in a continuously fluctuating marketplace.

Having examined a series of elements within the music environment we have found considerable upheaval in the marketplace. Diversification of an artist's career path, changing record company business models and a fluctuating global marketplace indicate a business sector in near constant change. This could be seen as a fertile proving ground for the entrepreneur.

The music entrepreneur

Etymology: Origins and meaning of the term 'entrepreneur'

The word 'entrepreneur' appears to have its origins in late fifteenth century France, evolving from the old French term 'entreprendre' meaning to under-take. Later it was introduced in literature by Cantillon but brought to greater attention by Say (Casson, 2003). The term 'enterprising' seems to have evolved around the early 1600s (Addison, quoted in Barnhart, 1988) to imply some initiative or larger scale engagement than the more established 'manager', which was commonly associated with business starting in the early 1700s. Connotations of 'enterprise' were for some time partially negative (as in scheming, over-ambitious or foolhardy). The description of an individual as an 'entrepreneur' is relatively recent by comparison. First noted in 1828 (Barnhart, 1988), the term was often used to describe theatrical managers or promoters (impresarios).

What makes, defines or motivates an entrepreneur is still the subject of debate. In the early twentieth century, Joseph Schumpeter effectively opened the discussion by identifying the entrepreneur as an innovator and the prime mover in economic development (Schumpeter, quoted in Casson, 2003). Later, however, Chell investigating three popular definitions created by other researchers (the 'outsider', those 'shaped by their environment' and the 'key traits and characteristics' models) found all to be inadequate (Chell, 1985). More recently, and more directly relevant for our purposes, work addressing business development in the arts has identified non-economic motivational factors (Stichfield, Nelson and Wood, 2012). Additionally, discussing the term 'cultural entrepreneur', Swedburg, citing Schumpeter's comparisons of the artist to the entrepreneur, 'would rather argue (in Schumpeter's spirit) that economic entrepreneurship primarily aims at creating something new (and profitable) in the area of the economy, while cultural entrepreneurship aims at creating something new (and appreciated) in the area of culture' (Swedburg, 2006). In this, arguably, he clearly draws a key distinction between those motivated by finance and those motivated by passion, a theme that we will see evolve throughout this book. In agreement with this, most modern dictionaries listing the term 'entrepreneur' in its purely business sense normally include specific reference to the words 'risk' and more importantly 'profit'.

The primary objective, then, of an entrepreneur, again by definition (in the purely business sense of the word), can be said to be the generation of profit. Many young people engaging in the music industries have other drivers. They may want to create an event, or a website, or a body of work which attracts interest from one sector of the general public and/or to fulfil a perceived need within a market. The primary motivator may not be financial gain. Hence the term 'entrepreneur' with potentially (in the UK at least) a somewhat negative public perception, purely business orientation and profit-seeking connotations may not seem entirely appropriate or fitting to the way those undertaking entrepreneurial activity in music view themselves.

To attempt to apply any reliable 'litmus test' for who is or who is not a music entrepreneur is therefore something of a minefield. However, to progress our research we required defining characteristics to label as smoke which would hopefully lead to entrepreneurial fire. Hence, at the risk of further confusing the debate rather than trying to clarify it, certain elements appeared to us to be regularly recognized when discussing this subject. Innovation (or creativity), for example, is often presented as a significant indicator (Schumpeter, quoted in Casson, 2003; Drucker, 2007), as are risk-taking (Drucker, 2007) and ambition or the determination to succeed (McLelland, 1987). Profit-making (Casson, 2003), while not specifically measured (for reasons discussed throughout this book), was considered as a potential future motivator. Academics overlap and vary in their support of each of these elements but they are commonly discussed. These were, therefore, amongst the elements we considered when analysing our emerging music developers.

In our interviews we found that a number of respondents expressed a reluctance to associate themselves with the title of entrepreneur: 'I definitely see myself as an ideas person and a project manager but less as an entrepreneur; LeeFest is about making things happen, not just making money' (Denny, 2014). Others, however, experienced no such reticence: 'Yes – I am an entrepreneur working within a company' (Gorman, 2013). However, some other interviewees perceived themselves as operating as a type of generic 'agent' or 'manager' (not to be confused with the music industries-specific terms of 'booking agent' and 'artist manager') where they were responsible for gaining income for a line manager/business owner as opposed to working directly for themselves. It was also identified by many of those interviewed that the standard view of the entrepreneur was not entirely appropriate to the music industries. Many of our respondents indicated that, for example, they were *not* primarily working to make profit. This observation would indeed be at odds with the economic basis of the word and dictionary definitions of an entrepreneur.

Even though it may not be entirely precise in this particular instance and may not be the exact definition of choice for many we interviewed, the term is closer to what we wish to discuss than any other. In this book we have, therefore, in the absence of any more appropriate terminology, chosen to work with the key term 'entrepreneur'. The terms 'project manager' and 'businessperson' fail to stress the pioneering and innovative elements of the work involved, 'ideas person' implies nothing further beyond the concept stage and 'self-employed' ignores the fact that many entrepreneurial activities are undertaken by those who are actually employed by others.

It should also be pointed out that most of those interviewed were working on several projects simultaneously. In some of these projects, they were the project manager or 'leader'. In others, they were assisting associates who were developing their own projects. Within a portfolio career, these different kinds of entrepreneurial practices are often standard. Practitioners are at times an entrepreneur and at others an entrepreneurial employee or co-worker.

Finally, in a more general sense, entrepreneurship as a career option appears to be rising. In 1975, 8.7 per cent of the UK workforce (1.9m people) was self-employed (this would include entrepreneurs). By 2014, this figure had risen to 15 per cent (4.6m people), a growth which has continued unrestrained throughout the financial recession which began in 2008. While not completely definitive in any way (not all self-employed persons are necessarily entrepreneurial), the background statistic does imply general growth amongst those taking their career into their own hands (ONS, 2014).

Which skills might the music entrepreneur need?

Having discussed the essential attributes of an entrepreneur we now need to consider whether an entrepreneur wishing to work within the music industries demonstrates any different or additional characteristics. As we have already seen, there is often reluctance amongst UK music entrepreneurs to embrace the term. On many occasions, the feeling was that they were developing their ideas out of passion where their concept of the word 'entrepreneur' was intrinsically associated with financial profit. There is indeed a dichotomy here. You have chosen to work in the arts but you need a functioning knowledge of business. This idea leads us to what some have seen as the essential contradiction at the heart of all creative industry.

Art versus commerce: Striking a balance

The inherent dichotomy between art and finance (key debates include how art is valued and priced; whether artists should also be managers or entrepreneurs; the corporate control of artworks and art marketplaces) experienced by many of the interviewees we spoke with has been addressed over a period of time by a series of writers including, notably, Frith (2001) and Caves (2002). Whilst a fuller examination of this dichotomy is beyond the scope of this book, it is worth discussing here briefly, as it helps to further contextualize the role and significance of entrepreneurship within the music industries. Aggestam (2007), for example, discusses a group of creative business developers whom she classifies as 'art-entrepreneurs', a term which would clearly include those working on music projects. 'An art-entrepreneur is defined as an individual who has an entrepreneurial mindset in response to two triggers . . . extrinsic, that is, contextual and business-driven; and intrinsic, that is, involving internal desire to create something aesthetic and focused on a sense of personal achievement.' If applied to the music industries, this definition understands entrepreneurs as having an inherent, personal need to develop projects that allow them to express themselves artistically or to freely exploit artistic opportunities while they simultaneously attempt to develop their career within a structured business environment.

In turn, this dichotomy can create tensions between the lateral freedom of expression and creation (whether of a song, a recording or an event) and the linear necessity for these artefacts to be presented in a particular format to be as attractive to the buying public as possible in order to make money. The music entrepreneur will therefore need to find a balance between the two to progress.

Self-belief: Opportunity/motivation

Casson, who writes extensively on entrepreneurship, states that in business generally, 'the entrepreneur believes that he is right while everyone else is wrong'. They have 'a different perception of the situation' (Casson, 2003). It could therefore be argued that an entrepreneur essentially sees an opportunity where others do not. Others may perceive the enterprise to be too complex, to have too many inter-dependent elements or simply to be too much work, producing too poor a profit margin. The entrepreneur does not see these problems, instead seeing the opportunities and the challenges.

Regarding what motivates the entrepreneur, McLelland (1987) identifies three key drivers: achievement, authority/power and affiliation (building bonds with others). The achievement incentive is defined as proving oneself capable and thereby progressing one's career (French, 1955, quoted in McLelland). This element, alongside altruism (wishing to improve matters, change circumstances for the better), which can arguably be considered a form of achievement in itself, clearly came across in our interviews. The second element (authority/power) was rarely evident in the responses we received, indicating perhaps a more enlightened, pioneering approach within music, again at odds with the popular perception of the entrepreneur as being primarily profit (or status) focused. Affiliation was implied in terms of networking but not directly stated. Most of our interviewees tended to work alone or to lead a team. It is possible, then, that music entrepreneurship is driven by the desire for affiliation within a business network rather than an immediate group of co-workers.

Our interviewees identified a range of opportunities and motivations. Some wished to counter a perceived gap in the market – 'The issue we hoped to address was the lack of distribution options for unsigned and independent musicians' (Gray, 2014). Equally, others were motivated by the desire to see positive change – 'Our company is built upon the premise that we want beer to be better at venues. It is shocking that fans pay a lot of money for tickets to see a fantastic artist, but are forced to drink very poor quality alcohol from a plastic cup for vastly inflated prices. This really needs to change' (Riley, 2013). The opportunity was often presented as an issue the entrepreneur wished to resolve.

Challenge/determination/failure as a learning experience

An entrepreneur also sees and is attracted to the challenge involved in undertaking a project. This challenge could be to overcome public scepticism or previous failure, to provide a service or product to fulfil an identified need, to prove to herself/himself that she/he can do it or simply to prove others wrong.

This notion of challenge was a common thread running through the interviews we conducted, as we found that the young music entrepreneur sees these as challenges and learning opportunities, *not* problems. When questioned, almost without exception, entrepreneurs stated that they would change nothing about their entrepreneurial history, citing challenges (including failure) as learning experiences. 'I can't think of anything I would change. I have learned from my mistakes and taken something from every job in the industry that I've had' (Barnes, 2013); 'I probably wouldn't change anything really' (Riley, 2013).

This discovery in turn came to be one of the defining entrepreneurial qualities of those people we spoke to. Most shook their heads, laughed or exhaled loudly when asked to expand on their answer, as one does when recalling experiences which were less than enjoyable, but most agreed that the negative experiences were the ones from which they learned the most. 'None, as every mistake/balls up/embarrassing incident is crucial learning' (Gorman, 2013). The young entrepreneurs we met seemed to expect difficulties to occur and accepted them as an everyday part of their work. More than this, they often identified the problems and challenges as *the* essential learning experiences. 'I embrace failure as a guiding path to success because it tells me where not to go . . . don't be afraid of failure. Success by the way of luck doesn't tell you anything' (Bothra, 2014).

As we shall see, the negotiated and often improvised solutions employed to overcome these challenges provided essential learning experiences for the emerging entrepreneur and, in many cases, new business contacts who helped to expand their network of associates, which in itself was identified as a key to development and progress. In fact, the acceptance of failure as a key learning tool rather than a stumbling block became a key theme within the interviews. In essence, learn from your mistakes and keep going.

Networking

Almost all of our case study interviewees identified networking (social and professional) as a key entrepreneurial ability. 'The power of networking is phenomenal' (O'Callaghan, 2014). 'This industry is all about who you know' (Barnes, 2013). The messages from our interviewees included: an individual in music is not able to function as an island; an entrepreneur's network of contacts is her/his employment radar and roster of potential assistants, the web of potential entrepreneurial activities and the other music professionals an entrepreneur meets and gets to know will be able to inform them of potential opportunities, appropriate work or become business partners themselves.

This echoes Scott (2012) in his identification of 'cultural intermediaries', the individuals within the arts who rise to a position of networking importance (gatekeepers as referred to by Caves, 2002), who can greatly assist an emerging artist (or not). Networking may well allow emerging professionals to become part of this group, which, of course, would be highly beneficial to their own careers as well as others.

Importantly, our interviewees did not believe you needed to be a larger-than-life character to engage possible contacts in conversation or to grow your network. 'Networking skills are pretty damn important. That's not necessarily being the world's most outgoing and friendly person, because for some of us that's never going to happen. What it does mean though is having the confidence to talk to someone and express yourself' (Riley, 2013). Also, 'I was uncomfortable with networking to begin with, but it's like gearing up for a stage performance – you start with small talk – you need to make sure you know what you're talking about. Some key personnel can be quite bullish or off-putting but you don't need to talk to the top person – you just need to get a contact at the company' (O'Callaghan, 2014).

Finally, being cautious and selective in identifying your potential network contacts is important. 'Young entrepreneurs are more selective in their networking and there are huge amounts of character analysis. They will suss out a contact and then approach them – they're looking for a reciprocal approach – what's to gain/share? If you take an empathetic approach you will be more approachable yourself' (O'Callaghan, 2014).

Exchanging not buying

Music entrepreneurs, due to the nature of the music industries, can (and actually are required to) work in different ways from the more general definition of an entrepreneur. We found many instances of young music entrepreneurs facing the difficulty of requiring specialist professional assistance. Lee Denny, promoter of LeeFest, for example, described a situation where at short notice he required legal assistance for development of the festival with the local council. Without financial means or detailed legal knowledge, he became worried that the event would not be able to continue. The solution came in meeting a legal expert who was happy to assist at low cost in return for being identified with the festival and gaining an introduction to others in the events industry who might also require his help. This exchange of services, mutual low cost/no cost assistance, appeared to be commonplace in music where emerging artists do not have the capital to afford studios, photography and other essential promotional tools required as part of their development. In effect, therefore, they develop a type of barter economy.

Scott (2012), for example, describes such 'cultural entrepreneurs' as having high artistic aspirations, but meagre financial resources instantiating a kind of 'barter economy'. 'As these DIY producers lack sufficient economic capital to pay professionals to produce complex products (recordings, videos, promotional material) and events (live performances, tours) they initiate contact with other established (or unestablished) cultural entrepreneurs who have the requisite skills and resources – designers, video makers et al. Due to similar professional standing in their industries, these cultural entrepreneurs all work for exposure, experience, friendship or interest.'

This idea is echoed in the interview with Steve Broadfoot where on a number of occasions when raising awareness of his product LugPlugs (hearing protection for the music industries), he exchanged quantities of the product for the profile gained from those seen using them. Equally, he was assisted by former contacts in the live music industry to further his business as they understood that this sector of the music industries requires an awareness of the potential damage to audience hearing (Broadfoot, 2013).

Passion/work ethic

The final thread in the responses we garnered was passion for what you do coupled with a strong work ethic. 'If you love your business you will not stop thinking of ways to make it bigger and better. To be an entrepreneur in the music business or any business you can never switch off the love you have for what you do' (Nyah, 2014). When asked for the most valuable attributes for a young entrepreneur, one quality consistently came to the fore: 'Passion. Whatever aspect of the music industry you wish to work in, passion will give you the drive and determination to achieve your dreams. A raw passion combined with talent will fuel learning' (O'Callaghan, 2014); 'Genuine passion for music, enthusiasm' (Barnes, 2013).

As we will see in the conclusions, this became one of the key findings of our research. Emerging music project developers routinely cited the love of what you do as a primary motivator, totally distinct from (and mostly ignoring) the drive for financial gain. In this, our music entrepreneurs were almost unanimous: you need to have passion for your project/business in order for it to succeed.

Summary: Characteristics of the music entrepreneur

The music entrepreneur, then, can potentially be seen to require a range of skills in order to maximize her/his chances of success (self-belief, networking skills, bartering and negotiating, understanding and learning from failure, passion). Can the emerging music entrepreneur be educated to instil these abilities? The QAA (Quality Assurance Agency) Scotland report, Creating Entrepreneurial Campuses, states: 'as a result of research over the past 25 years there is now a body of knowledge and skills about entrepreneurship which underpins entrepreneurship education and training that is now readily available to enhance the chances of entrepreneurial and personal success' (QAA, 2014). This brings us full circle back to what education can do to develop the emerging music professional.

Conclusions: Entrepreneurship in music education

I identified at the start of this chapter that music lecturers face significant initial resistance to business thinking. The community element within education, allowing groups of students (emerging performers, songwriters, producers, managers, record label personnel and events promoters) to interact and learn from each other notwithstanding, our original question was do *all* of these different types of music students need entrepreneurial skills? The evidence appears to indicate that perhaps they do. Accordingly, within my own experience, introducing business skills and project management as an essential part of the course for every music student (performance, business or production) has been a key principle within the programmes I have developed since the early 1990s. From the start of my work in education, it was obvious to me that sending musicians and music producers in particular out into the world armed with only artistic and/or technical ability and a certificate, was insufficient for sustaining a career in the modern music industries. This would often cause problems for many of them, as they failed to understand the necessity of skills such as financial planning, time and resource management, and setting objectives when all they wanted was to work 'in music'.

Thus, it could be said that it is important for music industries educators to deliver what students *need* as well as what students *want*, even if they do not yet know they need it. In a group of industries that appear to depend on entrepreneurship, educators are perhaps failing students if they do not teach them how to develop the planning and communication abilities that will assist them in developing a professional career. In this regard, it would appear, business development skills are fundamental for anyone entering any sector of the music industries and it is therefore the duty of programme leaders to ensure those skills are embedded in the teaching, content and delivery.

This principle is also being examined from a music education perspective in the US. Manhattan School of Music president, Robert Sirota, has commented that, 'just adding a business course or two in isn't enough to keep up with the times'. His vision is to foster 'a new generation of performing musicians who function more like individual small businesses' (cited in Miller, 2007). Derek Mithaug, Career Development Director at Manhattan's Juilliard School, demonstrating that US music students are more like their UK counterparts than their professional countrymen, states that the term 'entrepreneur' still elicits the wrong reaction from students. 'We try to avoid that word' he says. Mithaug does, however, understand the need for these skills in music education. The Career Development Office he directs only opened its doors in 2000. Before that 'there was no office, no nothing' (Miller, 2007). By 2007 about 25 per cent of Juilliard students were participating in the school's professional mentoring programme. This figure may well increase over time, but is this enough?

Many of the entrepreneurs interviewed for this book experienced the benefits of further or higher education (college or university) as part of their learning. Not all studied on music-specific programmes, but many gained valuable knowledge from the business aspects of their chosen course. 'At college and university I completed an HND [UK college qualification] in Business and Music Industry Management, a BA (Hons) in Management, Business and Administration, and an MBA in Music Industries. I think that these qualifications gave me a good grounding in a variety of subjects that have been important, for example law, specifically music industries related, finance and management but so much of the work I have done in my professional career could just not be taught' (Gray, 2014).

'I have an NC [UK college qualification] in Music and Promotions from North Glasgow College and a BA (Hons) degree in Commercial Music from Westminster University. Both these courses were hugely valuable and the fact they were recognized within the music industry meant that I was given work experience opportunities which may have been harder to get if I had just tried to get a job in the music industry straight from school' (Barnes, 2014).

'I went to college and did an HND in Music Performance and Promotion (specialising in Business) before going straight into the third year BA (Hons) Commercial Music degree at university, staying on for a further year to gain honours. This was hugely valuable to me, and I most certainly would not be where I am now without having studied in this way' (Gorman, 2013).

UK courses designed to prepare students specifically to enter employment in the business sectors (music publishing, artist management, concert promotion, for example) clearly require business skills education as a central foundation. However, performance and production courses do not always necessarily see themselves as being required to focus so much on business and entrepreneurial skills. A brief examination of the content of a series of college and university performance and production courses, undertaken as part of the research for the Music Education Directory (UK Music, 2013), reveals that as little as one business or career development module per year (in some cases as little as 10 per cent of overall teaching) is considered acceptable for these student cohorts, often less.

Given that as many as 24,000 students are emerging from music courses each year in the UK alone (UK Music, 2013) and current employment in the music industries is around 100,000 (UK Music, 2013), it becomes clear that entrepreneurship teaching is vital within these courses to support employment generally if not specifically. We cannot expect functioning organizations in music to expand continuously or retire around a quarter of their workforce annually to make way for incoming graduates. The US, however, does seem to be making progress in this direction. Harding, writing in Beckman (2011), states: 'The answer . . . is for emerging professional musicians to acquire . . . a set of skills . . . not possessed naturally or learned formally. This knowledge. . . [is] embodied in one discipline: entrepreneurship.'

Slowly, it would appear, music education in the UK and the US is moving towards the understanding that entrepreneurship is an important part of student learning. These territories have two of the most developed sets of music industries in the world. They may just be beginning to see the value of music entrepreneurship education.

Notes

1 See Williamson and Cloonan (2007). This article argues for the use of the term 'music industries' (covering all industrialized music activity but primarily in the recording, live and publishing industries) to avoid confusion caused by the repeated conflation of the 'music industry' with 'the recording industry'.

2 Debate continues amongst researchers over the definition of these industries. Caves, for example, uses the term 'creative industries' (2002), where Hesmondhalgh selects 'cultural industries' (2007). Given that 'creative' can be seen to imply on-going innovation where 'cultural' could be interpreted as 'that which already exists', we believe that the former term is more appropriate for the purposes of examining the possible underlying entrepreneurial activity. Hence we will use the term 'creative industries' throughout this book to describe the broader field which the music industries sit within.

3 DCMS. The UK government's Department for Culture, Media and Sport.

4 Fairwood Music (Publishing) represents songwriters; their catalogue includes work by David Bowie, Rizzle Kicks, Tina Turner and Katie Melua.

5 Over a thirty-five-year career, Mick Glossop has produced acts as diverse as Van Morrison, Suede, Sinead O'Conner and Public Image.

References

Aggestam, M. (2007), 'Art-entrepreneurship in the Scandinavian music industry', in C. Henry (ed.), *Entrepreneurship in the Creative Industries*, Cheltenham: Edward Elgar, pp. 30–53.

Anderson, C. (2008), *The (Longer) Long Tail: Why the Future of Business is Selling Less of More*, 2nd ed., New York: Hyperion, pp. 1–14.

ArcTanGent (2014), 'ArcTanGent Festival', available at: http://arctangent.co.uk/ [accessed 19 May 2014].

Barnhart, R.K. (1988), *The Barnhart Dictionary of Etymology*, London: H.W. Wilson, p. 78.

BBC 6 Music, http://www.bbc.co.uk/programmes/b00c000j

Beckman, G.D. (2011), 'Why music entrepreneurship and why in college music education?', in G.D. Beckman (ed.) *Disciplining the Arts*, Lanham, MD: Rowman and Littlefield Education, pp. 17–24.

Billboard (2012). 'How the K-Pop Breakout Star Harnessed the Power of YouTube, SNL and More to Become Music's New Global Brand', available at: http://www.billboard.com/articles/columns/k-town/474456/psys-gangnam-style-the-billboard-cover-story?page=0%2C1 [accessed 22 June 2014].

Billboard (2001), 'Napster, RIAA Spar In Court', available at: http://www.billboard.com/articles/news/77473/napster-riaa-spar-in-court [accessed 22 June 2014].

Cantillon, R. (2010; 1755), *An Essay on Economic Theory*, Auburn, AL: LVMI.

Casson, M. (2003), *The Entrepreneur: An Economic Theory*, Cheltenham: Edward Elgar.

Caves, R.E. (2002), *Creative Industries, Contracts Between Art and Commerce*, 2nd ed., Cambridge, MA: Harvard University Press.

Celtic Connections (2014), 'Celtic Connections Festival', available at: http://www.celticconnections.com/ [accessed 19 May 2014].

Chell, E. (1985), 'The entrepreneurial personality: A few ghosts laid to rest?', *International Small Business Journal* 3: 43–54.

Department of Culture, Media and Sport (2001), Creative Industries Mapping Document 2001, London: DCMS.

Drucker, P.F. (2007), *Innovation and Entrepreneurship*, Oxford: Butterworth-Heinemann.

Frith, S. (2001), 'The popular music industry', in S. Frith, W. Straw and J. Street (eds.), *The Cambridge Companion to Pop and Rock*, Cambridge: Cambridge University Press, pp. 26–52.

Harrison, A. (2008), *Music the Business: The Essential Guide to the Law and the Deals*, 4th ed., London: Virgin Books.

Hesmondhalgh, D. (2007), *The Cultural Industries*, 2nd ed., London: Sage Publications.

Howkins, J. (2007), *The Creative Economy*, 2nd ed., London: Penguin.

Ingham, T. (2012), 'Revealed: The true value of "360" deals to labels', available at: http://www.musicweek.com/news/read/360-deals-spark-76m-income-for-labels-in-2011/052043 [accessed 16 May 2014].

International Federation of Phonographic Industries (2007), *The Recording Industry in Numbers 2006*, London: IFPI.

International Federation of Phonographic Industries (2012), *The Recording Industry in Numbers 2011*, London: IFPI.

International Federation of Phonographic Industries (2014), *The Recording Industry in Numbers 2013*, London: IFPI.

Jones, R. (2013), '360 deals are "immoral", says Neil Warnock', available at: http://www.musicweek.com/news/read/neil-warnock-360-deals-are-immoral/053740 [accessed 16 May 2014].

Karubian, S. (2009), '360° deals: An industry reaction to the devaluation of recorded music', *Southern California Interdisciplinary Law Journal* 18: 395–462.

Lindvall, H. (2011), 'K-pop: how South Korea turned round its music scene', available at: http://www.theguardian.com/media/organgrinder/2011/apr/20/k-pop-south-korea-music-market [accessed 18 May 2015].

Mahr, K. (2012), 'South Korea's Greatest Export: How K-Pop's Rocking the World', available at: http://world.time.com/2012/03/07/south-koreas-greatest-export-how-k-pops-rocking-the-world/ [accessed 16 May 2014].

Matthews, C., http://www.cerysmatthews.co.uk/bio.php [accessed 25 November 2014].

Miller, K. (2007), 'Teaching musicians to be entrepreneur', *Business Week*, 28 March 2007.

McLelland, D. (1987), *Human Motivation*, Cambridge: Cambridge University Press, pp. 223–372.

Music Week (2005), 'BPI in new anti-filesharing push', available at: http://www.musicweek.com/news/read/bpi-in-new-anti-filesharing-push/028602 [accessed 22 June 2014].

Office for National Statistics (2014), 'Self-employed workers in the UK – 2014', available at: http://www.ons.gov.uk/ons/rel/lmac/self-employed-workers-in-the-uk/2014/rep-self-employed-workers-in-the-uk-2014.html#tab-Self-employed-workers-in-the-UK

Passman, D. (2013), *All You Need to Know About the Music Business*, 8th ed., New York: Simon and Schuster, p. 63.

Pfanner, E. (2013), 'Music Industry Sales Rise, and Digital Revenue Gets the Credit', available at: http://www.nytimes.com/2013/02/27/technology/music-industry-records-first-revenue-increase-since-1999.html?_r=0 [accessed 22 June 2014].

Quality Assurance Agency Scotland (2014), *Creating Entrepreneurial Campuses*, QAA: Gloucester.

Scott, M. (2012), 'Cultural entrepreneurs, cultural entrepreneurship: Music producers mobilising and converting Bourdieu's alternative capitals', *Poetics* 40: 237–55.

Stinchfield, B., R. Nelson, and M. Wood (2013), 'Learning from Levi-Strauss' Legacy: Art, Craft, Engineering, Bricolage and Brokerage in Entrepreneurship', *Entrepreneurship, Theory and Practice* 37: 889–921.

Swedberg, R. (2006), 'The cultural entrepreneur and the creative industries: beginning in Vienna', *Journal of Cultural Economics* 30: 243–61.

Sweney, M. (2011), 'Global recorded music sales fall almost $1.5bn amid increased piracy', available at: http://www.theguardian.com/business/2011/mar/28/global-recorded-music-sales-fall [accessed 16 May 2014].

UK Music (2013), *Music Education Directory 2013*, available at: http://www.ukmusic.org/skills-academy/music-education-directory/ [accessed 22 June 2014].

UK Music (2013), *The Economic Contribution of the Core UK Music Industry*, London: UK Music.

Williamson, J. and M. Cloonan (2007), 'Rethinking the "music industry"', *Popular Music* 26 (2): 305–22.

Young, S. and S. Collins (2010), 'A view from the trenches of music 2.0', *Popular Music and Society* 33 (3): 339–55.

YouTube (2014), https://www.youtube.com/results?search_query=gangnam+style [accessed 21 December 2014].

3

From DIY to D2F:

Contextualizing Entrepreneurship for the Artist/Musician

*Holly Tessler and
Matthew Flynn*

Introduction

Whilst entrepreneurship has always been a part of the music industries' activity, it is important to understand how the role and nature of entrepreneurial activity has evolved as the music industries themselves have changed over time. The first section of the chapter looks at entrepreneurship from a historical perspective, with particular attention to its relevance to the recorded music sector through the rise of DIY (do-it-yourself) recording in the post-Punk era of the 1970s. The second section examines how the collapse of the traditional recorded music business model in the mid-to-late-1990s created new opportunities for independent musicians and labels and established new, more entrepreneurial business practices, most notably the 360-degree contract. The third section of the chapter looks at the impact digitalization has had on entrepreneurship in the music industries, affording aspirant musicians and labels opportunities to record, produce and distribute their music by means and through channels beyond the traditional music industries' infrastructure. This digital 'musicscape' (cf. Roberts, 2013; Lashua and Cohen, 2010; Oakes, 2000), which includes new media like the streaming service Spotify, new applications like Bandcamp and new financing options like the crowdfunding site Kickstarter all require musician-entrepreneurs to acquire a suite of technical, legal and business skills to navigate these and other online environments. The musician Tommy Darker (cited in Songhack.com, 2014) has coined the phrase 'musicpreneur' to describe this set of skills.

The primary issue this chapter seeks to explore is the implications for musicians in having to exist within the intersections of creativity, industry and entrepreneurship. Is this interconnectedness ultimately good for music and/or musicians? What are the issues faced by aspirant musicians when simple market entry now demands they run their fledgling bands like entrepreneurial businesses?

Part 1: Entrepreneurship and DIY

A useful place to begin consideration of the role and significance of entrepreneurship in the music industries is with the Punk era of the 1970s. Punk established in the late 1960s and early 1970s, the first swathe of entrepreneurial UK independent record labels, including Immediate, Virgin and Chrysalis, like their US predecessors, predominantly operated in a style not terribly different from the traditional major label business model. But by the mid-1970s, the political and civil unrest permeating throughout many of the UK's larger cities began to manifest itself in the popular music and culture of the age. The anger and frustration felt by many young people reflected their increasing dissatisfaction with traditional social hierarchies and political and governmental power structures. The lyrics and titles of songs like 'Anarchy in the UK' and 'God Save The Queen' by the Sex Pistols, plainly illustrate the desire for change amongst young musicians and music fans. Similarly, Punk's simple and unadorned musical constructs not only sought to move away from the overblown excesses of Progressive Rock, but also encouraged anyone interested to pick up a guitar and learn three chords (Laing, 1985).

Even more significantly, however, Punk's aesthetics motivated a differently inflected set of business and industrial practices which helped to establish an entirely new entrepreneurial paradigm: DIY, or do-it-yourself. At the heart of the DIY movement was a shared love of Punk music and the ideals it celebrated. The lines between musician, fan and entrepreneur grew increasingly blurred as activities like distributing fanzines, running small, specialist record shops, promoting Punk nights at neighbourhood venues and, of course, forming bands, helped to create alternative and often tightly-knit local Punk communities. Most relevant to this discussion, however, the people involved in Punk/DIY created a hybrid network of labels/studios/shops and sometimes venues that were operating wholly apart from the well-trodden paths established by the majors: Rough Trade, Beggar's Banquet, Probe and Factory amongst them. These enterprises enabled Punk (and latterly other non-mainstream genres of popular music) to travel beyond London, to regions of the UK where often the only option for purchasing or even hearing new music was in high street shops. But perhaps inevitably, Punk's growing popularity eventually nudged it into the mainstream, where major label investment sought to develop the genre's full commercial potential, which in turn, catalysed its decline in both credibility and popularity amongst its original fanbase. Prominent Punk fanzine creator, Mark P publicly and famously commented that, 'Punk died the day The Clash signed to CBS' (cited in Montague, 2006: 438). However, Hesmondhalgh (1997), citing Laing (1985) and Frith and Horne (1987), rightly asserts that to characterize the Punk movement in such polarizing terms would be too simplistic a description. Both aesthetically and industrially, Punk was a more nuanced and complicated genre than its often celebrated popular history affords, with working-class mixing with middle-class, art-school sensibilities blending with dole-queue politics. Remaining intact after Punk's seeming decline were the origins of a new kind of music entrepreneurship: 'an independent distribution network which would run in parallel with, and in opposition to, the distribution facilities of major record companies' (Hesmondhalgh, 1997: 257).

From Punk to post-Punk

A small number of independent shops and labels that began during the Punk era remained in business through the 1980s, and increasingly moved to redress the market gap left by the majors. Working with independent wholesalers and distributors, indie shops would often meet consumers' demand for music in niche genres or specialist areas (Hesmondhalgh, 1997). Where indies succeeded, they did so through an explicit, entrepreneurial local knowledge of niche music. These shops would offer customers opportunities to purchase music that could not be found on the high street: rare and/or deleted recordings, imports, alternative genres, sometimes even live or bootleg releases. Most notably, they would also allocate space for releases by unsigned local acts, thus often becoming a hangout or hub for local musicians.

Following the pattern established in the Punk era, many of these indie shop owners would meet local demand for access to recording facilities by allocating space for the setup of small, rudimentary studios. In this way, as Hesmondhalgh (1997) describes, indie music shops became a locus for the establishment of an entirely new and independent sector of recorded music. Shops such as Beggar's Banquet and Probe were record label, distributor, retailer and music meeting place all in one. Where major labels and high street shops sought to attract the mainstream and indiscriminate, indie shops aimed to target the local and the knowledgeable music fan.

Hesmondhalgh identifies three key ways in which the post-Punk era influenced music entrepreneurship; namely the 50/50 profit split, contract duration and artistic autonomy (1997: see pp. 260–3 for more detail). One of the most positive outcomes of the post-Punk independent sector was that for fans who were looking for sounds beyond those found on the high street, these innovative business and creative practices created an entirely new space for local musicians who existed both geographically and aesthetically outside London's musical mainstream. However, just as with Punk itself in the 1970s, post-Punk's success ultimately proved its downfall. By the early 1980s, a number of indie labels were enjoying substantial success, most notably, Factory Records' signing of Joy Division, Rough Trade's signing of The Smiths and Mute's signing of Depeche Mode. As with The Clash's 1977 deal with CBS, the more popular post-Punk acts became, the more pressure there was to produce a more mainstream sound. And the more mainstream a sound, the bigger the lure to sign a major-label deal. By the 1990s, so many post-Punk acts had become so successful with their 'alternative' sound, a new genre of so-called 'indie' music began to emerge, focused less on innovative aesthetic and entrepreneurial activities and more on the particular sound and look that the designation of 'indie' had now come to embody (Hesmondhalgh, 1997). However, as Hesmondhalgh points out, to simply dismiss the post-Punk independent sector's lasting contribution to the music industries as that of only being a conduit to the majors, preparing initially niche acts for an eventual global audience, would be to fundamentally misunderstand the entrepreneurial nature of the independent sector as a whole. The nascent dance music and rave scenes that emerged in the UK at the end of the 1980s, in the same way that post-Punk indie was co-opted by the mainstream, reaffirmed the entrepreneurial nature of the independent sector.

From the late 1970s to the early 1990s, indie labels exhibited innovation and entrepreneurship in a number of significant ways. First, labels identified and redressed a gap in the marketplace that was unmet by major label practices and activities. Second, despite some examples to the contrary, such as the Stone Roses' protracted battle to get out of their deal with Silvertone (Harrison, 2008: 108–9) generally the indies developed more 'humane' contractual dealings with acts signed to their labels instead of relying on outmoded and unfair long-term deals. Rather than aiming to maximize profit and minimize expenditures, independent labels would work sympathetically with acts to deliver a recording that was creatively fulfilling, seeking to balance aesthetics and finance through a more controlled and rational approach than majors typically had. Lastly, by working in relatively more artist-friendly terms, the independent sector influenced the business practices of major labels, specifically in the creation of the 360-degree deal. Read collectively, all of these independent-sector activities both empowered and compelled musicians to become meaningfully engaged with the business and industry of music-making.

The development of the UK independent sector offered musicians access to markets previously unavailable to them. Operating under the tag of 'bedroom producers,' musicians using increasingly affordable digital samplers and computer software could self-produce dance music tracks without the need to spend extensive periods of time in costly recording studios. Digitization was democratizing the means of music production and the digital sounds produced were reaching large audiences at illegal raves, organized by entrepreneurial promoters in and around the UK's major cities and at holiday destinations like Ibiza. And whilst some musicians became involved in the entrepreneurial practice of label ownership, fanzines, gig promotion and the like, for many, the risks remained solely creative ones. DIY enabled musicians to grasp the principles of the record business beyond the major label oligopoly, but despite the DIY ethos, Jones' assertion that the 'music industry is how the people who make up music companies work with and through the efforts of musicians to make a profit on the investment of time, money and effort they expend on taking musicians and their music to market' (2012: 11) remains broadly accurate.[1]

Part 2: Major labels and 360-degree deals

One of the most lasting effects both the Punk and post-Punk indie movements had on the music industries was to change the nature and understanding of the interactions between creativity and commerce. Working within a DIY environment necessarily compelled musicians to be inherently more entrepreneurial in their activities. Beyond composing, writing, and recording songs, local and unsigned Punk- and post-Punk-era musicians also needed to consider the *business* of being a musician. The nature of many indie-label deals meant that there was often little or no marketing budget to promote an act or an album. And without an accountant or business manager, it was often down to the act itself to look after its royalties and other earnings. The more autonomous and short-term elements of independent record deals meant that acts were largely free to explore and create their own opportunities – a development that was not lost on the major labels of the period.

By the 1990s, a series of corporate bankruptcies, mergers and acquisitions meant that there were just five major record companies operating in international markets: EMI, BMG, Sony, Warner and Universal. In this period, this so-called 'Big 5' enjoyed an oligopoly over all aspects of recorded music, controlling an estimated 90 per cent of the global music market

(BBCWorldService.com, 2014). But the Big 5's dominance did not come without its share of problems. Where once signing a deal with a major record label was the ultimate goal of most aspirant pop acts, by the 1990s, many major-label deals were seen as increasingly unfair to the acts who signed them. High-profile legal action taken against the majors by Prince and George Michael brought into the public sphere the often stringent and limiting conditions contained within some major-label recorded music contracts. At the same time, in the United States, the majors were also battling with retailers and consumers, who, through a series of class-action lawsuits, alleged that the major labels had not only conspired to keep the prices of recorded music albums unfairly high (at an average of about US$15 in the mid-1990s) but also pressured major retail chains to keep from offering consumers promotional discounts or sale prices (Borland, 2000). Read together, by the 1990s the traditional business practices of the major labels had alienated acts, retailers and consumers alike. Thus, it is hardly surprising that when digital and online technologies reached speeds and capacities that made downloading and filesharing a reality, there was a tremendous backlash against major labels from all sides. Where the Big 5 once enjoyed a virtual stranglehold on all aspects of production, distribution and consumption of recorded music, emerging Internet technologies and companies meant the majors' influence and power was now greatly diminished. At first, the power to upload, download and share files at will was perceived to be a potentially democratizing force – enabling anyone with access to a computer, the Internet and requisite software to record, produce, release and promote their own recordings, seemingly rendering the need to sign a contract with a major label all but irrelevant. And of course, with peer-to-peer and filesharing programs like Napster and later LimeWire and Kazaa, consumers were no longer left with their only option being to purchase expensive albums when all the music they could ever want was now accessible (freely) online. It was clear this 'digital watershed' had brought fundamental change to the all aspects of the record industry and the old ways of doing business would be upended.

Unsurprisingly, the major labels were loath to embrace the changes that the digital era heralded. MusicNet and PressPlay, the Big 5's initial, half-hearted attempts to sell their music online belied their resistance to even realistically consider the potential opportunities this new digital marketplace might hold. This is the period of 'un-entrepreneurial resistance' referred to by Alison Wenham (Wenham, 2014). Whilst the majors dithered, a series of new online enterprises emerged, bringing with them an entirely new conception of how the music industries could function in both the physical and digital worlds. Most notably, Apple successfully launched iTunes. Whilst ubiquitous today, iTunes was, in its 2003 launch, significant for a number of reasons. First, iTunes provided for both the music industries and consumers an easy-to-use, affordable and legal alternative to filesharing. Where the Big 5 simply wanted all unregulated online activity to cease, Apple embraced the entrepreneurial opportunity to develop an entirely new business model: the 'a la carte' system. Whilst not without its drawbacks, providing consumers with an opportunity to purchase individual tracks and not just whole albums provided music fans a means of legally owning music that was an easier, faster and more reliable option than peer-to-peer-driven filesharing. Third, iTunes was an early example of the kind of integrative thinking that has come to drive the creative industries in the twenty-first century, allowing consumers to seamlessly link up devices (like computers, tablets and mobile phones), applications (like iTunes) and content.

Where the majors effectively missed their opportunity to help create their own space in the digital marketplace, the broader concepts of integration and convergence did not escape their attention. Where many artists, indie labels and even music fans celebrated the seemingly inevitable demise of the major labels,[2] the labels themselves took a new, holistically and entrepreneurially motivated new approach to how they might re-invent their role in these 'new' music industries. One way the majors have, at least in part, rebounded from diminishing album sales is through the use of the 360-degree deal. A new way of understanding the role of record companies, 360-degree deals provide more favourable terms for artists, including elements like an increased royalty rate, shorter contract duration and more creative control. In exchange, the label receives revenue from every one of the artist's income streams: recording, publishing, touring, merchandising, endorsements and the like. Whilst the costs and benefits of 360-degree contracts are debatable, the point most germane to this discussion is the fact that 360-degree deals have created a necessarily more entrepreneurial environment within the music industries.

Where once album sales were the primary driver of much music industry activity, today, they are just one element within a much broader creative industries environment where music is not only a product in and of itself, but increasingly integrated with other entertainment and media products: video games, streaming audio, film and TV programmes, advertising, web channels and YouTube videos. For consumers, this kind of media integration and content convergence means that music can be accessed anywhere. For labels and publishers, integration and convergence means there is an ever-increasing number of new opportunities to promote and exploit songs and sound recordings. Owning and exploiting the 'basket of rights' (Frith, 1988: 57) affiliated with every aspect of an artist's commercial activity is now essential for profit maximization. But what does this integrated creative industries environment mean for musicians? Echoing the DIY ethos of the Punk era, the wide-open spaces of the digital marketplace has, in effect, required all aspiring artists to become entrepreneurial start-up businesses. As Rodgers observes, 'The proliferating range of digital platforms for the marketing, promotion and distribution of music offers seemingly endless possibilities for creative artists (both established and aspiring) to access an audience to a level that would have been inconceivable less than a generation ago' (2013: 177). But the opportunities to connect directly with fans/consumers places expectations upon musicians historically beyond their purview. Whilst DIY culture may have generated a less esoteric understanding of record business amongst musicians, much of the value was still created through the entrepreneurialism of the people working in the independent labels. Even something as simple as having an active presence on a site such as Bandcamp demands that self-sustaining musicians demonstrate a suite of creative and technical skills, including writing, performing, producing and mastering music, designing artwork, marketing and promotion and understanding contract and copyright law and accountancy. Developing each new non-musical skill potentially distracts musicians from focusing on their core competencies of writing and performing music. The remainder of the chapter considers the issues faced by today's aspiring musicians who are confronted with the challenges of integrating the often conflicted and contested intersections of music, creativity and entrepreneurship.

Part 3: From DIY to D2F

For musicians and artists operating outside the existing 'Web of major and minor music companies' (Negus, 1992: 27), digitalization and the Internet have created new entrepreneurial opportunities for music to be heard. Ready and affordable access to digital recording technologies has enabled all musicians wishing to do so to produce their own recordings (Anderton, Dubber and James, 2013). Although established bands like Marillion had for sometime entrepreneurially extended their careers beyond the termination of their major label deals, using mail-order newsletters and distribution to sell direct to their existing fanbase, digital platforms adapted the business model so that aspiring acts no longer needed labels to distribute their music.

D2F (direct-to-fan) opportunities emerged at the end of the 1990s, with online stores such as CD Baby affording DIY musicians direct access to international markets for the first time. CD Baby's success heralded the emerging shift from physically distributed micro (Strachan, 2007) and indie labels, to online D2F digital platforms in two significant ways. First, CD Baby founder Derek Sivers was a musician who adapted his creative, technical and business skills to develop a website that provided an Internet solution to a music distribution problem he personally experienced (Sivers, 2010). The aptitude to learn programming and web design, or partner with someone who could would become one of the distinctive characteristics of the twenty-first-century digital music entrepreneur. Second, digital democratization of physical distribution shifted notions of independence away from the increasingly mainstream indie label operation, down to the level of the individual artist and musician. As producing and pressing CDs was still time, cost and technologically prohibitive for most musicians, the emergent MP3 technology enabled aspiring artists and acts to instantaneously, directly and virtually freely distribute their music direct to fans.

One such company to understand and exploit this emerging D2F marketplace was MP3.com, which pioneered the initial rush of unsigned artists onto digital distribution platforms. However, it was the advent and rapid rise of MySpace that firmly established D2F culture into the emergent twenty-first-century music industries. The mainstream media painted the success of bands such as the Arctic Monkeys and Lily Allen in the UK, and Hawthorne Heights in the US, as synonymous with, and tenuously credited to, their D2F engagement on MySpace. Although MySpace's demise was almost as quick as its rise, as it was usurped by Facebook, its heyday of 100m global users ushered in the social media dynamic to music production and consumption and fully realized the D2F business model.

The euphoria and hyperbole surrounding early D2F opportunities led Jenny Toomey, indie artist and director of the Future of Music Coalition, to claim, 'The only relationship that matters now is between the artist and the fan' (Toomey cited in Kott, 2009, p. 217). Digitalization had put the power of DIY's hybrid network of labels, studios and shops in the hands of every aspiring musician. In doing so, it also removed any remaining quality filter to market access. YouTube phenomenon Rebecca Black and her video for the song 'Friday' typified the 'new' Prosumer (Tapscott and Williams, 2008; Rojek, 2011: 11) market and renewed popular music debates around equating quantity with quality (*NME*, 2014). YouTube's 'broadcast yourself' vision encapsulated the removal of almost any risk to creating and publishing audio-visual recordings. The perceived removal of risk compared to the potential reward afforded by having the chance to go 'viral,' saw artists rush to market in an attempt to capitalize on new opportunities. The need to go viral, as a precursor for success, was so pervasive and compelling that by the end of the first decade of the twenty-first century, the Internet had become the fulcrum for artistic existence.

The competition for early market traction saw platforms offer artists contractual terms that made the short-term, 50-50 indie label deals look restrictive by comparison. Dependent on the cost of the set-up fee, platforms offered 80 to 100 per cent shares of sales or royalties in favour of the musician and most deals were non-exclusive, operating on a rolling basis and terminable by the artist with thirty days' notice. The rush to market by the platforms was met enthusiastically by artists, who for too long had been denied market access beyond their local music scenes. Long-held DIY ideals of democratization and Internet freedom drove early platform uptake. But once online, the community-spirited and self-styled entrepreneurialism and collaboration between artists and indie labels, was supplanted by ideologies that served the content agendas of the platforms. Whereas reclaiming the means of production was a politicized ideal in the DIY era, under D2F it was assumed to be an ever-present part of the creative process and the sole responsibility of the artist. Likewise, where indie labels had worked with the aesthetic sensibilities of the act, the D2F artist had total autonomy, but also responsibility to write, record and release whatever he wanted as often as he chose. Finally, where independent record deals meant acts were largely free to create their own opportunities, in the D2F model, artists had little choice but to create their own opportunities.

It is the subtle, but key distinction between being 'free to' and the imperative of 'having to' create opportunities that demands artists in the D2F paradigm adopt a fundamentally sharper entrepreneurial mindset than their DIY forbears. Having total entrepreneurial, as well as artistic, responsibility is the price for the artist friendly contractual terms and market access opportunities afforded to artists by digital platforms. The enthusiasm for this unashamed entrepreneurial spirit is evident in the shift in the nomenclature from describing an artist without a record or publishing deal as 'unsigned' to 'independent'. Even the 360-degree deals offered by major labels allude to a cultural, if not contractual, reclassification of the artist's status in the industry, away from exclusively contracted performers on recordings, towards joint venture partners in business endeavours. The benefits of the perception of artist credibility and authenticity of the autonomous entrepreneurial D2F approach was not lost on the major record labels either. Using a strategy tagged 'organic growth', new signings were often presented to audiences as unsigned D2F artists. This meant that labels could test market acts before fully committing further resources. But it also enabled them to cheaply develop dedicated fanbases they could later leverage when seeking support for the act in the mainstream media.

Foreshadowed by the entrepreneurial innovations in dance music that emphasized single tracks and playlists, building brands, the power of loosely aligned communities, consumer choice and social authorship (Toynbee, 2000: 162) D2F is the digital evolution of DIY. The entrepreneurial opportunity independent artists have to add value to their projects and careers, comes with the responsibility of using digital platforms effectively and advantageously. Not unlike the more familiar platform of the stage, where artists craft performances for the acceptance of audiences, each digital platform can be viewed as another instrument the artist must learn to play to be heard.

Part 4: Playing the platforms

Almost all digital platforms adopt the 'long tail' (Anderson, 2006) business model, meaning any artist can have a presence in the marketplace. The long tail theorizes that selling one download of a million tracks is as profitable as selling a million downloads of one track. Therefore, having as much choice as possible available online enhances the platforms' chances of turning a profit. Platforms incentivize artists to license their entire catalogues of recordings with favourable shares of sales royalties and low-cost sign-up fees as outlined in the previous section. Therefore, artists need to understand the processes that turn resources into outputs offline and adapt them online. Most importantly, the primary currency online is content. Artists need to become adept content creators going beyond the fundamental products of songs, recordings and performances to regularly deliver updates, pictures, videos, events, blogs, vlogs, comments and contribute to the conversation (cf. de Zengotita, 2005; Lanham, 2006; Dubber, 2007). Almost all artists use one or a combination of social media, including Facebook, Twitter, YouTube, Instagram, Pinterest, Mailchimp, Tumblr and the like as a way of communicating with and marketing and promoting to fans. Being effective on social media demands artists coordinate campaigns that link various platforms to each other. They need to learn, understand and apply marketing, PR and promotional techniques to build, manage and use databases of followers and friends. Social media, whilst not defined as a specific D2F platform, is generally where attention is initially sought. Interactive features like views, likes, plays, shares and comments both add to and measure the value of an artist's content. Artists cannot begin to monetize their content until it is in the conscious awareness of audiences. As Falkinger observes, 'The cost of attention-seeking is incurred because being present in buyers' minds is profitable' (2008: 1601). First and foremost D2F artists have to be entrepreneurial attention seekers, engaging and sustaining the audiences' awareness of them and their music.

Whilst social media platforms circulate content and capture attention they do not directly facilitate sales. Download stores like iTunes and Amazon, streaming services such as Spotify and Deezer, and hybrids like LastFM, whilst dominated by signed artists, are readily accessible to D2F artists. The delivery of digital tracks into sales platforms through aggregators, such as AWAL, The Orchard and MusicKickup is one of the key innovations of the D2F era, affording all musicians the legitimacy of being available in mainstream online stores. However, as Stern observes, 'the MP3 in most cases was not in any direct sense acquired for a price' (2012: loc 4287). The opportunity the MP3 afforded also heralded the devaluation of recorded unit format. Not unlike the problems faced by the major record labels, even if D2F artists were present in the minds of buyers, they would struggle to see a return on their investment, let alone a profit. Fortunately, digitization also offered new income streams through business-to-business and previously inaccessible publishing income.

Every platform facilitates direct and indirect income generation through the sales and use of the D2F artist's music. Consistent with Wikstrom's (2009) assertion that the music industries are best understood as copyright industries, for all these platforms and services, D2F artists need to understand copyright ownership, registration and administration and the contracts that define royalty splits of sales, publishing and performance income. Monetizing the attention their content receives in the same way as signed artists is feasible for D2F artists, but demands explicit knowledge of complex music industry structures.

Circumventing the complexity of industry structures is partly the appeal of platforms such as Reverbnation, MusicGlue, Topspin, Soundcloud and Bandcamp, all of which are self-referentially D2F. These platforms blend MySpace's profile-page approach with a PayPal account purchase feature, facilitating direct sales of physical and digital recordings, concert tickets and merchandise, in exchange for a percentage share of sales. They offer the complete collapse of the control of distribution by anyone other than the artist. Bandcamp, in particular, emulates the all-in-one record label, distributor, retailer and music meeting place once the domain of the independent record store. In championing niche genres and hosting a taste-making front page, Bandcamp also seeks to replicate the community spirit of the indie record store. Its strap line, 'Discover amazing new music and directly support the artists who make it' (Bandcamp, 2014: online) imbues the spirit of Punk, post-Punk DIY and independence, selling itself as an ideal entrepreneurial antidote to aspiring musicians locked out of the 'system'. These platforms enable D2F artists to closely monitor, respond to and capitalize upon the impact of the attention paid to their content. Aware audiences are turned into active fans by purchasing music, merchandise or tickets, supplying database information or advocating for artists across their own social media networks. This active engagement affords artists the opportunity to deepen their connections with fans.

The D2F platform that best represents the depth of connection between artist and fan is the patronage of artists by fans on crowdfunding sites such as Indiegogo and Pledge music. These platforms enable D2F artists to leverage their close connections with fans by allowing them to play a part in the production phase of projects. Somewhat distinctively, the notion of crowd funding sells the process as much as it does the actual product.

Like the indie labels that preceded them, D2F platforms demonstrate entrepreneurialism in offering alternative routes to market that quickly monetize D2F artists' content. Furthermore, unlike platforms such as iTunes and Spotify, that adhere to conventional copyright structures that are licensed and regulated by performing rights organizations (PROs), many D2F platform contracts demand users opt out of third-party royalty collection. The D2F platform circumvention of established copyright practices, in the pursuit of profit maximization, is another distinctive feature of these platforms' digital entrepreneurialism. However, the risk for all D2F platforms is whether their services are compelling enough to artists and fans to produce sufficient sales to make a profit.

The entrepreneurial logic of the long tail business model for the digital platforms means the aggregate success of artists already 'signed up' encourages more and more artists to play on the platform. As the major record labels recognized in the 1970s, repackaging their existing catalogues was a relatively risk-free endeavour that capitalized upon initial up-front risks already taken. Moreover, unlike the record labels, beyond building and improving the platform, all the risk of investment in content lies solely with the artist. In addition to offline areas such as gigs and scenes now offered by digital platforms appear more tangible to musicians than the rarity of signing a record deal. Therefore, D2F musicians' beliefs in defying the odds persist. So much so, the perception of self-determination on behalf of the artists means these platforms avoid the level of scepticism and animosity artists previously had for labels. The entrepreneurial genius of successful digital platforms is that they have commodified the proto-markets' 'vain hopes of glory' (Toynbee, 2000: 27–9) by positioning themselves as less an opportunity and more a necessity for aspiring artists. But has the ability and opportunity to be heard really changed the entrepreneurial landscape for musicians?

Part 5: The D2F entrepreneur

Where Anderson's long tail theory frames D2F markets as better entered than not, Elberse (2013: loc 1461) describes the music industry as a 'winner takes all' market, 'where large numbers of buyers are willing to pay a little more for the services of one performer over another'. Next Big Sound is one of several platforms that measures the social media reach of artists. Its 2013 industry report suggests that around 80 per cent of music-based activity on Facebook, Twitter and YouTube/Vimeo is driven by the top 1.1 per cent of mega- and mainstream signed artists, with the 90 per cent of D2F artists responsible for only 3 per cent of traffic. Viewed from this perspective, a 'winner takes all' analysis remains consistent with long-standing assertions that the majority product of the music industries is one of failure (Jones, 1999: 26; Knab and Day, 2013: 15). However, on his blog, 'How much do musicians really make on Bandcamp?' (2014: online), D2F artist Steve Lawson suggests that in the D2F era the *perception* of failure may have changed. After reaching the milestone of £10,000 worth of sales since opening an account on Bandcamp in 2009, Lawson, whilst acknowledging the £4,000 made in 2013 is below the minimum wage, compared to the work put in, remained optimistic 2014 would return enough profit to at least cover his rent. Moreover, for most musicians, as one element of a portfolio career (Myles, 2010: 321) that also includes performances, teaching, studio sessions and the like, Bandcamp offers an efficient additional income stream to small scale cultural practitioners (Strachan, 2007: 246) who, 'by maintaining financial as well as artistic control . . . are able to retain their copyrights and any profits made' (Anderson, Dubber and James 2013: 36). The basket of rights (Frith, 1988: 57) that has been entrepreneurially appropriated as the 360-degree deal by the major labels is equally exploitable by entrepreneurial D2F musicians, who equally need to view their careers from a 360-degree perspective. However, D2F has moved musicians' interactions with the companies they contract with to enter markets from face-to-face music companies to digital interface technology companies. More importantly, as Jones (2012) emphasizes, the importance of music companies was the investment on the part of people within the music companies, not just the music companies themselves. The value-adding function that was traditionally provided by people in music companies has, in the D2F approach, become the responsibility of the musicians themselves. The risk for the D2F artist is in the sunk costs of the consistent production of content and the time spent developing and expanding the suite of technical, legal and business skills necessary to have a presence and be present.

If questions of 'how?' and 'how often?' fans use music and engage with artists defines the D2F artist, the challenges of creating and capturing value and generating growth are similar to challenges faced by start-up D2F platforms. Initially, growth outputs appear easily measurable through an artist's page views, likes, plays and the like. However, Ries (2013: 77) identifies these as 'vanity metrics': data that gives the appearance of a thriving project but provides little indication as to the value of the interaction between artist and fan. Valuable fans are those who are deeply connected, listen repeatedly, regularly buy and drive the conversation on behalf of the artist. In online Prosumer communities the social authorship (Toynbee, 2000) of the fan is the position between producer and other consumers, as Brown and Sellen observe, 'Friends act as a form of collaborative filtering for new music' (2010: 54). This is not so much mediation but *me*-diation, where fans construct their own online identities through visibly and vocally supporting certain acts.

To succeed, D2F artists need to identify and differentiate the high-value fans in amongst the wider, passively attentive audience and concentrate on growing active fan numbers and levels of engagement. Potentially, artists who can use and learn from data and metrics will have the entrepreneurial advantage over the competition. However, the key distinction and advantage between D2F platforms and artists here is that the platforms can use the metric data entrepreneurially to continually iterate and innovate the design and function of platforms towards enhanced success. As Dan Croll, who took a D2F approach to securing a record deal with Decca, observes, for artists, 'once it's out, it's out' (2014: personal communication), meaning once produced and uploaded, recordings of songs and associated image and video content are unrecoverable and are likely fixed in the minds of audiences. Thus, choosing musically what to, and strategically when to, upload, effectively acting as their own A&R, is a significant entrepreneurial characteristic of the D2F artist.

There are several high-profile examples of D2F artists who have successfully demonstrated high-value growth. Using a combination of a million YouTube followers, iTunes and social media, Alex Day delivered three chart hits in 2011–12: 'It's basically perseverance. [I]'ve been doing it six years, and only in the last year have people really started paying attention to my music. I make sure I upload at least one video a week, keep my stuff consistent and entertaining, and don't talk about music all the time because people would get bored' (Day, 2012). Likewise, Kina Grannis is a YouTube artist based in the US who turned down a deal with Interscope Records in favour of remaining independent (Grannis, 2013), a choice that illustrates the creative and business autonomy D2F artists can exercise in their decision-making by being part of digital communities. This example typifies the importance of the perception of belonging in online communities. The D2F artist's entrepreneurial goal is to monetize a greater proportion of the attention they are paid. The larger and more active the fanbase, the lesser the risk to the artist and his or her projects. The ability to leverage the audience as a commodity (Manzerolle, 2014) would appear to be a key entrepreneurial characteristic of the D2F artist.

In the D2F era, the clash between the long tail business model of social media, sales and D2F platforms and the 'winner takes all' model of D2F artists has fostered an entrepreneurial environment where every artist has opportunity and can define success on their own terms. However, in terms of sales, the sheer volume of sales required in the digital platforms means that in a 'winner takes all' market, the vast majority are losers, who simply work to create content for the platforms for less than the minimum wage. As the record industry moves away from a unit sales model towards streaming, where no one fails to sell but the winners take less (*The Trichordist*, 2014) all new artists, both signed and D2F, will have to compete with an ever-burgeoning catalogue to win the fight for audience attention.

The latest technologies in the shape of digital and D2F platforms want aspiring musicians to believe they can sustain a career through spending their time building a direct relationship with the fan. However, artists are increasingly burdened with the business of music at the expense of making it. Yet the catalyst for success of the majority of the D2F success stories was, and remains, a song. From DIY to D2F, the song remains the entrepreneurial engine that drives the music industries and underpins any artist-fan relationship. The entrepreneurial activities a musician must prioritize and specialize in are songwriting, or working with songwriters to deliver performances of songs. Beyond that, be it self-sustaining in fan communities built through D2F platforms, seeking the investment of the people in the music companies, being a pioneer of the next latest technology or 'simply' delivering mind-blowing performances, twenty-first-century musicians have more choice now than ever as to how they enter markets. However, as the only way to capitalize upon their songs and performances is to seek to profit from opportunities replete with risk, they have little choice but to be entrepreneurial.

Conclusion

What this chapter has demonstrated is that despite social, cultural and technological change, entrepreneurship within the music industries remains inextricably bound up with notions of creativity and community. In the 1970s, the DIY ethos of Punk drew together musicians and fans, united by a shared set of ideals and beliefs. It was out of those local music-making communities that venues, shops, and labels to support Punk music emerged. Similarly, the post-Punk era of the 1980s and 1990s celebrated and united fans and musicians who existed outside the 'mainstream', as defined by the acts signed to and promoted by major labels and broadcast on radio. Through the post-Napster digital watershed, the Internet and digital technologies were meant to be a great democratizer, effectively allowing a local and/or unsigned act to record, release and sell its music direct to fans, without need for mediation by labels, publishers or managers. At the same time, however, the D2F environment has undeniably altered the nature of what it means to be a musician – to be creative. As evidenced through examples like Alex Day, independent musicians must now be in equal measures technicians and business people, adaptive to not just one overarching online world, but simultaneously responsive to the digital vagaries and intricacies of multiple platforms. Thus, elements essential to entrepreneurship more broadly, qualities like adaptation, innovation and knowledge through failure, have proven themselves central to evolving spatial and temporal notions of music entrepreneurship. In the same way the music industry – singular – has been superseded by the music industries – plural – it can be argued that musicians are no longer 'only' musicians but are necessarily required to be musician-entrepreneurs, or indeed, 'musicpreneurs'. As technologies and platforms continue to grow and change, musician-entrepreneurs will need to have the array of skills to keep up with the demands of an ever-changing environment. Where community was once delimited by geography, it now resides globally as well as locally, virtually as well as actually. In an era when 'successful' acts still need to hold on to 'day jobs' (Ewens, 2014), it becomes clear that a career as a 'musician' is no longer easily defined. Creativity and industry, entrepreneurship and community are increasingly bound up within new cultural and economic constructs that continue to blur the once-distinct lines between professional and amateur, creator and supporter, fan and performer.

Notes

1 While it is outside the scope of this chapter, it is worth noting that parallels can be drawn between the UK and US Punk and post-Punk scenes in cities like New York and Los Angeles in the

same time periods. For further reading see Moore (2004) and Goshert (2000).

2 See, for instance, Thom Yorke's 2010 comments calling major labels a 'sinking ship' (cited in Kreps, 2010).

References

Anderson, C. (2006), *The Long Tail: How Endless Choice is Creating Unlimited Demand*, London: Random House Business Books.

Anderton, C., A. Dubber, and M. James (2013), *Understanding the Music Industries*, London: Sage.

Bandcamp (2014), Bandcamp homepage, available at: https://bandcamp.com/ [last accessed 24 November 2014].

BBC World Service, 'Global Music Machine: Dominating The Music Industry', available at: http://www.bbc.co.uk/worldservice/specials/1042_globalmusic/page3.shtml [accessed 24 October 2014].

Borland, J. (2000), 'States target record labels with price-fixing suit', available at: http://news.cnet.com/States-target-record-labels-with-price-fixing-suit/2100-1023_3-244195.html [accessed 24 October 2014].

Brown, B. and A. Sellen (2006), 'Sharing and Listening to Music', in K. O'Hara and B. Brown (eds), *Consuming Music Together: Social and Collaborative Aspects of Music Consumption Technologies*, Netherlands: Springer, pp. 37–56.

Croll, D. (2014), The Musician's Career. Conversation after the Music Masterclass at the Liverpool Institute for Performing Arts. Personal communication, 15 November 2014.

Day, A. (2012), 'Over 500,000 Songs Sold, 3 New Releases & Close to 100 Million YouTube', available at: http://www.tunecore.com/blog/2012/07/alex-day.html [accessed 24 November 2014].

de Zengotita, T. (2005), *Mediated: How the Media Shape the World Around You*, London: Bloomsbury Publishing.

Dubber, A. (2007), 'Twenty Things You Must Know About Music Online', retrieved 18 July 2014, from New Music Strategies, http://newmusicstrategies.com/wp-content/uploads/2008/06/nms.pdf

Elberse, A. (2013), *Blockbusters: Why Big Hits – and Big Risks – are the Future of the Entertainment Business*, London: Faber and Faber (Kindle).

Ewens, H. (2014), 'Loads of Huge UK Rock Bands Still Have Day Jobs: Longreads or Whatever', available from: http://noisey.vice.com/en_uk/blog/our-favourite-bands-and-their-day-jobs [accessed 12 November 2014].

Falkinger, J. (2008), 'Limited Attention as a Scarce Resource in Information-Rich Economies', *The Economic Journal* 118: 1596–1620.

Frith, S. and H. Horne (1987), *Art Into Pop*, London: Methuen.

Frith, S. (1988), 'Copyright and the Music Business', *Popular Music* 7 (1): 57–75.

Goshert, J.C. (2000), '"Punk" after the pistols: American music, economics, and politics in the 1980s and 1990s', *Popular Music and Society* 24 (1): 85–106.

Grannis, K. (2013), 'Finding Community Through the Internet', TED: available at: https://www.youtube.com/watch?v=Cqg0HHp6W2U [accessed 24 November 2014].

Hardy, P. (2012), *Download!: How the Internet Transformed the Record Business*, London: Omnibus Press.

Harrison, A. (2008), *Music the Business: The Essential Guide to the Law and the Deals*, 4th ed., London: Virgin Books.

Hesmondhalgh, D. (1997), 'Post-Punk's attempt to democratise the music industry: The success and failure of Rough Trade', *Popular Music* 16 (3): 255–74.

Jones, M.L. (1999), 'Changing Slides: Labour's music industry policy under the microscope', *Critical Quarterly* 41 (1): 22–31.

Jones, M.L. (2012), *The Music Industries: From Conception to Consumption*, London: Palgrave Macmillan.

Knab, C. and B.F. Day (2013), *Music is Your Business*, 4th ed., Seattle: Four Front Media.

Kott, G. (2009), *Ripped: How the Wired Generation Revolutionized Music*, New York: Scribner.

Kreps, D. (2010), 'Thom Yorke: Major Labels Are a "Sinking Ship": Radiohead frontman offers advice to aspiring musicians in new textbook', available at: http://www.rollingstone.com/music/news/thom-yorke-major-labels-are-a-sinking-ship-20100609 [accessed 24 October 2014].

Laing, D. (1985), *Three Chord Wonders*, Milton Keynes: Open University Press.

Lanham, R.A. (2006), *The Economics of Attention: Style and Substance in the Age of Information*, Chicago: Chicago Univeristy Press.

Lashua, B.D. and S. Cohen (2010), 'Liverpool musicscapes: Music performance, movement, and the built urban environment', in B. Fincham, M. McGuinness and L. Murray (eds), *Mobile Methodologies*, Basingstoke: Palgrave Macmillan, pp. 71–84.

Lawson, S. (2014), 'How Much Do Artists Make On Bandcamp', Solo Bass and Beyond blog, 4 January, available at: http://www.stevelawson.net/2014/01/how-much-do-artists-make-on-bandcamp-thoughts-on-reaching-a-milestone/

Manzerolle, R.V. (2013), 'Technologies of Immediacy/Economies of Attention: Notes on the Commercial Development of Mobile Media and Wireless Connectvity', in L. McGuigan and V. Manzerolle (eds), *The Audience Commodity in the Digital Age*, New York: Peter Lang, ch. 11.

Montague, E. (2006), 'From Garahge to Garidge: The Appropriation of Garage Rock in The Clash's "Garageland" (1977)', *Popular Music and Society* 29 (4): 427–39.

Moore, R. (2004), 'Postmodernism and Punk Subculture: Cultures of Authenticity and Deconstruction', *The Communication Review* 7 (3): 305–27.

Musicweek.com (2014), Creative industries worth £71.4bn to UK economy, DCMS report available at: http://www.musicweek.com/news/read/creative-industries-worth-71-4bn-to-uk-economy/057292 [accessed 20 April 2014].

Myles, A. (2010), *Beyond Talent: Creating a Successful Career in Music*, 2nd ed., New York: Oxford University Press.

Negus, K. (1992), *Producing Pop*, London: Arnold.

Negus, K. (1996), *Popular Music in Theory*, Cambridge: Polity Press/Blackwell.

Next Big Sound (2013), '2013: The Year in Rewind', available at: https://www.nextbigsound.com/industryreport/2013/ [accessed 24 November 2014].

NME (2014), '50 Worst Music Videos Ever', available at: http://www.nme.com/list/50-worst-music-videos-ever/253198/article/253216 [accessed 24 November 2014].

Oakes, S. (2000), 'The influence of the musicscape within service environments', *Journal of Services Marketing* 14 (7): 539–56.

Ries, E. (2011), *The Lean Start Up: How Constant Innovation Creates Radically Successful Businesses*, London: Penguin.

Rogers, J. (2013), *The Death and Life of the Music Industry in the Digital Age*, New York: Bloomsbury Publishing.

Roberts, L. (2014), 'Marketing musicscapes, or the political economy of contagious magic', *Tourism, Leisure and Hospitality Management* 14 (1): 10–29.

Rojek, C. (2011), *Music Pop Culture*, Cambridge: Polity Press.

Sivers, D. (2011), *Anything You Want: 40 Lessons for a New Kind of Entrepreneur*. USA: The Domino Project, Do You Zoom.

Songhack.com (2014), 'Tommy Darker's "Musicpreneur" Movement', available at: http://www.songhack.com/blog/the-musicpreneur-movement-an-interview-with-tommy-darker/ [accessed 24 October 2014].

Spotify (2014), 'How We Pay Royalties', available at: https://www.spotifyartists.com/spotify-explained/#how-we-pay-royalties-overview [accessed 24 November 2014].

Strachan, R. (2007), 'Micro independent record labels in the UK: Discourse, DIY cultural production and the music industry', *European Journal of Cultural Studies*, 10 (2): 245–65.

Sterne, J. (2012), *MP3: The Meaning of a Format*, Durham and London: Duke University Press.

Tapscott, D. and A.D. Williams (2008), *Wikinomics: How Mass Collaboration Changes Everything*, London: Atlantic Books.

The Trichordist (2014), 'Breaking Spotify Per Stream Rates Drop. Artists for an Ethical and Sustainable Internet', blog, 17 November, available at: http://thetrichordist.com/2014/11/17/breaking-spotify-per-stream-rates-drop-as-service-adds-more-users/ [accessed 24 November 2014].

Toynbee, J. (2000), *Making Popular Music: Music, Creativity and Institutions*, London: Bloomsbury Publishing.

Wikstrom, P. (2009), *The Music Industry: Music in the Cloud*, Cambridge: Polity Press.

3A

Example Case Study?: The Professional Musician

Allan Dumbreck

The second part of the book will examine the music industries as a series of inter-dependent business sectors. Each chapter will begin with a discourse considering a review of the current literature and, where relevant, evidence of entrepreneurial activity within the sector and continue by examining one or more case studies of individuals developing their career in that field. Throughout each chapter the reader will be introduced to some of the key debates and theorists relevant to that sector and to the case study personnel.

However, we felt it might be appropriate to present an initial case study ahead of the fuller chapters to summarize some of these concepts to familiarize the reader with the structure of the case studies and the directions in which our research has taken us. Throughout this mini-chapter we will therefore direct the reader to more thorough examinations of the central discussions within the chapters of the second part. In this way, it is possible to navigate the second part of the book in terms of emerging themes and relevant theory rather than the series of business sectors a musician or artist might encounter as laid out sequentially in the chapters.

To begin our case study examples we thought it would be wise to examine one of the most recognized positions in professional music. As discussed within the last chapter, live performance and later recorded music have, from the earliest commercial phases, been dependent on the jobbing or session musician. The consumer is aware of the vocalist, the star, the front person or featured artist but can also see and hear a number of other instrumental players on the recording, on the stage and in the video. These professional musicians are often career performers who spend their entire working life perfecting their playing skills and mastering new genres and often new instruments to keep themselves fresh and relevant for each new successful artist and successive style. The work can be very demanding, the career gaps can be demoralizing and the financial returns inconsistent but the experiential rewards and potential for success (however that is defined) draw significant numbers into this arena.

As already identified in Chapter 2, the 2013 UK Music report into the core value of music to the UK economy found that around 68,000 of the 101,860 full time equivalent positions in the UK music industries were musicians or composers (66.7 per cent, UK Music, 2013). Clearly these career routes (musician, artist and songwriter) are by far the most popular and possibly the most attractive to young people wishing to enter professional music. Hence it makes sense to examine this sector as an example case study to set the tone for the remaining case studies in part two.

Case study: Ross McFarlane (professional musician)

Ross McFarlane is currently the drummer with the internationally successful mainstream act Texas. He has also performed and recorded for The Proclaimers and Jon Fratelli, and was a member of the band Stiltskin which achieved

European success with their song 'Inside' which was featured as a soundtrack for one of the Levi's jeans commercials in the early 1990s which acted as a springboard for the revival of many classic pieces of music from the 1960s and 1970s and on this one occasion for a new act with an original song. He started by explaining how he graduated from local bands to working with signed artists.

'I was in a band called Unity Express and we were doing local gigs supporting a lot of bands. Then my friend got a job as a keyboard player with Worldwide which was a Precious Organisation band (artist managers for then successful act Wet, Wet, Wet) and I auditioned and I joined them. That was the start of quite a busy period. At that time (late 1980s) Glasgow was really busy and lots of bands were getting signed. We supported people like Donovan and Crowded House and Curiosity Killed the Cat and we did gigs with the Wet's, did an arena tour with them, so that's how I got into it and obviously that was a calling card and I pushed on from there.'

In this Ross demonstrates the value of an emerging performer's industry network of fellow musicians and business professionals in getting shortlisted for interviews and auditions. He was able to access an audition for a successful act because he knew an existing member. Networking has already been identified in Chapter 2 as a key element to success in music. Developing one's professional network to make positive contact with, and impress, 'cultural intermediaries' (as described by Scott, 2012) or 'gatekeepers' (as identified by Caves, 2002), is clearly vital to entrepreneurial progress. These key personnel who can assist access to professional music (promoters, agents, managers, journalists for example) are easier to approach though a common acquaintance or through having worked with someone they already respect (Scott, 2012). This ability is addressed in several case studies in the second part of the book, notably Goc O'Callaghan (Chapter 5), Ally Gray (Chapter 8) and Richy Muirhead (Chapter 11).

Ross then discussed his approach to developing a career in professional music which some may find unconventional: 'the start of my career was always [to be] in the shop window, playing gigs and meeting people. I was always a bit younger than everybody else at that time, you know, so that was my way in. I also did drum tech for Ted McKenna who is a really famous Scottish drummer and he worked with great acts, so that was a great education as well. I met him through a mutual friend who was a keyboard player . . . and I just called him up and asked if he was ever needing a hand with his kit and he called me back a week later and I worked with him for a year and a half; that was great, going to gigs and festivals. I found out what a stage manager was, a production manager, catering, road crew, it was an education.'

Like many professional musicians, this unpaid internship initially replaced formalized qualifications for Ross. Many of the emerging professionals we interviewed have benefited from a formal, higher level education, a number of others have taken a more direct route into professional music. The role of education in music entrepreneurship is examined in the case studies of Sumit Bothra (Chapter 4), Caroline Gorman (Chapter 9) and Steve Broadfoot (Chapter 11). Music specific courses have been examined by Cloonan and Hulstedt (2013) and are discussed in Chapter 4. The value of entrepreneurial skills teaching in education has been investigated by a series of researchers and reports (including the QAA report into entrepreneurial campuses, 2014) and is addressed in Chapter 2.

When asked about the point where his career began to take off, Ross is clear: 'probably the biggest defining moment would be the number one hit single with Stiltskin, it obviously makes you a name, it gives you an industry name as well as a musical name so you get recognized within the industry and you get recognized amongst your peers . . . with drum endorsements, with record companies.' The timing of this opportunity was also important: 'it's an age thing with some people; there is a window when you are a certain age, I was 23, 24 so it was a great age to get in and start a career . . . the musician's biological clock is ticking where they feel they have a shelf life and that took a lot of anxiety out of me, because I was worried about money and I wanted to maintain this life and it was difficult, signing on and doing pub gigs to pay for it and if you have a full time job you can't practise or go away [on tour], so I was always pretty broke but optimistic. So that was great ... an internal voice was like "you can do this, you have done this", and doing that [Stiltskin] for me meant I didn't need to do much else to prove it to myself, so I had the confidence.' The advantage of belief in oneself in the early stages of career development may clearly be a significant factor. The importance of confidence and self-belief to the music entrepreneur has already been encountered in Chapter 2, highlighting the work of Casson (2003) and McLelland (1987) amongst others, and is touched upon in the case study featuring Steve Broadfoot in Chapter 11.

In common with many other emerging music entrepreneurs, Ross identified his home life when discussing what initially inspired him. 'Firstly, it would be my family, massively, and they still do. I am the youngest of four and I was brought up in a real crazy household, my brothers and sister left Scotland when they were young and went to Los Angeles. It was that time in the 1980s when it was booming and a lot of people were moving to America and to London so there was a big exodus of the creatives. So that was quite inspiring to me because I was at school in Scotland and they were in America and my sister was in London. There was always music in the house and my brothers were brought up with the Glasgow Apollo and this great Punk period, so there was always great music around and I think just the luck of being the baby of the family, just the way the cards were stacked. And also just the travel sense ... they would come home and it seemed really glamorous and other world-like and I thought that looks great and it inspired me.' Family and home background is a key area in many studies of entrepreneurial confidence and behaviour. Writers on this topic include Kariv (2013), discussed in Chapter 6 and Henderson and Robertson (1996) in Chapter 9. Many of our young professionals referred to this as a vital element of their entrepreneurial growth, notably Princess

Nyah in Chapter 4, Chantal Epp in Chapter 6 and Mindy Abovitz in Chapter 11.

Again, like other successful music professionals, Ross had experienced non-music employment prior to becoming successful. 'I was a landscape gardener for about a year. It made me want to get into the music industry because I didn't want to do that! I worked in a stationery warehouse as well . . . through one of these YTS Schemes and I was in bands at this point. It was of value though, everything is a learning curve; it gave me a real work ethic to get up and get out and do things. I bought a really expensive . . . top of the range drum kit because I had a job. I wasn't making much but it gave me a system of value, you know, economics, because later on in my career things were thrown at bands, I was working with big sponsorship deals and big drum kits. When I bought the drum kit at seventeen it was £2,500 and I remember it was the drum shop in the city centre and I went up and paid it every week and most of my wages went to that as well as a bit to my mum and dad, and it was a real bind but once I had paid it off it was a great feeling. So there was [an understanding of] economics and value I had gained and I think that has all stayed with me, nothing for nothing. It gave me a really good value system for money and a bit of respect as well. It just filtered down, you know; you get out of your bed, you go down to your work and you put a day's graft in, whether it be music or whether it be lecturing or whether it be car valeting, a job's a job.' The possible advantages of working in non-music employment (but perhaps in a related area) are addressed in all three of the case studies in Chapter 11.

When it came to addressing the key theme of this study, 'what is an entrepreneur?' and more pointedly, 'do you consider yourself to be an entrepreneur', Ross identified himself to be in the positive middle ground where he may not use the term when talking about himself but he recognizes the elements of entrepreneurship in his own activity and career development. 'I don't have a problem with the word. I think back in the day it had a few connotations and I think there is a conflict in the music industry . . . I think that it means capitalism and maybe even, in Britain, Thatcherism. It means get rich quick; it means bosh, bosh, bosh, loads of money. Or big business, huge companies squashing the little companies. But I think yeah, we are entrepreneurial, we are entrepreneurs and it is not a socialist industry. Not to get all political but it is an industry based on commerce, big sales and big money, and there is a lot of money in the industry, even still. Any big tour I have been involved in has had a lot of money in it. We employ people, we are a business and I think people get frightened of that word.' The economic value of the live music market is examined in Chapter 5. Much of this value derives from the 'experience economy' (also Chapter 5), and discussed in the writing of Auslander (2011), Pine and Gilmour (1999) and Darmer (2008), also highlighted in Chapter 5.

'Am I an entrepreneur? I've never called myself an entrepreneur but if I analyze it and look back there is entrepreneurialism or entrepreneurship, there are definitely elements of it. It's an individual level and then it becomes a business level, but yeah, I think we are entrepreneurs, creatively, just even by having to get up in the morning and phone people, ideas, see it through, write songs, contacts, putting people together and all that sort of stuff – it's part of it. I think we are entrepreneurs. I wouldn't necessarily call myself an entrepreneur but I wouldn't have a problem if someone said "could you describe yourself as an entrepreneur?" I would say absolutely.' Attempts to define entrepreneurship (generally and in relation to music specifically) are addressed in several chapters. Debates raised by Schumpeter (1934), Aggestam (2007) and Swedburg (2006), for example, are referenced in Chapters 2 and 4. The degree of acceptance (or rejection) of the term 'entrepreneur' by our case study personnel is again prevalent throughout the book but can notably be found in Chapters 4, 8 and 11.

Progressing to one of the central questions which drove our research, 'everyone who works in music is, in some way, an entrepreneur – yes or no?', Ross had this to say: 'They might not know it; it might be on a subconscious level but yeah. You could always take out entrepreneur and put business in its place, it's a more friendly word, good business, and good financial management. I think entrepreneurship is here whether we know it or not on a subconscious level . . . as soon as you start booking studios and organizing bands.'

In this response, Ross replicates a theme which many UK-based music professionals raised with us. The idea that while they might not necessarily agree or accept the terminology, most of those working in the music industries in Britain are indeed in some way entrepreneurial. The reticence which many others in the same position voiced may be put down to historic viewpoints or possibly media-reinforced stereotypes but in reality when examined impartially their activities and behaviour are those of the entrepreneur. This leads to one of our primary conclusions in Chapter 12.

The remainder of this book dissects professional music into a series of sectors to make investigation clearer. We aim, as we have already stated, to analyze work patterns and progression routes throughout the music industries to try to understand whether this represents entrepreneurship or not. The opening chapters have laid out the landscape and this first case study has addressed some of the broader issues involved while bringing one of the most familiar job descriptions in music under the spotlight. Part two will now examine other parts of this landscape and, in search of evidence of entrepreneurship in career development, will discuss the concept with a series of young professionals.

References

Aggestam, M. (2007), 'Art-entrepreneurship in the Scandinavian music industry', in *Entrepreneurship in the creative industries*, C. Henry (ed.), Cheltenham: Edward Elgar, pp. 30–53.

Auslander, P. (2011), *Liveness. Performance in a Mediatized Culture*, London and New York: Routledge.

Casson, M. (2003), *The Entrepreneur: An Economic Theory*, Cheltenham: Edward Elgar.

Cloonan, M. and L. Hulstedt (2013), 'Looking for Something New: The Provision of Popular Music Studies Degrees in the UK in the Twenty First Century', *IASPM@ Journal* 3 (2): 63–77.

Darmer, P. (2008), 'Entrepreneurs in music: the passion of experience creation', in J. Sundbo and P. Darmer (eds.), *Creating Experiences in the Experience Economy*, Cheltenham: Edward Elgar, pp. 111–33

Henderson R. and M. Robertson (1996), 'Who wants to be an entrepreneur? – Young adult attitudes to entrepreneurship as a career', *Career Development International*, 5 (6): 279–87.

Kariv, D. (2013), *Female Entrepreneurship and the New Venture Creation: An International Overview*, New York: Routledge.

McLelland, D. (1987), *Human Motivation*, Cambridge: Cambridge University Press, pp. 223–372.

Pine, B.J. and J.H. Gilmore (1999), *The Experience Economy*, Boston, MA: Harvard Business School Press.

Schumpeter, J. (1934), *Theory of Economic Development*, Cambridge, MA: Harvard University Press.

Swedberg, R. (2006), 'The Cultural Entrepreneur and the Creative Industries: Beginning in Vienna', *Journal of Cultural Economics* 30 (4): 243–61.

UK Music (2013), *The Economic Contribution of the Core UK Music Industry*, London: UK Music.

PART TWO

Sectors and Case Studies

4

Artist Managers and Entrepreneurship:

Risk-takers or Risk Averse?

John Williamson

Introduction

This chapter addresses two understudied and unresolved questions: what it is to be a manager in the music industries[1] and to what extent these managers can be viewed as entrepreneurs.

It will do this in four parts. The first will examine how managers have been portrayed historically in existing literature, drawing on academic, journalistic and insider accounts. The second will focus on entrepreneurial traits and types of entrepreneurship evident across the music industries and the extent to which these apply to management functions.

The core of the chapter comprises two contrasting case studies in music management and entrepreneurship, based on interviews with Sumit Bothra of ATC Management[2] and the artist and clothing designer, Princess Nyah.[3]

Finally, I will use these and my own background in artist management[4] to argue for the study of artist managers to be at the centre of future studies of the music industries, but will urge caution in the uncritical use of the term entrepreneur when it comes to describing the work of all managers.

The changing nature and reputation of artist managers

To build a reliable picture of artist management from previous accounts of the profession is impossible because of a combination of ignorance and sensationalism. While academic accounts have opted to largely overlook the role of artists' managers, journalists and some of the managers themselves have tended to focus on the most hysterical, debauched, voracious and plain exploitative examples of the profession. This leaves a considerable gap in the literature to attempt a serious, contemporary account of what is an increasingly important, economically significant and professional occupation. However, that may not be immediately apparent from the evidence so far.

Within the field of Popular Music Studies,[5] accounts of the music industries have tended to over-privilege the recording industry to the exclusion of other activities. The nature of the music industries before 1999 can justify an obsession with the workings of record companies in, for example, the early work of Negus (1992, 1999), Shuker (1994) and Longhurst (1995) but though some of these key texts have been updated (Shuker, 2001, 2007, 2012; Longhurst, 2007; Longhurst and Bogdanovic, 2014) to reflect substantial recent changes in the music industries, they still pay scant or no attention to the role of managers. If this suggests that studies of the work of managers are a gaping void in Popular Music Studies, there is some cause for optimism. Guy Morrow (2009, 2013) and Martin Cloonan (2015) have used their experiences as managers in Australia and Scotland respectively to write about both the profession in general as well as their own experiences, while Mike Jones has used his experience of being managed[6] to offer the most nuanced overview of artist management so far. Here he makes the crucial observation that 'artist managers occupy the only position in the Music Industry[7] which interacts with all other areas of activity and the individuals involved with them' (2012: 91).

However, the increased interest in the study of managers only offers a starting point. While Jones provides a succinct and convincing account of artist management from the 1950s onwards, and the fragile relationships that underpin it, he offers less insight on the contemporary changes in the profession. In much the same way as he describes how the managers of the early 1960s (when recording replaced live performance as the main source of incomes for many artists) had to reinvent their business practices, managers in the twenty-first century have been subject to another 'seismic upheaval' (ibid: 88).

At the core of this is the decline in the financial power and human resources of the record companies. Marc Marot, who was Managing Director of Island Records during the 1990s and who is now CEO of Crown Talent Management,[8] describes his company's role now as 'providing all sorts of services I would never have dreamt of thirty years ago, and that is all because record companies are so shrunk to the bone that they simply cannot offer these services anymore' (interview, 9 April 2014).

In the absence of such expertise within the record companies, a greater burden has been placed on artists and their managers to not only guide and administer their careers but also to facilitate, among other things, the organization and release of recordings; raising funds for recording and touring; the production of videos and artwork and executing marketing campaigns, all of which would have previously been done in conjunction with specific record company departments. So while academic study of managers has yielded little by way of meaningful understanding of the scope and diversity of the job, it is only one source of both historical and contemporary perspectives. Managers have also been discussed in more journalistic accounts as well as in a number of autobiographies of former managers.

In the first category, the two best accounts of the first generation of pop and rock managers were both published in the late eighties. Simon Garfield's *Expensive Habits* (1986) presents a wider view of the history of what his subtitle calls 'the dark side of the music industry' in which managers feature prominently. One chapter recalls some of the most breathtaking examples of chicanery, with the stories of Elton John, The Beatles, Gilbert O'Sullivan, The Who and The Rolling Stones, all used as examples of sharp or naively incompetent managerial practice. More specifically, Johnny Rogan's *Starmakers and Svenaglis* (1988) remains the most detailed account of the first generation of famous/notorious British artist managers from Larry Parnes[9] onwards.

The managerial perspective has also been reflected in a series of entertaining memoirs written by former managers of, among others, The Rolling Stones (Loog Oldham, 2001, 2003, 2014), The Yardbirds and Wham! (Napier Bell, 2001, 2014), Echo and the Bunnymen (Drummond, 2001) and the Jesus and Mary Chain (McGee, 2014), but these, while anecdotally rich, are largely one-sided and frequently self-serving accounts and offer little detail when it comes to the day to day nature of management.

None of these do much to rescue the somewhat dubious reputation of managers in the music industries, which has been shaped by a mixture of sensational stories, mythologizing and artists' accounts of horrific rip-offs. That these are now less frequent[10] and that managers now enjoy a slightly higher professional status can be attributed to two factors: the formation of professional organizations and the wider recognition of the economic importance of the creative industries by governments.

The formation of the Music Managers' Forum (MMF) in 1992 was the first major move in this direction in the UK and it has, since its inception, worked to bring a new level of definition, professionalism and organization to artist management. Faced with frequently having to explain what artist managers actually do, the MMF's Jon Webster has attempted to describe what he calls 'an outwardly simple but incredibly complex task' (2013: 10) as a 'combination of administration, communication, negotiation and enabling', but admits that 'within those four words exists a wealth of detail' (ibid). While these categories go some way to covering the extent of the job, it hardly provides the type of job description that may be found in other occupations. Instead, the nature of artist management, the nature of the job varies hugely depending on the individuals, the companies and the artists involved. In recent years, the MMF has grown in size and influence, with its agenda now concentrating on developing trade and training,[11] but significantly, much of the narrative surrounding this has been bound up in notions of entrepreneurship.

Like other music industries' organizations, the MMF has benefited from the increased interest of governments in the wider creative industries. In UK terms, this can be traced to the election of the Labour government in 1997 and its formation of the Department of Culture, Media and Sport (DCMS). DCMS commissioned a series of mapping exercises of the various industries, including music, and, having ignored them in the first survey (1998) placed 'management, representation and promotion' (1998: 4) among the 'core activities of the music industry' in the second (2001: 1). This was perhaps the first 'official' recognition of artist managers and inevitably came with both benefits and some strings attached. While such exercises have attempted to quantify and value various sectors across the creative industries, it has so far been impossible to meaningfully survey both the number of artist managers working in the UK and the value they bring to the wider economy.

One consequence of this was that much of the discourse surrounding management (and the music industries more generally) began to stem from attempts to recognize the value of the creative industries in the wider economy. Therein, entrepreneurs were considered important drivers of the economy and entrepreneurship took a more prominent place in academic, industrial and journalistic accounts of the music industries.

The next part of the chapter will explore these in more detail and with specific reference to the place of managers.

Locating the artist manager as an entrepreneur

The subsequent case studies will offer some examples of the different types of artist manager, but it is important to contextualize the debates around management and entrepreneurship by attempting to reconcile definitions of what is understood by the term entrepreneur with the lived-in experience of managers themselves. This can be done by looking at broad definitions, those modifications more specific to the music industries and the activities of the managers themselves. Throughout this it is important to note that 'the nature of the entrepreneur and entrepreneurial process have defied consensual definition' (Chell, 2007: 5) while efforts to narrow down the various aspects and types of artist manger are equally elusive.[12]

Twentieth-century accounts of entrepreneurs usually begin with the work of the Austrian economist, Joseph Schumpeter (1934), but similar figures had previously been identified, albeit under different names[13] by economists going back to the start of the industrial revolution. Schumpeter saw entrepreneurs as innovators, involved in 'carrying out new combinations' (ibid: 74) and the 'creation of new goods/services/sources of supply' (ibid). This has remained a pillar of understanding of what it is to be an entrepreneur, with the most significant adaptation or critique coming from Kirzner (1973) whose work focuses on the alertness of entrepreneurs in identifying market conditions or opportunities, but argues that they are not necessarily directly involved, as per Schumpeter, in the supply of the new goods or services they have identified.

Recurring themes of risk-taking, profiting from uncertainty, opportunism, alertness, innovation and creativity all feature prominently in accounts of entrepreneurship, but these characteristics do not always sit comfortably with those entrepreneurs working within the creative (or music) industries. To account for this, various modifications of the definitions of entrepreneurship have been produced to reflect different parts of the economy, such as corporate entrepreneurship (Birkinshaw, 2003) and, social entrepreneurship (Mair and Ignasi, 2006) to highlight the different types of entrepreneurship at work in large corporations and the third sector respectively.

To this end, the most helpful labels applied to entrepreneurs within the creative industries have been 'impresarios' (Becker, 1982) or cultural entrepreneurs (Swedburg, 2006). For Becker, the impresario is seen as a more benign capitalist, with an interest in the development and continuation of the art as well as the generation of profit, while Swedburg's cultural entrepreneurs 'do something new and appreciated in the area of culture' (2006: 260) as opposed to ordinary entrepreneurs who do 'something new and profitable in the area of the economy' (2006: 260). Indeed, the downscaling of the importance (or presence) of profit in both accounts is significant and matches the rhetoric of many of those involved in entrepreneurial ventures in the music industries. For example, the CEO of the British recording industry's trade body, the BPI (British Phonographic Industry), claimed recently that the 'British music sector is risk-taking, innovative and at the cutting edge of trends' (Taylor, 2013).

Although such descriptions of entrepreneurs involved with aspects of art and culture are helpful, they remain problematic. Both Becker and Swedburg's models work best when applied to a particular type and level of entrepreneur, usually an individual or small business owner. While many managers and management companies still fall into this category, the sector has become increasingly corporate in recent years, with the majority of major artists now managed by a small number of companies, each with a large number of managers and even larger number of artists on their roster. For example, Artist Nation[14] now boasts of having over fifty managers and 200 artists including many of the largest acts in the world, including Madonna, U2, Lady Gaga and Rihanna. While entrepreneurial behaviour does take place within large companies and corporations,[15] there is growing evidence that, at the top end of the management industry, practices are now increasingly anti-entrepreneurial. Instead of risk-taking, those involved are largely concerned with the avoidance of risk.

The case of Artist Nation and one of its major clients, U2, is an example. Having already worked with Live Nation on touring and merchandising since 2007, their long-term manager, Paul McGuinness of Principle Management, was bought out by Live Nation in 2013 and the band has subsequently been managed by Madonna's manager, Guy Oseary of Artist Nation (see Carroll, 2013).

A quick survey of their recent career would suggest that by taking large advances against both future touring income (from Live Nation in 2007) and sales of their most recent album, Songs of Innocence (from Apple in 2014) while participating in assorted legal tax avoidance schemes (Lynskey, 2014) hardly represents a risk-taking venture.

Emboldened by huge success, Carroll is almost certainly correct in his assertion that 'the job of managing a band like U2 at this stage of their career is more about administration than anything else' (Carroll, 2013).

U2 may represent an extreme case as one of the world's most economically successful acts, but between them and the unknown artist at the start of their career is a whole spectrum of both entrepreneurial and decidedly non-entrepreneurial activity taking place under the guise of artist management.

The following case studies examine two managers at different stages of their careers, with unique backgrounds and outlooks, who fall within that spectrum. Each will examine their backgrounds and activities in the music industries as well as their sense of what it is to be an entrepreneur before attempting to draw some wider conclusions.

Case study: Sumit Bothra (ATC Management)

Sumit Bothra, who is a partner in ATC Management, has been involved in the music industries since working as a college rep for Virgin when at university in Pennsylvania during the mid 1990s and has been a manager since 2002, firstly with his own company, Embargo Management, which merged into ATC, a company formed by Radiohead co-manager, Brian Message, in 2010.

Having gained experience in promotion, marketing, records and publishing while working for Sony (in the UK) between leaving university and 2002, he has managed acts like The Boxer Rebellion and Fink, as well as composers (e.g., Nitin Sawhney and Erran Baron Cohen) developing a strong interest in the use of music in film, TV and video games in the process. At ATC, he now also manages PJ Harvey and The Staves in addition to some of his long standing clients.

While he considers himself an entrepreneur, Sumit separates this from his experience in the music industries and attributes this outlook to a combination of factors that pre-dated his involvement in music: primarily his parents and his American education.

His early life was somewhat nomadic. Born in Leeds, he moved to Saudi Arabia at the age of six and he attended an American school before returning to the UK to complete his GCSEs. During this period, he launched his first entrepreneurial venture: a café in Harrogate, before continuing his education in the USA, firstly at a boarding school in Virginia before getting on to a business and technology course at the University of Pennsylvania.

'Generally Indian parents aspire for their children to become professionals,' he suggests, 'especially if they are professionals themselves – doctors, accountants, that sort of career path. So they have always pushed me to excel and challenge myself, and I was privately educated.'

Sumit qualified with a prestigious degree from the Wharton School of Business and the University of Pennsylvania's School of Engineering, and while his university life was the gateway to his career in the music industries, this was not entirely down to his academic qualifications.

Firstly, he came to the attention of Virgin Records in LA when he began organizing fund raising events at the university. This resulted in him being offered work as a college rep for the label and for a year while studying he promoted Virgin acts to press and radio stations in the Tri-State area. Secondly, he met and interviewed a number of music business personnel as part of his dissertation project, including the then CEO of Sony Music, Paul Burger, who was to give him his first full-time job in the recording industry. This meant that, on completing his degree, he returned to London, where he headed a new college marketing department within Sony.

When he now describes how he was able to convert his passion for music into paid employment he says he 'just fell into it'. This may be true, but his approach to both study and entrepreneurial outlook had much to do with this. The latter was greatly influenced by his time in the USA and his naturally entrepreneurial instincts ('it has to be in your DNA') were further enhanced by the attitudes of his contemporaries at university.

'Americans tend to think that anything is possible,' he says, 'and that is something that I found missing when I moved back to England. I came from a school where I would say "we should talk to Pepsi" to get them involved and the answer would be "that's a great idea, phone Pepsi reception, find out who the head of marketing is, get their e-mail and set up a meeting".

'In the States, being an entrepreneur is a highly competitive industry in itself because everyone sees themselves as an entrepreneur. Even the cab drivers are entrepreneurs – they have all got a hustle whereas here I just didn't find anyone who had a hustle and the people that I did find were the ones I associated with because I enjoyed that!'

Considering his work as a manager more specifically, Sumit accepts that not everyone involved in the music industries is an entrepreneur but argues that 'generally, those who are incredibly successful in creating, innovating and executing new ideas are the entrepreneurs in the industry'.

Besides innovation, the second entrepreneurial trait to which Sumit assigns great importance is the willingness to take risks, and as a result, to accept failure as a possible outcome.

'You have to try things,' he says, 'and see what happens. And not be afraid of the risks. In fact, I embrace failure as a guiding path to success. The two go hand-in-hand. For me, you create in the hope of success but I'm happy with failure or success. Sometimes failure is great.'

However, when pressed, there is evidence that he is not fully comfortable with the idea of being seen as an entrepreneur, especially when it comes to associations with accumulating money at the expense of artistic endeavour. To this end he qualifies his definition of entrepreneurship saying that 'my definition of an entrepreneurial mindset is not about how much money that person has in the bank, but about using your mental capacity', and points to his relationship with his artists as evidence of the need to balance artistic and commercial concerns.

'I have a very strategically minded brain,' he says, 'which I suppose is advantageous in the capacity of a manager because one of our challenges is always how to manage commerce and art in a way that is credible and meaningful to an artist. So I guess one of these areas that is a strength of mine is being able to walk the line between the world of art and commerce with my artists. I see myself as a partner of theirs – I don't really see it as a manager–client relationship.'

Sumit's example can be used to raise a number of issues of wider interest to those studying both artist management and entrepreneurship which can be grouped under two broad headings: the background and education of artist managers, and the changing nature of artist management and the role of entrepreneurs within it. Previous studies of artist managers have tended to focus on either the nature of the job or the individuals involved in it. Few attempts have been made to look more broadly at the characteristics of those working as artist managers. Here, the disparate and scattered nature of the job has made any kind of longitudinal study difficult, but it is perhaps worth making some general points about gender, race and background in artist management in the UK.

The first thing to note is that management has been and is largely the preserve of white males. There has been considerable progress in this respect since Rogan's (1986) study of managers, all of them men. While there have been a number of notable British female managers dating back to the 1960s including Vicki Wickham[16] and Gail Colson,[17] it is only in the last decade or so that a growing number of female managers including Sarah Stennett (Sugababes, Rita Ora, Iggy Azalea), Hilary Shaw (Girls Aloud), Mairead Nash (Florence and the Machine) and Carol Crabtree (MD of Solar Management) have enjoyed large-scale, commercial success, often, significantly, with female artists. Even so, their achievements are frequently under-recognized and are never mythologized in the same way as some of their male contemporaries. In spite of this shift, the current board of the MMF has two women out of twelve members and its advisory board has one woman out of eight (http://www.themmf.net, accessed 13 October 2014).

Being of Indian parentage, Sumit is part of another minority among artist managers, but as with matters of gender, there is some evidence that there is a small recalibration of management away from the white, male hegemony.

This can be partly attributed to education and some of the opening up of opportunities presented by the wider availability of courses, which offer either direct or indirect routes into the music industries. Sumit's background in business studies and technology is a combination of two possible routes into artist management, but the most significant change here is the rapid growth of higher education courses which focus either exclusively or partially on study of the music industries (see Cloonan and Hulstedt, 2013). These come in a variety of guises with modules and courses spanning both the music industries and entrepreneurship. Examples include courses in Popular Music, Management, Performance, Commercial Music, The Music Industry, Music Business Management and Music Production (ibid) covering various aspects of the music industries, while these are linked in courses like Creative and Cultural Entrepreneurship (at Goldsmiths), Music: Innovation and Entrepreneurship (at the University of the West of Scotland) and Creative Entrepreneurship (at the University of East Anglia). In addition, less formal courses and advice on artist management are available through workshops and seminars provided by industry organizations, including the MMF (the Musicians' Union) and the rights' collection agencies.

This has undoubtedly produced a cadre of managers who are more informed and better equipped to enter artist management as a career than was the case in the past. The number of examples within the broader music industries in this book testifies to this but specifically within artist management, Simon Bobbett (LIPA graduate), manager of The Wombats, and Tim Brinkworth (MA Music Innovation and Entrepreneurship, UWS), manager of Mercury Music Prizewinners Young Fathers, stand out.

However, Sumit's account of 'just falling into' management is particularly resonant. His degrees did not qualify him to be a manager and he could have equally pursued many other routes with them. Historically, many artist managers have shifted seamlessly from other occupations when presented with the chance to manage what were often their friends or contemporaries. Most had no or little specific training. Jones observes that there is 'no guide or template' (2012: 95) for artist managers and that 'the only real course is trial and error' (ibid), citing the example of New Order manager, Rob Gretton, who he describes as 'not a svengali, rather someone who identified tasks and followed them through' (ibid).

Educators face a dilemma when teaching about artist managers and their role. While the professionalization of artist management brings with it many advantages (not least recognition and respect in and beyond the music industries), there is also a danger that attempts to teach what it is to be an artist manager (where, whether in universities or elsewhere, the advice is rarely free) exclude the type of maverick or what Sumit calls an 'innate' entrepreneur, who is instinctively, and without training, able to navigate their way through the music industries.

The important point from Sumit's case is that becoming an artist manager is not dependent on a particular type of education or qualification, but rather an ability to think strategically that can be acquired through many different types of education. Indeed, he recognizes that most of the information required to be a successful manager is now available either online or by making contact with those who have or are doing the job already, but this alone is insufficient preparation for the range of unexpected situations that can arise in the course of day-to-day management.

If these observations have centred on the work of individual artist managers, it is also important to reflect on what Sumit's experience says more generally about the nature of artist management as a profession.

His success has been largely down to the ability to work collaboratively and successfully with both his artists and those in the wider music industries. His involvement as a director of the MMF and the growth of his business from 2003 to 2014 illustrate some of the issues facing a twenty-first-century manager. Having initially set up his own management company, the larger pool of resources to draw on within ATC Management has given him a platform to develop the careers of a diverse and not overly commercial roster of artists.

However, while the organization of artist management has changed, the basic model of engagement has changed little since the contracts The Beatles signed with Brian Epstein over fifty years ago (see Jones 2012: 86). In general, the artist employs a manager to 'advise upon, organise and administer all aspects of an artist's career, including seeking out and creating contracts and opportunities' (Bagehot and Kanaar, 1998: 1) and pays them usually in the form of commission, occasionally in the form of a salary. However, the individual deals vary hugely based on the circumstances and market conditions facing both artist and manager. Equally variable are the expectations artists and managers have of each other.

The complex nature of both the many negotiations that underpin the music industries and the demands and market position of individual artists are what determines the business structure best suited to individual artist/manager relationships. The second case study presents one such scenario: where the artist is also the manager.

Case study: Princess Nyah (self-managing artist)

Princess Nyah is a London-based artist and clothes designer – a DIY artist, who has spent the last six years building her own profile in a number of different areas. As well as self-managing her musical career,[18] she has also set up her own record label (Royletease) and runs Binghi's Boutique, a clothing line which has grown from selling limited edition slogan t-shirts on MySpace in 2008 to now being distributed through ASOS and other major retailers, gathering endorsements from the likes of

J. Cole en route. She has adopted and embraced the concept of the branded artist; a multi-faceted role that requires more than one face to succeed.

In many ways, she represents a more familiar type of entrepreneurship as someone who is young, running small businesses and operating across a number of different fields. She has a college degree in Media Studies, and retail management experience, which she highlights as important in shaping her approach to managing her music career.

'I worked in a sports shop for a number of years as a manager and this heavily influenced me in becoming an artist that takes on the job of a manager too. While working in retail I was infused with music on a daily basis, people selling their own mix CDs outside the store every day. I was able to learn the art of team spirit, having your staff and team respect you and be motivated.'

Perhaps unsurprisingly given the approach she takes, Nyah finds fewer problems in asserting herself as an entrepreneur, describing it as 'communicating your craft to the masses', from an informed position when it comes to dealing with those in the music industries.

'Long gone are the old books of how to break into the music industry,' she says. 'The biggest labels struggle to break brand new artists, with things like "X-Factor" and other reality shows focused on music. It is hard to compete if you think of doing things by the book.'

Indeed, her first-hand description of being a music entrepreneur matches, in many respects, the more general descriptions discussed previously, with one major difference: that she is actively involved in selling her own goods and services, rather than those belonging to someone else.

'Having an understanding of how to extract money from the business is really important,' she explains, 'and being able to follow your gut and take risks when sharing your music with the world is all a part of being a music entrepreneur.

'You have to understand that your music is your truth that then becomes a product. That is vital in communicating with your key consumer and also that you have to separate your creativity from your business mind. Being two people, delving into two roles, understanding that your product is something you sell and that you are not selling yourself is tough, but it is what makes for an entrepreneur.'

There are two aspects of entrepreneurship where she echoes Sumit's comments – that it is innate and that accepting and learning from failure is important, yet it is hard not to feel that the investment and faith she has in her own work makes the music itself more important in her entrepreneurial vision.

'I think there are many valuable attributes a young entrepreneur must possess,' she says, 'and self-belief is the most common. If you love your business you will not stop thinking of ways to make it bigger and better. It's in your blood and DNA. If for a minute you forget you have a business, or other things take precedence in your life like the money or material things, then being an entrepreneur is not for you.'

She admits that 'many people are not prepared for this and it knocks their confidence when things don't go as they imagine,' but to counteract this she values collaboration and networking. Evidence of her effectiveness in this field is apparent in her appearance at an event called 'Think Like A Boss' at the Houses of Parliament on International Women's Day (2014) and in conducting her own music master classes at the Liverpool Institute for the Performing Arts (LIPA) and other music schools around the country.

Elsewhere, her outlook and career has less in common with Sumit. Where he has drawn on his education and the organization of business relationships with artists and others in the music industries, Nyah has drawn more from her experience outside the music industries (in retail management) and relies on more informal support networks than those which are governed by (for example) industry organizations, management contracts or partnership agreements. She talks of the importance of having a mentor and how she looks up to Sarah Stennett[19] of Turn First as a management role model.

Nyah's career can be seen as something of a juggling act between the twin demands of being a musician and a manager, whereas for Sumit his focus is primarily on business rather than creativity. In addition to this, she finds herself in part of an industry that, according to Sarah Stennett, is 'clearly still male dominated' (see Jones, 2013) which brings with it its own particular set of problems, which have been described by Claire Boucher (aka Grimes) in the *Rookie Yearbook* (2014).

Nyah and Boucher have, along with their art, developed and used a range of entrepreneurial traits and managerial skills, acquired as a result of access to technology and information that has often been gained from beyond traditional educational and music industries channels, with other female artists and businesswomen playing an important part in their career paths. Boucher argues that 'just because someone has more qualifications than you doesn't mean they're better than you. We live in the age of technology, so you can Google anything you don't know how to do. The only thing you can't Google is how to be creative and unique. Your thoughts have more value than a degree or a parent in the same field or whatever' (2014).

This perspective, which privileges creativity over business but acknowledges the close relationship between the two, and highlights the empowerment of the artist who is in control of their own affairs, is one that offers an important counterpoint to the historic narratives around artist managers, which have frequently revolved around great men (and they were nearly always men) and their business deals.

Conclusion

One of these men, Colonel Tom Parker, the first hugely successful pop manager, declared categorically in the 1950s that he was *not* an entrepreneur. 'Entrepreneurs wear tuxedos,' he proclaimed. 'And the only time I wore one was when I had to wear one as a waiter. I rented one for 10 bucks, got 15 bucks for the evening's work, so made 5 bucks profit' (Roxon, 1959). Parker offers a confused notion of both what it is to be an entrepreneur and how he saw artist management, but, in 1959, with the world's biggest star on his books and a contract that paid him between 25 to 50 per cent of Elvis Presley's income, Parker could be forgiven for thinking that artist management was easy, lucrative and almost entirely risk free. However, in the period since, the role of the artist manager has been obfuscated by a series of technological and organizational changes in the music industries, while both the notion itself and various definitions of what it is to be an entrepreneur have moved in and out of fashion.

The managers interviewed for this chapter find themselves taking risks, seeking opportunities and juggling the frequently contradictory needs of art and commerce. Both see themselves as entrepreneurs, albeit coming from very different backgrounds, with different relationships to both the business and artistic elements of their work. The contrast between the organization in which Sumit works (ATC) and the small businesses run by Princess Nyah is also marked in terms of both economic and cultural capital.

Rather than being able to draw wider conclusions from their cases and generalize about the nature of artist management and entrepreneurship, they serve to highlight the problems of scope (in what it is to be an artist manager) and definition (in what it is to be an entrepreneur) and offer examples as to the huge range of roles performed by managers in the music industries.

This spectrum of managerial activity and the acceptance that what it is to be an entrepreneur has 'defied consensual definition' (Chell, 2007: 5) are both inadequately covered in much of the existing work in the field of artist management and combine to highlight the need for a better, more nuanced understanding of the entrepreneurial aspects of artist management among both researchers and the managers themselves. With this mind, I will end the chapter by drawing simultaneously on my experience as a researcher and an artist manager to offer three observations and two questions that may be starting points for further investigation.

The first is for those researching the music industries. Previous accounts of the music industries have concentrated on recordings and, to a lesser extent, live music. Artist managers are, however, the point at which most of the key decisions in the music industries are made. Therefore, for researchers to get a better picture of how the music industries work, there is no better starting point than to ask managers: quite simply, they know more about how things work across *all* aspects of the music industries.

The second extends this plea for more research, but argues that to produce a new account of the music industries from the perspective of artist managers requires careful consideration of what type of artist manager to study. Existing accounts are dominated by successful, white, male managers usually working with either pop or rock artists. To fully understand artist management also needs to involve the experiences of, for example, unsuccessful managers or those just starting out, female managers, artists managing themselves, part-time managers (who have other careers), those working in management outside of commercial pop and rock and to look at examples from beyond the UK and USA.

The final point relates to the artist managers themselves and their willingness to be identified as entrepreneurs. The chapter has shown that while many entrepreneurial traits and processes are bound up in some of the routines of artist management, the extent varies, depending on a whole range of factors, not least of which is the attitude and career point of the artists being managed. As a result, some artist managers may view themselves as entrepreneurs while indulging in some decidedly non-entrepreneurial activity (for example, risk management and avoidance). Others may match many of the characteristics of entrepreneurs but find themselves reluctant to embrace the term because of the negative connotations it has acquired in some circles since its embrace by neoliberal governments in the early 1980s. Chell argues that entrepreneurship has been, in many places, driven by a political ideology where only economic value counted and that measurement of success depended on 'who is doing the counting and for what purpose' (ibid: 19).

This requires further adaptations of existing definitions of entrepreneurship in the creative industries to encompass those aspects of the work that are more concerned with the art than the economics. Of crucial importance for managers is that by working with artists who do not always behave in entirely economically rational ways, the extent to which they can behave as entrepreneurs is often limited. Terms like 'art entrepreneurs' and 'cultural entrepreneurs' may come closer to explaining their position, but it is worth remembering that often the artist manager is merely a conduit for the more entrepreneurial inclinations of their artists, outsourcing the real risk to other individuals or organizations. And while it is both tempting and entertaining to view managers as wildly entrepreneurial, the truth is usually more prosaic. For some artists, all they seek in a manager is what Cloonan describes as 'a safe pair of hands' (2015) to handle the non-creative part of what they do. In such cases, our understanding of the work of artist managers is bound up in finding the answer to two unresolved questions: Are they entrepreneurs or administrators? Risk takers or risk averse?

Notes

1   See Williamson and Cloonan (2007). Here we argue for the use of the terms 'music industries' (covering all industrialized music activity but primarily in the recording, live and publishing industries) to avoid confusion caused by the repeated conflation of the 'music industry' with the 'recording industry'. We developed these ideas in Williamson and Cloonan (2011).

2   ATC manage, among others, Nick Cave, PJ Harvey, Jessie Ware and Laura Mvula.

3 See http://www.princessnyah.com. Princess Nyah as well as managing her own career as a recording artist and performer, also runs the clothing brand, Binghi's Boutique.

4 During the 1990s, I managed bis, El Hombre Trajeado and Swelling Meg. More recently, I managed Belle and Sebastian and their associated side projects (God Help The Girl, Stevie Jackson) between 2006–12.

5 As a field of academic study, the origins of Popular Music Studies is often dated to the formation of IASPM (International Association for the Study of Popular Music) in 1981.

6 He was a member of the successful group, Latin Quarter, managed by Marcus Russell of Ignition Management (who also manages Oasis).

7 Jones defines the 'Music Industry' as distinct from the music industries and music industry (2012: 10–11).

8 Crown Talent manage a range of musicians including Jesse J and Ella Henderson, but also has clients in broadcasting, sport and fashion.

9 Described by Rogan as 'the most famous British pop manager of the fifties (1986: 19), Parnes managed Billy Fury, Marty Wilde and many early British rock 'n' roll acts.

10 See Addley (2012) for the recent travails of Leonard Cohen.

11 See http://www.themmf.net for more details.

12 Rogan identifies thirteen types of manager in his 'paradigms of pop management' (1988: 14–18).

13 Cantillon refers to them as 'risk-bearers' (1755), for Adam Smith they were 'enterprisers' (1776).

14 Artist Nation is a division of the live music/ticketing conglomerate, Live Nation.

15 For a survey of definitions of corporate entrepreneurship see Sharma and Chrisman (2007).

16 Manager of Dusty Springfield and LaBelle.

17 Former manager of Peter Gabriel and The Pretenders.

18 Her first release, Frontline, was in 2009; her most recent, Champion, came out in summer 2014.

19 For a detailed account of Sarah Stennett's career see Jones (2013).

References

Addley, E. (2012), 'Leonard Cohen's poetic thanks as former manager and lover is jailed for harassment', *The Guardian* (online), http://www.theguardian.com/music/2012/apr/19/leonard-cohen-former-manager-jailed [accessed 1 September 2014].

Aggestam, M. (2007), 'Art-Entrepreneurship in the Scandinavian music industry', in C. Henry (ed.), *Entrepreneurship in the Creative Industries: An International Perspective*, Cheltenham: Edward Elgar, pp. 30–53.

Bagheot, C. and N. Kanaar (1998), *Music Business Agreements*, London: Waterlow.

Becker, H. (1982), *Art Worlds*, Berkeley and Los Angeles: University of California Press.

Birkinshaw, J. (2003), 'The Paradox of Corporate Entrrpeneurship', *Strategy and Business,* 30, http://www.strategy-business.com/article/8276?pg=0 [accessed 7 September 2014].

Boucher, C. (2014), 'Grimes Gives Advice on Making Music and How to be a Boss', *Elle Online*, http://www.elle.com/news/culture/lessons-from-grimes-on-how-to-be-a-boss [accessed 10 October 2014].

Cantillon, R. (2010 [1755]) *An Essay on Economic Theory*, Auburn, AL: LVMI.

Carroll, J. (2013), 'Just what is going on at U2 Inc?', *The Irish Times,* 27 November 2013, available at: http://www.irishtimes.com/blogs/ontherecord/2013/11/27/just-what-is-going-on-at-u2-inc/ [accessed 2 October 2014].

Chell, E. (2007), 'Social Enterprise and Entrepreneurship: Towards a Convergent Theory of the Entrepreneurial Process', *International Small Business* 25 (1): 5–23.

Cloonan, M. and L. Hulstedt (2013), 'Looking for Something New: The Provision of Popular Music Studies Degrees in the UK in the Twenty First Century', *IASPM@ Journal* 3 (2): 63–77.

Cloonan, M. (2015), 'Managing The Zoeys: Some Reminiscences', in N. Beech and C. Gilmore (eds), *Organising Music: Theory, Practice, Performance*, forthcoming, Cambridge: Cambridge University Press.

DCMS (1998), *Creative Industries' Mapping Exercise: Music*, London: DCMS.

DCMS (2001), *Creative Industries' Mapping Exercise: Music*, London: DCMS.

Drummond, B. (2001), *45*, London: Abacus.

Frith, S., M. Cloonan, M. Brennan and E. Webster (2013), *The History of Live Music in Britain, Volume 1 (1950–1967)*, Aldershot: Ashgate.

Garfield, S. (1986), *Expensive Habits*, London: Faber & Faber.

Hirsch, P. (1970), *The Structure of the Popular Music Industry*, Ann Arbor: University of Michigan Press.

Jones, M. (2012), *The Music Industries*, London: Palgrave.

Jones, R. (2013), 'We Never Give Up On Any Artist', *Music Week*, 13 December, pp. 13–15.

Kirzner, I. (1973), *Competition and Entrepreneurship*, Chicago: University of Chicago Press.

Leyshon, A. (2001), 'Time-Space (and Digital) Compression: software formats, musical networks and the reorganisation of the Music Industry', *Environment and Planning*, 33 (1): 49–77.

Leyshon, A., P. Webb, S. French, N. Thrift and L. Crewe (2005), 'On the reproduction of the musical economy after the internet', *Media, Culture and Society* 27 (2): 177–209.

Longhurst, B. (1995), *Popular Music and Society*, London: Polity.

Longhurst, B. (2007), *Popular Music and Society*, 2nd ed., London: Polity.

Longhurst, B. and D. Bogdanovic (2014), *Popular Music and Society*, 3rd ed., London: Polity.

LoogOldham, A. (2001), *Stoned*, London: Vintage.

Loog Oldham, A. (2003), *2 Stoned*, London: Vintage.

Loog Oldham, A. (2014), *Stone Free*, London: Because Entertainment.

Lynskey, D. (2014), 'U2: It's the job of art to be divisive', *The Guardian* (online), available at: http://www.theguardian.com/music/2014/oct/12/u2-job-art-divisive-interview [accessed 12 October 2014].

Mair, J. and M. Ignasi, (2006), 'Social Entrepreneurship Research: A Source of explanation, prediction and delight', *Journal of World Business* 41 (1): 36–44.

McGee, A. (2014), *Creation Stories*, London: Pan Macmillan.

Morrow, G. (2009), 'Radiohead's Managerial Creativity', *The International Journal of Research into New Media Technologies* 15 (2): 161–76.

Morrow, G. (2013), 'Regulating Artist Managers: An Insiders' Perspective', *International Journal of Research into New Media Technologies* 15 (2): 161–76.

Napier-Bell, S. (2007), *Black Vinyl, White Powder*, London: Ebury.

Napier-Bell, S. (2014), *Ta-Ra-Ra-Boom-De-Ay: The Dodgy Business of Popular Music*, London: Unbound.

Negus, K. (1992), *Producing Pop*, London: Edward Arnold.

Negus, K. (1999), *Music Genres and Corporate Cultures*, London: Routledge.

Rogan, J. (1988), *Star Makers and Svengalis*, London: Trans Atlantic Publications.

Roxon, H. (1959), 'I Met the Colonel', *Elvis Australia*, http://www.elvis.com.au/presley/article_imetthecolonel.shtml [accessed 15 August 2014].

Schumpeter, J. (1934), *Theory of Economic Development*, Cambridge, MA: Harvard University Press.

Sharma, P. and J. Chrisman (2007), 'Toward a reconciliation of the definition and issues in the field of corporate entrepreneurship', in A. Cuervo, D. Ribeiro and S. Roig (eds), *Entrepreneurship: Concepts, Theory and Perspective*, Berlin: Springer, pp. 83–105.

Shuker, R. (1994), *Understanding Popular Music*, London: Routledge.

Shuker, R. (2001), *Understanding Popular Music*, 2nd ed., London: Routledge.

Shuker, R. (2007), *Understanding Popular Music Culture*, 3rd ed., London: Routledge.

Shuker, R. (2012), *Understanding Popular Music Culture*, 4th ed., London: Routledge.

Smith, A. (1982 [1776]), *The Wealth of Nations*, London: Penguin Classics.

Swedburg, R. (2006), 'The cultural entrepreneur and the creative industries: beginning in Vienna', *Journal of Cultural Economy* 30 (4): 243–61.

Taylor, G. (2013), 'New Export Scheme to Promote British Music Overseas Now Open For Business', *BPI online*, http://www.bpi.co.uk/searchresult/new-export-scheme-to-promote-british-music-overseas-now-open-for-business.aspx [accessed 15 October 2014].

Webster, J. (2013), 'Introduction', in N. Riches (ed.), *The Music Management Bible*, London: SMT, pp. 9–10.

Williamson, J. and M. Cloonan (2007), 'Rethinking the "music industry"', *Popular Music* 26 (2): 305–22.

Williamson, J. and M. Cloonan (2013), 'Contextualising the contemporary recording industry', in L. Marshall (ed.), *The International Recording Industry*, London: Routledge, pp. 11–29.

Wilson, T. (2012), *24 Hour Party People*, London: Macmillan.

Websites

ATC: http://www.atcmanagement.com
Binghi's Boutique: http://www.binghisboutique.com
BPI: http://www.bpi.co.uk
MMF: http://www.themmf.net
Princess Nyah: http://www.princessnyah.com

5

Live Music

Kenneth Forbes

Outline

This chapter locates the entrepreneur within the live music sector and explores some of the entrepreneurial characteristics that can underpin success within this environment. In general, the live sector is mainly focused on the production and consumption of live music, performances or events. Possessing a relatively wide scope, it accommodates a variety of activities-enterprises, such as agent, promoter, venue owner, festival or tour organizer-manager, media-publicity representative, ticket administrator, sound technician, amongst numerous other associated roles.

Whilst debate surrounds the monopolization of key parts of the live industry by global conglomerates such as Live Nation-Ticketmaster (Sweney, 2013), live music's capacity to function at a myriad of levels (along with its increasing popularity and commercial potential) acts as an incentive for entrepreneurial initiatives. Undeniably, given the manner in which live music can matter to its audience (Frith, 2007), the sector is particularly open to new and innovative approaches across its established parameters.

This chapter possesses five main sections. Following an overview of the historical development and present status of the live industry, an outline is provided of the role of the entrepreneur within this sector. Two case studies are then featured before the conclusion to the chapter draws together the various discussion threads and offers some further guidance to the potential live music entrepreneur.

Introduction

As a key means of consuming music, live music is privileged by many for several reasons. If anything, it is one of the few music industry-entertainment sectors to commercially benefit from the digitalization of media content. This follows the inherent limitations within the digital environment, whereby the facility to produce perfect copies of texts functions to marginalize forms of uniqueness. The opposite scenario can apply to live performance. Certainly, its very essence vouches for its exclusiveness; it can only take place at a specific time/place, and it also involves a unique temporal simultaneity between the audience and artist (Auslander, 2011: 61).

Similarly, within experiences such as the live event, Pine and Gilmore (1999) refer to the way in which the various components of the experience itself combine to capture and elevate the tangible and sensory nature of the occasion. In essence, attending live music concerts can encapsulate and symbolize an experiential 'thereness' that is difficult to reproduce by any other means.

This uniqueness is a factor that has been recognized and capitalized on by the live sector, and, as a result, has led to a vast increase in the scale of the live music market (Frith, 2007: 6). In this instance, the UK collection agency PRS for Music (2012) calculated that the 2011 domestic revenues for live music (£1.6bn) were far greater than those generated by recorded music (£1.1bn), continuing a trend first established in 2008.

The sector's commercial viability has been stimulated by the growth of both the arena and festival circuits in the UK. In 2013, almost 8 million customers attended 1,136 live music performances within the UK arena circuit, representing increases of 25 per cent and 20 per cent respectively (Pakinkis, 2014). New additions to the arena network, such as the SSE Hydro (Glasgow) and First Direct Arena (Leeds), have both made major contributions to these totals. Similarly, the UK festival itinerary has increased dramatically since the beginning of the twenty-first century, with 682 UK music festivals of some description taking place during 2013 (Moore, 2013).

Whilst the main UK festival events like Glastonbury and T In The Park continue to attract media attention and large audience numbers, an upsurge in smaller (5,000–35,000 capacity) boutique-type festivals has also been evident, with events such as Latitude, Green Man and End of the Road, all gaining popularity (Moore, 2013). Overall, a report by the industries umbrella group UK Music (2013) calculated that the UK live industry attracted 6.5m domestic and international music tourists in 2012, with these customers spending £1.3bn in the process of attending both concerts and festivals.

Such developments represent a fairly recent trend. In the main, the UK live sector of the 1960s and 1970s embraced an amateur aesthetic. Encumbered by a badly maintained ad-hoc circuit of town halls, theatres, cinemas and ballrooms, run-down live locations, such as the Rainbow Theatre in London (1971–81) and the Glasgow Apollo (1973–85), represented what were considered to be key venues within the prevailing live sector. However, as stage productions grew larger and the demand for live music increased, the numerous shortfalls within this somewhat antiquated circuit became increasingly evident. This was addressed in part by the establishment of a UK arena network in Birmingham (1976), Glasgow (1985) and Manchester (1995), which aligned with increasing modes of professionalism and revenue generation within the live sector.

Progressions of this nature inevitably led to a few international conglomerates, such as Live Nation, controlling large numbers of venues, festivals and live promoters (Frith, 2007: 2). It has also led to commercial sponsors (O2, Carling, Tennents, etc.) establishing a presence within the live sector through the branding of venues and festivals (ibid: 7).

Whilst differences in scale exist between festivals and venues at the higher end of the scale and their small-medium equivalents, forms of mutual dependence prevail between the two entities. This is mainly due to the fact that large venues and festivals depend upon the existence of viable live music ecology at all levels, which largely provide them with a regular supply of breakthrough artists (Behr et al., 2014). However, research suggests that small-to-medium independent venues represent the weakest point of the live music ecology (Behr et al., 2014). Here lies a crucial challenge for the live sector.

Existing without the financial backing and infrastructure of their larger counterparts, independent grassroots venues and festivals can face problems that their greater equivalents can more easily accommodate. Accordingly, smaller independent festivals can more regularly go bust (*New Musical Express*, 2014) or be cancelled at late notice (Reynolds, 2014). Similarly, a number of small live music venues (affectionately known as the 'toilet circuit' in the UK) have been forced to close due to gentrification and under-investment (Harris, 2013). Other factors to impact on their sustainability include local licensing constraints, such as those involving noise abatement issues (Williamson, 2014).

Although prospective entrepreneurs must remain wary of such developments, sufficient scope exits, as the examples to follow will show, for new and innovative ventures to succeed. Engagement with, or at least recognition of, future trends within the live sector can also help form the basis of success. In this instance, the drift towards cashless music festivals assumes significance. Indeed, industry association UK Festivals predicts that cashless payments are on the verge of making a major breakthrough, with the totally cashless Standon Calling Festival of 2013 being the first money-free festival (2013: 26).

Cashless festivals provide several benefits for organizers and audiences. Festival management not only avoid cash-handling costs, they can also track and data mine the spending habits of festival-goers, thereafter adjusting their facilities to align with these patterns and therefore increase their overall revenue potential (Waddell, 2014). Similarly, fans that attend the cashless festivals no longer have to worry about possessing a ticket for admission, carrying sufficient cash or retaining a credit card.

In general, the widespread proliferation of music festivals and outdoor stadium concerts in the UK, Europe and North America has led to the creation of a highly popular (yet slightly precarious) live circuit tier that effectively splits the annual gig calendar in two. Between May and August, festivals and outdoor concerts predominate, whereas indoor concerts assume more importance during September to April. As the two case studies featured in this chapter will show, both circuits can present the live music entrepreneur with a wealth of opportunities from which success can emanate. Before we look at these examples in more detail, some further elaboration of the history of the entrepreneur within this sector will be offered to provide a foundation for the current models.

The role of the entrepreneur in the live sector

Until the late 1960s, several factors limited the extent of entrepreneurial activity within the UK live sector. A dependence on the increasingly dated pop package tour business model, inadequate technology, and the sector's fragile infrastructure were among the main reasons for the restriction of suitable opportunities. However, following increasing recognition of the commercial potential offered by live rock, a new breed of young promoter was attracted towards the live sector during the late 1960s and early 1970s (Brennan and Webster, 2011: 10–11).

One entrepreneur to emerge from this environment was the promoter Harvey Goldsmith. Unlike his predecessors who had operated within the realms of variety entertainment, he learned his trade as a Social Secretary during the mid-1960s within the burgeoning UK college-university live circuit. Goldsmith subsequently established his reputation by booking and promoting many of the then-emerging rock artists, several of whom went on to achieve global success during the 1970s. By 1976 he had become the UK's leading promoter, handling The Rolling Stones' landmark tour of that year, and, of course, went on to organize Live Aid in 1985.

Other notable promoters and live sector operatives also followed a similar path. As an example, Rod MacSween, Director of the International Talent Booking agency, was Social Secretary at Exeter University between 1969–72. This process continued through to the early to mid 1980s, when Stuart Galbraith of Kilimanjaro Concerts (Leeds University), Simon Moran of SJM Concerts (University of Sheffield), Mark Mackie of Regular Music (University of Glasgow) and Geoff Ellis of DF Concerts (Middlesex Polytechnic), all assumed equivalent roles.

Like many of their peers, these live industry entrepreneurs were initially drawn towards the sector by their passion for live music. In each case, their business acumen was largely gained through high levels of engagement with a wide range of innovative entrepreneurial initiatives that functioned to establish their respective profiles, as well as provide the foundations for success. Certainly, a quick glance at their career histories reveals a multitude of successful enterprises in which these entrepreneurs have been involved. For example, Goldsmith was a leading figure behind the establishment of the music charities the Princes Trust and the Teenage Cancer Trust, whilst Moran was responsible for the hugely successful comeback tours by Take That (2006, 2009, 2011) and The Stone Roses (2012–13).

However, closer inspection will also reveal that most have also experienced business failures at some point in their careers, whether it is cancelled or loss-making festivals (Ellis, Galbraith and Mackie), or other forms of financial disappointment (Goldsmith). Such occasional deviations from success can, nevertheless, form a crucial part of the learning process for entrepreneurs, and reflect the common business adage that failure must be experienced in some capacity in order to fully appreciate the (much more plentiful) achievements that will form the basis of their everyday endeavours.

Obviously, the live industry has moved on greatly since Goldsmith gained success, with the amount of competition alone marking a paradigm shift within the sector. Therefore, in the face of such competition prospective entrepreneurs need to be aware of the limitations of 'just' providing a standard service to potential customers, whether it be organizing a festival, promoting a concert or running a venue. Instead, a sense prevails that, to achieve the required impact, contemporary live music experiences should consist of multiple influential layers and be more responsive to the needs of the individual music fan.

A purveyor of this approach is Dominique Soma, the winner of the 2014 Young Creative Entrepreneurship Live Music Award. This prestigious British Council accolade was conferred as a result of Soma's active role in promoting live hip-hop events in South Africa through the Back to the City Festival and WeHeartBeat initiative (Shezi, 2014). Back to the City, held in Johannesburg, uses Freedom Day as a focus for a large-scale hip-hop event that brings together the local music community, and incorporates 'graffiti jams', DJs, dance competitions and live performances from both local and national artists. From humble beginnings in 2007, when 3,500 attended the event, the festival has grown considerably, to the extent that over 22,000 tickets were sold in 2014.

WeHeartBeat, Soma's main enterprise, is a monthly touring event that features rising hip-hop artists, and which engages with local DJs, producers and studios as part of the itinerary. It also encompasses regular 'meet and greets' between audience members and artists, as well as the provision of multimedia access for the virtual fan. Overall, Soma's entrepreneurial vision can therefore be seen to provide the ideal range of multi-layered experience that resonates with customers and other stakeholders.

Another successful enterprise that embraces a similar dynamic is Songkick, a personalized-localized concert recommendation app developed in London by university graduates Ian Hogarth, Michelle You and Pete Smith in 2007. The app has since achieved global success through 10m subscribers being recruited between 2012 and 2014 (with half of this total being based in the USA), and by also generating ticket sales of over $100m during the same period (Bradshaw, 2014). As part of this process, Songkick, which makes recommendations based on the subscriber's digital music collection and integrates with the music-media platforms YouTube, Sound Cloud and Spotify, has since established the largest global database of concert listings (Millner, 2013). Again, it can be seen that the potency of the live music aesthetic served as the initial driver to create the product, as co-founder Ian Hoggarth explains: 'The overarching philosophy of Songkick is that we believe an amazing concert experience can change your life. It has done for everyone who works here, and the reason we get out of bed in the morning is to try and make more people have those experiences. The reason that those experiences are so magical and so memorable is because of the connection between the artist and the fans. What makes a great concert is the atmosphere, and the atmosphere is the function of the artist and the fans, not just one of those two. It's that connection that matters' (Millner, 2013).

Overall, Songkick's capacity to align with live music's 'thereness', along with its Web 3.0 functionality and personalization, means that the app, like other successful live music enterprises, holds a multi-layered appeal for its many users. Indeed, achieving similar levels of engagement with customers is a facet that underlines the success of our case studies, which are featured in the two sections to follow.

ArcTanGent

Case study: Goc O'Callaghan (ArcTanGent Festival)

Our main live music entrepreneur case study features Goc (pronounced 'Jock') O'Callaghan, one of the three organizers behind the ArcTanGent festival. The festival, which is held just outside Bristol, launched in 2013 and has a capacity of 5,000, with eighty bands appearing on four stages over three days in late August. Before her involvement with ArcTanGent, O'Callaghan gained experience by organizing a range of smaller festivals. Overall, she regards her involvement with ArcTanGent as a means of fulfilling her life-long passion for music, and as a vehicle for accomplishing her dream to create memories for millions for people who attend her events.

Following the successful completion of a professional and commercial photography degree, where she specialized in music, O'Callaghan became disheartened by the experience of working for other festival organizers. This led her to 'take the plunge' and set up her own business, which proved to be both a frightening and inspiring experience: 'Running my own business with no background in business management was a baptism of fire, but an experience I am so glad to have had. By running your own business you are giving yourself the best education you could ever have, learning something new every day' (O'Callaghan, 2014).

The first ArcTanGent Festival in 2013 was regarded as a widespread success by the 3,500 festival-goers who travelled from Europe and North America to attend the event. The 2014 event was sold out and nominated for three festival awards.

Achieving a niche identity may represent the key foundations of any entrepreneur's business mantra, but, as the only global festival dedicated to the math-rock, post-rock and noise-rock music genres, ArcTanGent's 'niche-ness' is more than discernible. For O'Callaghan, 'Finding a niche in the market, and fulfilling the requirements of that niche' (ibid), represents a key characteristic of the music entrepreneur. Furthermore, whilst conceding that the role of the entrepreneur presents challenges, she also recognizes that it can, more importantly, produce rich and unique experiential rewards: '[It involves] working tirelessly to achieve your goal. It's about exploring new opportunities and challenging yourself every single day. It is also the best education available, not a day goes past when I don't learn something. There are often extreme lows and highs with being entrepreneurial. There are often days when it can feel like you're banging your head against a brick wall, when you are working so hard and yet feel like you are taking two steps backwards. However, this is compensated for by the massive highs; I cannot explain to you the feeling I had standing on the main stage as the headline act took to it. There I was with 3,500 people having the time of their lives, all as a result of the hard work that myself and the rest of the team had put in to making the festival happen. Never has a glass of champagne tasted so good!' (ibid).

Ultimately, O'Callaghan feels that the appeal of a small festival like ArcTanGent (which charged £70 for a weekend ticket plus camping in 2014) is framed by the clear dichotomy that exists between it and large, corporate music festivals, where overpricing and poor standards prevail: 'punters are becoming more savvy to being brainwashed by ill-placed big brand sponsorships and being overcharged for both the event ticket and all amenities on site. I mean who really wants to pay £6 for a generic warm, sub-standard beer in a paper cup? Especially after having forked out a couple of hundred quid for a ticket' (ibid).

'Becoming' an entrepreneur is a process that O'Callaghan believes follows a trajectory whereby, 'You start as an ideas person, move into project management, then you become an entrepreneur. I work with a group of friends, and we are entrepreneurial. There's no financial backing, we're not doing it for money – it's more of a lifestyle choice, it's *not* for financial security. You work fourteen hours a day for three weeks, then nineteen hours a day for three days but it's not like work. You have to keep learning. The step up from year one to year two in festivals is considerable' (ibid).

Already discernible within such reflections is that a high level of commitment is required to organize a live music festival. However, it also involves some additional components, as O'Callaghan indicates: 'A nine-to-five work life has never been something I have aspired to. In fact, I've actively rebelled against it. Why spend eight hours a day doing something you hate when you can spend sixteen hours a day doing something you love! It doesn't feel like work if you enjoy it' (ibid).

Consequently, this level of commitment *and* passion can function to emphasize that running a music-related business can symbolize a distinct music-as-life agenda. Ultimately, as in O'Callaghan's case, this can produce immense dividends for those concerned: 'If I were to put a fee on what I've learned in the last week alone it would be huge. I have had experiences I couldn't pay for' (ibid).

Such outcomes therefore emerge as noteworthy elements within enterprises of this nature. Accordingly, the concept of experience creation (Sundbo and Darmer, 2008) assumes significance and provides a basis for a deeper understanding of our featured entrepreneur's motivation and commitment. The 'experience' in question refers to the experience economy, a concept defined by Pine and Gilmore (1999), whereby an experience, be it of a leisure, cultural or tourist-related nature, is one where its distinct components and aesthetics combine to create the unique user *experience*. Sundbo and Darmer (2008: 4) regard the process of creating this experience (its design, management and organization) as a product in itself, and as one that enhances the final product consumed by the customer. In effect, the customer ultimately benefits by experiencing the fruits of the construction of the experience.

It is within such realms where O'Callaghan's experiential epiphany ('I cannot explain to you the feeling I had . . . I have had experiences that I couldn't pay for') function to underline the way in which the experience creation process can represent more than sufficient incentive for the entrepreneur. In this case, the long hours and lack of financial security matter little as such constraints and commitments helped to produce the final product; the successful live music festival. Of course, O'Callaghan's passion for music provides the initial impetus for this progression.

Certainly, further research by Darmer (2008: 113–14) on the Danish independent record sector suggests that similar forms of passion can represent a major entrepreneurial driver and also provide symbolic compensation for the lack of profits that can manifest in some cases. Why should music resonate to such an extent, given that, in some respects, it functions to fragment traditional models of profit incentive for the entrepreneur?

The answer perhaps lies within music's potential to reflect the human condition. In his study entitled *Music as Social Life* (2008: 1), the musicologist Thomas Turino illustrates that music's capacity to shape the social being is one of its prime functions: 'Musical sounds are a powerful human resource, often at the heart of our most profound social occasions and experiences . . . [however] music is not a unitary art form, but rather . . . this term refers to fundamentally distinct types of

activities that fulfil different needs and ways of being human
... musical participation and experience are valuable for the
processes of personal and social integration that make us
whole.'

Indeed, Darmer's (2008: 121) study identifies similar
sentiments within the Danish record label sector, where a
passion for music enabled the drive and commitment shown
by the entrepreneurs in question, with the author regarding
this process as symbolizing an extension of their social beings:
'... passion [about music] is an imminent part of ... their
lives. They cannot stop being passionate without stopping
being entrepreneurs and humans as well.'

In this respect, O'Callaghan's passion for music can be
regarded as being a 'natural' and true reflection of the live
music entrepreneur. Whilst similar passion-entrepreneurial
drive alignments may exist in other creative arts-related
sectors, music's ability to resonate within the human condition
means that this facet can be regarded as a meaningful and
compelling component that can bolster the successful live
music enterprise.

Of course, entrepreneurs do not exist in a vacuum; neither
do they emerge from one. Like any other entrepreneur,
O'Callaghan possesses previous work-life experiences and
now operates within an environment whereby these experiences
can resonate: 'Prior to running ArcTanGent I was a production
manager working in the experiential industry, often dealing
with event sponsorship on behalf of brands. This gave me great
foundations in being an accomplished project manager, dealing
with all the production requirements for campaigns. The
business I set up to run my first small festival and stages at
other festivals taught me the business acumen that is key to the
success of ArcTanGent: contracts, sales, marketing, promotion,
staffing, licensing, pretty much everything. As an entrepreneur
you have to be a jack of all trades to some extent; not that you
can do everything yourself, but you do need to know enough
about everything to ask the right questions to get things done'
(O'Callaghan, 2014).

O'Callaghan makes several valid points. Building on her previous experiences, she relates that levels of business acumen were acquired across a range of activities. The reference to being a 'jack of all trades' is a recognized prerequisite within such enterprises, yet it can serve to overwhelm the early-stage entrepreneur (especially if it involves unfamiliar legal or financial transactions). However, as O'Callaghan indicates, even with just a limited amount of knowledge on specific issues, entrepreneurs can use available networks to both gain further guidance, as well as establish effective working relationships: 'Your network is key – whatever you come across there is professional service sharing – the more you network the more you find people will help with advice and contacts. I was uncomfortable with networking to begin with, but it's like gearing up for a stage performance – you start with small talk – you need to make sure you know what you're talking about. Also, some key personnel can be quite bullish, and this sometimes can be off-putting, but you don't need to talk to the top person – you just need to get a contact at the company. Essentially, the power of networking is phenomenal; you never know how one of these contacts you have met will come in handy. [It] does produce a driven versus cautious approach – you learn who to talk to and what to say. There is more transparency due to social media. However, a rant on Facebook/ Twitter can be counter-productive due to its visibility. You are your own PR effectively' (O'Callaghan, 2014).

The extent of O'Callaghan's in-depth and articulate response provides clear indications about the significance that networking possesses within an enterprise of this nature. The validity of the oft-repeated business idiom, 'it's not what you know, but who you know' is perhaps debatable, but its underlying message essentially remains true within the live music sector. For O'Callaghan, networking proved to be an invaluable experience. After an initial reluctance dissolved, it was used as a tool to expand her entrepreneurial horizons through sharing knowledge and services with like-minded professionals in the live sector.

Again, the passion that drives O'Callaghan and other entrepreneurs in the live industry provides a foundation for these relationships to develop. Indeed, a study by Leek and Canning (2011) found that the degree of networking within passion-based industries, such as the live industry, was closely linked with the depth of social capital that can emerge as a result of this activity. Defined by Woolcock (1998: 155) as being the 'norms and networks facilitating collective action for mutual benefit', social capital can be regarded as a fundamental ingredient of success in the live sector. From this perspective, Anderson and Jack (2002) refer to the way in which networking within entrepreneurial circles acts both as a 'glue' and 'lubricant' among stakeholders. This process, suggest the authors (ibid), subsequently forms the basis of dynamic relationships that engender social capital, with mutual acquaintances acting as a catalyst for economic interaction.

In this instance, Boitnott offers several tips for networking among music industry entrepreneurs (some of which O'Callaghan is clearly following), whereby: 'Success in the music industry requires being a talented networker as much as being talented'. Whilst technology can pave the way for networking activity, the author suggests that 'face time' (in its original sense) is of prime importance for meeting key contacts, especially on a one-to-one basis at key networking events, such as conferences and trade exhibitions (Boitnott, 2014).

Boitnott also stresses the importance of establishing the correct contact (as being one that directly relates to your business requirements) within the host enterprise, as well as determining the most appropriate or preferred means of establishing and maintaining contact, be it by telephone, text, social network or in person (Boitnott, 2014). Obviously, maintaining these relationships also possesses importance, especially those contacts that may appear, initially at least, to hold limited potential. This follows research conducted by Granovetter (1973), which found that 'weak-tie' low-activity networks tended to be more profitable than 'strong-ties' as they hold the key to a wider range of social networks.

Whilst it can be clearly seen that O'Callaghan has established a wide range of successful business relationships, she admitted that, on occasion, some difficulties were experienced due to misconceptions about gender roles: 'With production staff in particular there's an assumption that you're male. I've experienced all sorts of responses. On one occasion I walked into a production office and introduced myself to the stage manager who said "Goc O'Callaghan? And you're a girl . . . AND THAT'S COOL!" However, there can be an underlying sense in some quarters that you can't "deliver" for some reason. Nevertheless, I climb the rigs and/or scaffolding and just get on with it – it's not a problem. We work with volunteers and students who are female – we had a female stage manager who had to tell an American band to cut their set to avoid over-running, but this presented no problems whatsoever. It depends more on the level of empowerment. In this case we had an 11pm curfew, and there would have been significant consequences if this hadn't been met.'

O'Callaghan identifies an issue where her gender can impact on her working relationships, albeit this may 'just' happen occasionally. However, in the UK and USA at least, current data on the issues surrounding gender equality in the live music sector is scarce and, in this respect, this may prove to be a fruitful area for future research. Nevertheless, historical research and anecdotal evidence from within the wider music industries framework, suggest there are sufficient grounds for O'Callaghan's concerns.

In the early 1990s Keith Negus (1992) suggested that female staff in the record industry generally assumed what were considered gender-specific occupations, such as those encapsulating secretarial and marketing responsibilities. More recently, in the keynote John Peel Lecture of 2013, the artist Charlotte Church referred to the male-dominated music business as possessing a 'juvenile perspective on gender' (Rogers, 2013).

Such views are framed by what Leonard (2007) regards as the fundamental issue intrinsic to rock music, whereby, despite recent improvements in equivalent fields, the genre continues to be understood as masculine. Additionally, Rogers, who conducted interviews with a range of female music entrepreneurs, also found that most had encountered direct or indirect forms of discrimination, with gender-role expectations being a key cause. However, faced by such occurrences, these entrepreneurs (as was the case with O'Callaghan) were incentivized towards confronting these gender misconstructions, thus, paradoxically, adding further to their entrepreneurial skillset (Rogers, 2013).

Mairead Nash, manager of Florence and the Machine, believes that gender issues are changing for the better within the music industries. Nash credits the digital environment for initiating this process, whereby it has served to democratize content provision and fragment the entrenched music industry, along with its associated gender-related workplace practices (Rogers, 2013). Recent indicators suggest that she may be correct. In 2012, the umbrella group UK Music launched a large-scale initiative to improve equality and diversity within the wider music industries (UK Music, 2012), thus raising awareness of gender issues. Furthermore, UK Government figures for 2013 show that a higher proportion of women (51.2 per cent) are employed than men in the 'music, performing and visual arts' sector (Ingham, 2014). Although further research has to yet confirm this, the live music sector may well be benefiting from such trends. Certainly, O'Callaghan serves as a prime exemplar of this trajectory.

Some final thoughts from O'Callaghan on the role of the entrepreneur serve to reiterate some of the main points made in the preceding discussion. Asked if she agreed with the statement that, 'everyone who works in the music industries is an entrepreneur', O'Callaghan was emphatic in her response: 'Definitely – without a shadow of a doubt. To stay a leader, even in a nine-to-five job in music you need to stay on top of things. It also relates to the accessibility of music. It's now a different world – young people are saturated in music.'

Again, clear indications are given about the level of commitment and passion that is required to maintain an entrepreneurial profile. It also signifies that, given the accessibility of music, enterprises must provide an additional level of experience for their potential customers.

Finally, the entrepreneur for this case study was asked to reflect on the relevance that her higher education (a degree in Professional and Commercial Photography, specializing in music) held towards her present role and whether higher education helped to provide a basis for successful music-related enterprises? 'Courses are now more open, accessible and authentic, although you don't need an education to work in the industry – it can almost be like playing dumb at times. However, if I could suggest one invaluable attribute for young entrepreneurs to possess, then that would be passion. Whatever aspect of the music industry you wish to work in, passion will give you the drive and determination to achieve your dreams. A raw passion combined with talent will fuel learning and consequently experience will be gathered along the way.'

Following her success at ArcTanGent, O'Callaghan is now looking to expand, with consideration being given towards establishing a similar festival in America.

In summary, our first case study shows that passion, enthusiasm and commitment can provide the initial foundations for the live music enterprise. It also indicates that the live music *experience*, whether it relates to the experience-creation or experience-realization, can prove to be a potent incentive for the entrepreneur.

Although located in a different sub-sector of the live music industry, our second case study shares some similarities with the one just described, not least its position as another entry-point location for the potential live music entrepreneur; the small live venue.

Case study: Joe Smillie, the Glad Café

Our second case study takes us to the Glad Café, a small live music venue that opened in Glasgow's Southside in 2012. The 120-capacity venue hosts and promotes a regular array of Indie, acoustic and electronic gigs, amongst other live events. Since opening, it has established a close working relationship with several of the city's leading promoters, as well as local and touring artists. Some of the luminaries who have performed at the Café include Norman Blake (Teenage Fanclub), Cate Le Bon, and The Trembling Bells. Framed by an arts-related DIY aesthetic, the venue also holds film nights, political debates, and small theatre presentations. As a result, most evenings in the Café's busy schedule have a live event of some description.

Whilst the Café could be regarded as being part of the aforementioned 'toilet circuit' venue tier based on its size alone, it is far removed from any such associations due to the high standard of its facilities. Certainly, as well as boasting an award-winning food menu, the venue also possesses a professional live set up with a thirty-two channel sound desk within pleasant surroundings for both audience and artists. The venture has adopted a social enterprise business model, where it re-invests any profits back into the business and undertakes local community obligations. In this case the venue has established the Glad Foundation that, among other functions, supplies low cost music lessons to local inhabitants. As a result, the Café possesses strong links with the local community.

Despite its high quality facilities and focus on aesthetics, the venue, like others within a similar urban setting, has also suffered complaints about noise pollution. Indeed, the complaints forced the Café to close for an entire month in January 2013 to carry out reproofing of the live room. Despite this slight setback, the venue has progressed to extend its live event portfolio and garner further plaudits from its many stakeholders.

Reflecting on the path that the venue has followed since its inception, co-owner Joe Smillie, a relatively young veteran of several Glasgow-based independent bands, offers some salient guidance to the potential live music entrepreneur. Smillie, who benefited from the award of a Popular Music degree from Napier University, feels that, like O'Callaghan, the live music experience still holds resonance for audiences and artists. However, Smillie is keen not to focus solely on 'live music', but more so on 'live events': 'I think if you had to depend on ticket sales for live music alone, then that could cause you some problems. For the venue, bar sales are obviously important. However, if you were just a promoter having to depend on the people coming through the door, then that could be a bit of a nightmare if they don't turn up in the numbers you expected. When we were planning the venue we asked some of our friends as to what type of live events they would like to see, and they wanted to see other things such as film shows, art shows and talks and things like that. To fill up the schedule "just" with music would be a bit ... you need some variety basically. Rather than appeal to one demographic with live music, you can appeal to five demographics by putting on a wider range of events.'

In many ways, Smillie is following the commercial trends established by much larger venues and promoters, whereby profitable new event genres (such as comedy and theatre productions, musicals, family shows, etc.) have been adopted as standard (Holt, 2010: 251–2). Even the live music events at the venue assume forms of distinctiveness above and beyond the 'ordinary' live gig. Unique collaborations, themed events and special 'one-offs', all help to make many of the music gigs at the Glad Café more of an event in itself. This further illustrates the importance for live music entrepreneurs to confront the issue of 'just' meeting the expectations of customers and other stakeholders. In essence, there are many other small live music venues in Glasgow, but none could be said to embrace many of the distinct characteristics that the Glad Café encapsulates through their live events.

Again, like O'Callaghan, Smillie is driven by his passion for live music and also recognizes that this aspect functions to make entrepreneurial activity within the music industries somewhat different from other business sectors. However, he emphasizes that this passion can be severely tested by the financial and legal elements involved when trying to establish a new enterprise within the live music sector: 'For us it was three years of hell trying to get the business off the ground and obtaining various grants and funding. A lot of this fell through and, in a way, we were glad this happened because we eventually found this current space, and this is so much better than the ones we failed to get before.'

Overall, Smillie regards the whole experience of establishing a small live music venue as being an immensely constructive one, which has functioned to apply a distinctly positive sheen to the entire enterprise: 'We've built up a good name here, and you get to deal with a range of people that enhance your day. So, yes, I certainly feel empowered in a positive way.'

Therefore, in a similar way to O'Callaghan's experiences at ArcTanGent, it can also be seen that both positive and negative aspects of the experience creation process assume the merits of a key entrepreneurial driver. Reference to the venue's 'good name' is something that is considered important by Smillie, and is one that he feels can be both helped and hindered by social media: 'I suppose one of the things that resonate is how important it is to maintain the good name of the Company, and how easy it is to have this damaged through things like social media. This is something you've got to be wary of.'

Smillie makes a valid point. There are, of course, several benefits to small enterprises possessing a solid social network presence, not least the ability to attract and maintain a digital relationship with its customers. A solid understanding of the way that customers communicate and connect provides the foundation of Solis' (2013: 31–32) concept of the 'C' generation and the '5-Cs' of communication; not so much an age group, more a cohesive demographic force that use technology such as smartphones and tablets as an extension of their existence within social networks to create, connect, consume, communicate and contribute (Solis, 2013). In recognizing that customer markets are shifting in the twenty-first century, Solis (2013) believes that the entrepreneur requires new skillsets to deal with this new type of connected consumerism.

However, as Amrom (2014) cautions, social networks can also possess several potential pitfalls. First, there is a danger involved in being overly tied to these networks as such practice can serve to overwhelm both the customer and the company's identity. Essentially, the key term here is social *presence*, not deluge. Clearly, as an open forum, social networking can also attract both positive and negative comments for the relevant enterprise. In this respect Amrom suggests that it is in the interests of enterprises to respond timeously to both positive and negative comments. This is particularly relevant in the event of negative posts, where a polite and persuasive response can serve to signal high standards of customer service to the person concerned, as well as other stakeholders. In effect, this does not represent damage limitation, more so it represents good customer service.

Overall, similarities with our previous case study are palpable, with a passion for live music, engagement with the experience creation process, and the focus on extending the expectations of customers, all resonating as key characteristics of the live music entrepreneur. We now draw together some of the discussion threads explored thus far within the conclusion to the chapter.

Conclusion

Overall, live music enterprises run by entrepreneurs like O'Callaghan and Smillie succeed due to the way in which they have tapped into live music's overall potency and uniqueness, as well as its capacity to build significant and meaningful relationships with stakeholders.

Central to our understanding of their achievements is the quintessential nature of the live music *experience*. As discussed earlier in the chapter, the live music experience represents an opportunity for the audience member to encounter instances of tangibility, social interaction and 'thereness' that cannot be replicated by any other comparable means. From the perspective of both entrepreneurs, especially O'Callaghan, the actual experience creation process proved to be the most rewarding activity overall. The significance of this process (both positive and negative) lies in the fact that it not only contributes greatly to the 'making of' the well-rounded entrepreneur, it also draws upon, and thereafter shapes, the live music experience of the audience member.

Parallels can therefore be made with the relatively new interdisciplinary research field of design anthropology. The field, which analyses practice associated with products that are designed specifically to meet the needs of those who will use them, also holds a strong affinity with the concept of experience. For Kilbourn (2013: 70) the required 'embeddedness' that the participant has to gain within practice in order to gain the relevant experience, skills and knowledge, requires them to 'embrace the experiential'. The author refers to this as a 'style of knowing'. In this instance, Cooper and Vlaskovits (2013: 119) regard this knowingness as a crucial factor for the entrepreneur: 'You simply cannot solve a problem if you do not deeply understand the problem you're solving and you cannot design a solution if you do not deeply understand those that will use it.'

Similarly, as is the case with our featured entrepreneurs, it can be seen that their desire to 'embrace the experiential' has greatly contributed towards the success of their respective enterprises.

If anything, passion permeates our two case studies. As discussed, this intense enthusiasm for live music can, perhaps more so than in other type of enterprise, help the entrepreneur to shoulder some of the initial difficulties that will no doubt be encountered during the formative period for the business. According to Christopher Small in his ground-breaking study *Musicking* (1998), music, especially live music, is not so much a 'thing', more so, as 'musicking', an inclusive activity that involves everyone (and everything) present. By extension, both O'Callaghan and Smillie can be considered to be 'musicker' entrepreneurs due to the manner in which they embrace the full content of live music within the local setting.

Like any case study, each contain unique elements that are unlikely to be represented in other enterprises, yet, within a wider context, common traits can also be identified between the two enterprises, as well as within the larger music-related entrepreneurial milieu. What may be unique about both enterprises (any enterprise for that matter) is that each will possess different networks and encompass a diverse range of business relationships. Of course, both O'Callaghan and Smillie are also part of larger teams, with each team member possessing their own unique profiles. However, as both entrepreneurs indicate, their success and viability depends greatly on their relationships within these teams, as well as with other operatives, most notably those within the live music sector (Behr et al., 2014: 19) or wider music industries (Jones, 2012: 150–2).

Finally, if, following the spirit of social networking, we attempt to encapsulate the essence of the desired characteristics of the live music entrepreneur in the form of a 'tweet-conclusion', then a tweet along the lines of the following would summarize this as: underpinned by a passion for music, our enterprise embodies the experiential aspect of live music. After all, live music matters.

#desiredcharacteristicsofthelivemusicentrepreneur

References

Amrom, D. (2014), 'How to avoid the pitfalls of social media marketing', *The Guardian*, 5 July (online), available at: http://www.theguardian.com/small-business-network/2013/aug/06/social-media-marketing-mistakes [accessed 7 September 2014].

Anderson, A.R. and J.L. Jack (2002), 'The articulation of social capital in entrepreneurial networks: a glue or lubricant?', *Entrepreneurship and Regional Development: An International Journal* 14 (3): 193–210.

Auslander, P. (2011), *Liveness: Performance in a Mediatized Culture* London and New York: Routledge.

Behr, A., M. Brennan and M. Cloonan (2014), 'The Cultural Value of Live Music from the Pub to the Stadium: Getting Beyond the Numbers', report (online), available at: http://livemusicexchange.org/wp-content/uploads/The-Cultural-Value-of-Live-Music-Pub-to-Stadium-report.pdf [accessed 10 September 2014].

Boitnott, J. (2014), '5 Tips for Networking Like a Rock Star', *Entrepreneur*, 25 September (online), available at: http://www.entrepreneur.com/article/237234 [accessed 1 September 2014].

Bradshaw, T. (2014), 'Songkick makes a noise with 10m subscribers', *Financial Times*, 27 May (online), available at: http://www.ft.com/cms/s/0/82635984-e5bc-11e3-aeef-00144feabdc0.html#axzz3EXByBTgl [accessed 19 September 2014].

Brennan, M. and E. Webster (2011), 'Why concert promoters matter', *Scottish Music Review* 2 (1): 1–25.

Cooper, B. and P. Vlaskovits (2013), *The Lean Entrepreneur*, Hoboken, NJ: John Wiley and Sons.

Darmer, P. (2008), 'Entrepreneurs in music: the passion of experience creation', in J. Sundbo and P. Darmer (eds), *Creating Experiences in the Experience Economy*, Cheltenham: Edward Elgar, pp. 111–33.

Frith, S. (2007), 'Live Music Matters', *Scottish Music Review*, 1 (1): 1–17.

Granovetter, M.S. (1973), 'The Strength of Weak Ties', *American Journal of Sociology* 78 (6): 1360–80.

Harris, J. (2013), 'Can the UK's "toilet circuit" of small music venues survive?', *The Guardian*, 22 February (online), available at: http://www.theguardian.com/music/2013/feb/22/toilet-circuit-venues-john-harris [accessed 10 September 2014].

Holt, F. (2010), 'The economy of live music in the digital age', *The European Journal of Cultural Studies* 13 (2): 243–61.

Ingham. T. (2014), 'Women outnumber men across UK jobs in music and arts', *Music Week*, 27 June (online), available at: http://www.musicweek.com/news/read/women-outnumber-men-across-uk-jobs-in-music-and-arts/058870 [accessed 1 September 2014].

Jones, M.L. (2012), *The Music Industries*, Basingstoke: Palgrave Macmillan.

Kilbourn, K. (2013), 'Tools and Movements of Engagement. Design Anthropology's Style of Knowing', in W. Gunn, T. Otto and R.C. Smith (eds), *Design Anthropology: Theory and Practice*, London and New York: Bloomsbury Academic, pp. 68–84.

Leek, S. and L. Canning (2011), 'The Role of Networking and Social Capital in Initiation of Relationships in Passion Based Service Networks', paper submitted to the 2011 IMP Conference, available at: http://www.impgroup.org/uploads/papers/7695.pdf [accessed 1 September 2014].

Leonard, M. (2007), *Gender in the Music Industry*, Aldershot: Ashgate.

Millner, J. (2013), 'Detour: Crowdfunding the Future of Live Music', *Tech City News*, 13 June (online), available at: http://techcitynews.com/2013/06/13/detour-crowdfunding-the-future-of-live-music/ [accessed 19 September 2014].

Moore, N. (2013), 'Boutique festivals: Small, but perfectly formed', *The Independent*, 21 May (online), available at: http://www.independent.co.uk/arts-entertainment/music/features/boutique-festivals-small-but-perfectly-formed-8625868.html [accessed 1 September 2014].

Negus, K. (1992), *Producing Pop: Culture and Conflict in the Popular Music Industry*, London: Edward Arnold.

New Musical Express (2014), 'London's Camden Crawl goes into liquidation', 3 July (online), available at: http://www.nme.com/news/various-artists/78312 [accessed 1 September 2014].

O'Callaghan, G. (2014), interview with Allan Dumbreck, London, 17 January.

Pakinkis, T. (2014), 'Back With A Vengeance', *Music Week*, 28 March, pp. 19–20.

Pine, B.J. and J.H. Gilmore (1999), *The Experience Economy*, Boston: Harvard Business School Press.

PRS for Music (2012), 'Adding Up the UK Music Industry 2011', report (online), available at: http://www.prsformusic.com/

aboutus/corporateresources/reportsandpublications/
addinguptheindustry2011/Documents/Economic%20Insight%20
11%20Dec.pdf [accessed 1 September 2014].

Reynolds, R. (2014), 'RockNess music festival cancelled', *The Scotsman*, 20 March (online), available at: http://www.scotsman.com/news/rockness-music-festival-cancelled-1-3347075 [accessed 10 September 2014].

Rogers, J. (2013), 'Girls allowed? The women on top in the music industry', *The Guardian*, 26 October (online), available at: http://www.theguardian.com/music/2013/oct/26/women-running-music-industry-feature [accessed 1 September].

Shezi, N. (2014), 'Young Creative Entrepreneurship Award Winner: Live Music', *Connect/Za* (online), available at: http://connectza.tumblr.com/post/81667369015/young-creative-entrepreneurship-award-winner-live [accessed 19 September 2014].

Small, C. (1998), *Musicking: The Meanings of Performing and Listening*, Middletown, CT: Wesleyan University Press.

Solis, B. (2013), *What's the Future of Business?*, Hoboken, NJ: Wiley.

Sundbo, J. and P. Darmer (2008), 'Introduction to experience creation', in J. Sundbo and P. Darmer (eds), *Creating Experiences in the Experience Economy*, Cheltenham: Edward Elgar, pp. 1–12.

Sweney, M. (2013), 'Live music industry sets off alarm bells over ticket and artist monopolies', *The Guardian*, 29 January (online), available at: http://www.theguardian.com/music/2013/jan/29/live-music-players-alarm monopolies [accessed 1 September 2014].

Turino, T. (2008), *Music as Social Life*, Chicago and London: University of Chicago Press.

UK Festivals (2013), 'The Festival Awards Market Report 2013', UK Festivals, 6 December, available at: http://www.festivalinsights.com/wp-content/uploads/UKFA2013_SHOWGUIDE_MarketReport.pdf [accessed 1 September 2014].

UK Music (2012), 'UK Music launch equality and diversity drive', 8 February (online), available at: http://www.ukmusic.org/news/uk-music-launch-equality-and-diversity-charter

UK Music (2013), 'Wish You Were Here/Music Tourism's Contribution to the UK Economy', October 2013, report (online), available at: http://www.ukmusic.org/assets/general/LOWRESFORHOMEPRINTING.pdf [accessed 10 September 2014].

Waddell, R. (2014), 'Ka-Ching! Cashless Wristbands at Music Fests Means Big Bucks', *Billboard Biz*, 8 September (online), available at: http://www.billboard.com/biz/articles/news/touring/6244053/ka-ching-cashless-wristbands-at-music-fests-mean-big-bucks [accessed 10 September 2014].

Williamson, C. (2014), 'Manchester's Night and Day Café served with noise abatement notice', *Music Week*, 26 August (online), available at: http://www.musicweek.com/news/read/night-and-day-caf-served-with-noise-abatement-notice/059403 [accessed 10 September 2014].

Woolcock, M. (1998), 'Social capital and economic development: towards a theoretical analysis and policy framework', *Theory and Society*, 27 (2): 151–208.

Useful sources

IQ Magazine – online magazine dedicated to the global live music industry. http://www.ilmc.com/index.php/iq-magazine/iq-mag

Live Music Exchange – an industry-academy initiative that provides an 'online hub for anyone interested in live music' (highly recommended). http://livemusicexchange.org

Music Tank – an information hub for the UK music industries including the live sector. http://www.musictank.co.uk

UK Music – live music group. http://www.ukmusic.org/about-us/our-members/uk-live-music-group

6

Entrepreneurship and Music Technology Practitioners

Helen Reddington

This chapter will examine changes in the practice of record production, and the role of entrepreneurship as part of the skillset of the successful recording professional. In the recording studio, just as in every other sector of the music industry, change management (both technological and practice-based) has always been part of the ethos, and the successful development of the interfaces between amateur, semi-professional and professional activities is a vital part of this process. The recording industry itself has always demonstrated the effects of technological determinism[1] in that developments in the technologies of recording and distribution have an active effect on the music itself. This has manifested itself right from the start, for instance in everything from the length of the average single, still at roughly 3 minutes 45 seconds as dictated by the size of the actual shellac (later, vinyl) record, to the effects of multi-tracking which frequently made a recorded song into a commodity object that was almost impossible to recreate live (Theberge, 1997: 169). An understanding of the close relationship between creativity and future developments in audio technology is therefore vital to a studio professional.

The technical side of studio practice, in common with other areas of the music industry, is augmented by a combination of the practitioner's positive personality traits, their network and luck. Aggestam summarizes these as a 'harmonious set of skills' (2007: 32) that include 'intangible assets such as know-how' (Leadbeater and Oakley, 2001: 17). This chapter will, through the case studies of two different informants, balance their experiences and opportunities to demonstrate some of the challenges that can be experienced within the recording profession, drawing across different life stories that include setbacks as well as situations that have contributed to positive career moves. These case studies illustrate different perspectives on the ways that entrepreneurship skills can be used in music production: one from a sole practitioner approach that demonstrates the integration of business and music-technology skills, and the other from the supply of an adaptable and practical music engineering 'toolkit' to a mainstream commercial organization.

Key concepts and issues

Each of the case studies has been chosen to illustrate issues that the studio professional is likely to experience in the earlier stages of their career; one producer has set up her own fledgling music production business based on her activities as a cheerleader, and has been chosen to exemplify just how adaptable one needs to be at the micro level of practice. Chantal Epp's company, Synergy Sounds, illustrates the way that 'entrepreneurs are agents of change' (Leadbeater and Oakley, 2001: 11) as she uses the internet not only to gather material but also to distribute her product. Her commercial activities reside firmly in the 'long tail' described by Chris Anderson, because she services a niche market that has a clearly delineated and possibly finite number of potential clients (Anderson, 2006, 2009). In contrast, the other interviewee, a recording engineer, uses *herself* as a resource, building a role for herself within the network of large commercial studios in the London area. Helen Atkinson is a more conventional studio engineer, but again, changes in the technology of recording mean that the niche she has created as a skilled live engineer allow her to engage in new forms of distribution (direct from live to iTunes, for instance), and she uses entrepreneurial skills to capitalize on both her technological and her interpersonal experience.

Rapid changes in technology add further opportunities and stresses to the practice of the studio professional, not only in the recording and mixing processes themselves but also in the methods of communication between artists, producers and engineers and, of course, in distribution methods. Listening and consumption habits are in a constant state of flux as they have been since the invention of recording; notably, the globalization of the music industries facilitated by the internet in the last thirty years has led to a rationalization of methods and aesthetics that could potentially temper the quest for innovation, currency and future proofing. As Prior observes: '. . . the ubiquity of digital technology is inseparable from the rise of globalisation and the expansion of free-market capitalism increasingly reliant on rapid modes of communication' (Prior, 2009: 83). Negus (1992: 151) discusses the 'chaos and disorder' of the music industries in the 1990s and the 'conflict between commerce and creativity or art and capitalism (ibid: 152); add to this the acceleration of technological development, and the 'anticipatory approach' Negus describes becomes a vital part of survival. Recently, the quality expected by listeners has changed according to issues such as cheap portable listening on mobile phones, the subcultural capital factor of being a new vinyl collector and audiophile, and more recently, the desire of young bands to emulate their parents' record tastes (for instance, for rock bands like Led Zeppelin) that is causing the slow emergence of new analogue studio facilities to service this market.[2]

An understanding of place is also essential, even in the age of globalization. Cultural clusters exist in physical form, sometimes in quite concentrated locations (often around defunct heavy and light industry locations such as redundant dockland areas – Leith in Edinburgh and London's East End, for example) and they exist parallel to a global internet of opportunity (and competition). Local scenes, often encouraged by local and national regeneration funding, frequently combine music performance and recording venues, design studios, café, bar and club culture and other activities such as technological start-ups and craft activities, to form recognizable 'moments' of significant creative bursts. But scenes can also be diasporic in nature; these case studies demonstrate a shift away from defined locations and towards a wider networked community of clients that is held together by efficient use of communications technology.

As we shall see, the two producers interviewed here each exhibit different engagement with the Internet: one depends on it not only for marketing, but also for content, as she has to constantly refresh the sources of the digitized music that she uses for her mash-ups. The other uses the net as a tool for sending her finished mixed and mastered products direct to iTunes, working on location 'in the box' (in this case, a laptop that captures live performances). Although at first glance, Chantal could be defined as a creative professional and Helen an expert facilitator, the activities of both of them are more complex than this; Chantal's activities could be defined as postmodern: the redefinition of the meaning of existing music for a different purpose, thus creating a new artefact altogether. Helen's work is much more modern in nature: the acquisition of skills to service creative professionals. However, at the heart of the work that both of them do is a need to form social networks and a 'confident and committed view of the world' (one of Leadbeater and Oakley's definitions of the entrepreneur, 2001: 23). Computer technology is vital to both of them, and Chantal's business in particular illustrates what Hesmondhalgh identifies as a 'genuinely novel feature of the cultural industries since the 1980s', the fact that '. . . large and small companies are increasingly interdependent and mutually entangled in complex networks of licensing, financing and distribution' (2007: 301).

A young person entering higher education or indeed an apprenticeship, needs to possess a combination of skills, some of which may be self-taught, some peer-shared and some obtained from school or other less formal educational organizations. There can be a conflict between the ambitions of the individual and the practicalities of what is required by potential clients; just as in the artists' side of the industry, the concept of the star or the 'auteur' (Benjamin, 1936, 1999) can be a driver for the individual producer to acquire new hardware, software, practical skills and most importantly, develop a commitment in terms of time that straddles the amateur/professional divide.[3] For a producer who is used to working completely on their own and being in control of their output, it is sometimes difficult to adjust to the fact that from a business perspective, being a supplier supersedes being a creative.

The realities of the employment market for any musician are extraordinarily tough, for not only is there a surfeit of well-qualified studio engineers and budding producers emerging from British universities and vocational courses every year, but there are also those who have entered the employment market via the more traditional apprenticeship route, plus self-taught producer/engineers operating at a subcultural level who achieve success via routes such as pirate radio and DJ-ing. In addition, there is a simultaneous shrinkage of opportunity (for mid-range studios) and expansion of opportunity (for small-scale home production) afforded by the increase in laptop production (see Theberge, 1997: 231–5, and Wolfe, 2012). In addition, of course, the collapse of the traditional structures of music selling that has been under way for the last twenty years has made the music industries jittery and averse to change.

However, as the first case study shows, it is possible to start up a viable business by combining a set of skills with a driving personality and an ability to respond to the needs of a niche market. Indeed, it is encouraging to find that there is still a need for a broad base of studio-related skills that is serviced mainly by adaptable people who have branded themselves as specialists.

This may at first appear to be a conundrum, but I have found that the focus of the specialist often needs to be backed up by change-management and broad-based skills such as patience, reliability, the ability to juggle work commitments to prioritize urgent work without losing smaller clients (who may become bigger clients in time), and the ability to cross hardware and software platforms with ease. This is essentially a 'say yes to everything' mentality that is demonstrated, for instance, by the successful mastering engineer Mandy Parnell's willingness to transport a portable mastering kit to Iceland to re-master Bjork's 'Biophilia' album at short notice and at speed, sometimes working thirty-six hour days to complete the work by the deadline.[4]

Entrepreneurial activity is essential to the development of the recording industry for many different reasons; recorded music is the soundtrack to so many human activities; it is generation-specific, culture-specific and may even on occasions be gender-specific. It provides both cultural capital (Bourdieu, 1973) and subcultural capital (Thornton after Bourdieu, 1995), and it is often at the margins of music production where budding entrepreneurs are active and that innovation and experimentation occur. Leadbeater (1999: 23) cites the frequency with which cultural entrepreneurs in general dedicate themselves to their activities without thought of financial investment, particularly at the outset (with the accompanying problem of lack of capital, planning and manpower that can cause a small business to collapse). Opportunities can abound for those with good social skills and the 'radar' to recognize innovative music production technology that will have staying power in the future; an ability not only to predict the obsolescence of studio equipment, but also simultaneously to recognize the value of the burgeoning interest in particular vintage sounds and practices allows the successful practitioner to surf the changes that keep the industry alive. For instance, at the time of writing, the recent resurgence of vinyl as a medium for carrying recorded material has led to a parallel need for genre-appropriate mastering techniques and equipment;[5] the clients also need access to a cutting facility and a specific approach to sleeve-design, packaging and distribution. An engineer with a good understanding not only of the different sonic identities of different music genres, but also the routes that the music will take from the studio to the listener, will be able to create a business opportunity from the umbrella of knowledge that they have assembled through informal networking and peer sharing. This type of through thinking used to be the domain of efficient managers, but is now part of the ethos of any studio practitioner as a key survival skill in the music industries.

However, as with any activity in the creative industries, the risk factors are high because the entrepreneur is dealing with an audience as their market. The tensions between production and consumption are exaggerated because the tastes and activities of audiences depend on so many different cultural factors (Hesmondhalgh, 2007: 36). Likewise, the industry itself is a 'web [sic] of working practices, dialogues and articulated relationships' (Negus, 1992: 154) that has to be negotiated often with a hefty dose of lateral thinking.

To summarize: the production side of the music industries has always been an area that has developed alongside rapid technological change. Experimentation and the development of new techniques are built into practice, and producers/ engineers who are amenable to change and able to follow seemingly random pathways between the client (the artist/ record label) and the end user (the audience) swiftly, efficiently, decisively and with creative sensitivity, are more likely to thrive than those who possess an interest in audio for audio's sake.

Case study: Chantal Epp (Synergy Sounds)

The subject of the main case study in this chapter is the music producer Chantal Epp, who graduated from the University of Westminster's BA Commercial Music course in 2013. As a final year project, she developed a cheer-music company, Synergy Sounds, which has thrived since she left university. A cheer-leader herself, she was bedridden after a severe injury and could no longer take an active part with her team. Bored, she realized that there was no existing supplier of custom cheer music in Britain and she resolved to fill the gap in the market by starting her own company through which she actively created and produced the tracks to order for teams across the UK. She already possessed music technology skills and the means to source material for her mash-ups; added to her business acumen, and with time to think through the project, she turned a period of enforced inactivity to her advantage.

I asked Chantal to describe the unusual nature of the business she runs: 'I was a cheerleader at university and I got injured. I was the captain of my squad at the time, at uni, and my coach said, "Oh, why don't you do the music for the team, for the competition?" I'd had some previous experience with a producer, I'd done some recording with him, so I had basic understanding of how the studio works, and just developed it from there. I've found a niche market for my work.'

In terms of setting up the company, her role-model was her mother, who had set up her own dental practice and runs it as a successful business; she had worked for her mother for six years and learned many of the business skills that she needed from the experience. Encouraged both by her coach and by her music technology lecturer at university, Mike Exarchos,[6] who developed her programming skills in the space of two months, she used the enforced isolation of recovering from her injury to practical effect.

She had initially proposed the cheer-music business idea to her coach, but he was not interested in following it up as part of his own business. Market research had shown her that there was a market for this genre of music; there were only two or three other companies producing cheer music in the UK. The start-up costs were very low because she already had access to a laptop with music software installed on it, backup support from Mike and other lecturers at the university, and perhaps the most important commodity, ample time in which to learn the specific techniques she would have to use to create the music. Citing her own impatience as a key factor in the decision to 'go it alone', she decided to capitalize on the previous studio experience that she'd had not only in a recording studio but also as an intern in a music supervision company: 'I did a couple of weeks with Matthew Marsden who's a producer in Kingston, Surrey, and he taught me a little bit about Pro-Tools. I just basically made some music, he recorded me and then I also learnt a bit about the production side. And I did some work with PRS and music licensing as work experience; I did a week of music supervision with Platinum Rye.[7] It was suggested that I could go into music supervision because there, I'm finding music that fits a brief.'

Chantal still works part time, now at CueSongs,[8] a company co-founded by Peter Gabriel, where she is involved with music supervision, manages YouTube channels, and so on. Not only does this contribute to her own productions by allowing her to hone her skills at 'feeling' the music, but it also gives her access to a constant supply of new music to use in her cheer music mash-ups. She continues: 'I like to create stuff that's different, not mainstream pop; I like everyone's mixes to be original, something where I can get instrumentals and a cappella, and add the individual touch to it.'

Chantal's interests at school had been focused on music, mainly classical, and an inspirational music teacher had encouraged her to apply to the University of Westminster's Commercial Music BA course after A levels because of her interest in the business side of the music industry. In many ways, she has created the ideal company to match her interests, and she feels a real sense of achievement as the business gradually builds and grows.

In this respect her music skills, ability to learn and interest in business make her approach to being a producer very much of the modern age. As an entrepreneur, she is aware that the landscape will be constantly changing and she will need to adapt accordingly. For instance, cheerleading is relatively new to the UK (although in the USA, where it originated, it is much more common and so there are many more companies supplying music to the teams). She has a strong awareness of the potential future for her music: 'In terms of the cheerleading industry itself, it's a massively growing sport in the UK, Canada, and all over the world; it's huge. Europe is very behind; it's [most popular in] America, and then Canada and then the UK – so Canada's three years behind America, we're five to seven years behind, and then Europe is ten years behind. I think there's definitely scope to expand into it. There are not very many cheerleading teams in Europe. That's what's so great about a niche market: they can only go to you because there are so few companies that provide what they need.'

Within five years, Chantal feels that she will have developed her business enough to meet the inevitable competition head-on. The growing popularity of the sport in the UK was demonstrated in 2013 by the broadcast of a TV programme by the BBC called 'My Team the Cheerleaders',[9] and there is currently a campaign to make cheerleading an Olympic sport.

There is more to the company than pure business, however. Chantal has a strong identity as a composer/producer and there are frustrations at the focus on chart music that the teams demand in their mash-ups. She is at the mercy of what the teams want but has a strong desire to change this: 'There's a music company in America called Cheer Sounds,[10] who did this brilliant marketing on Facebook, so even people who weren't cheerleaders saw it. They made [an original] poppy kind of song advertising their business, which was basically like a cheer; it had the right tempo and the right length and it was really cool: "We're Cheer Sounds, we make original music". I think that might take off and the teams might want original music; I haven't heard any teams use a mix like that, yet. But it's still a new area.'

More recently British teams have been featuring voice-overs that reinforce the team identity; again, Chantal is watching this trend to see where she should move in terms of her own aesthetic approach: 'Back in December less than 50 per cent of the teams had voice-overs and now there's probably 60 per cent, or maybe 70 per cent of the teams starting to use them, so I assume that will grow and when that's run its course something new will come in: and it'll be cool if it's something more original: like the team's own actual song, rather than a mash-up of [other] songs.'

Chantal's customer base began locally to service her own university team, and then developed through a network of teams; by knowing the genre of music thoroughly because of her own active involvement with cheerleading, she is able to create tailor-made music for each client. There is a standardized tempo (with slight variations) of 145 bpm and with a sonic style that she describes thus: 'Highly energetic, dance-y, tons of sound effects ... I mix different instrumentals together, underneath different a cappellas of songs: a mash-up of eight to ten songs in one two-and-a-half minute track; each song has to be in a different section of the routine. I program my own drumbeats.'

She has to work quickly and to order for specified competitions, and at the moment is developing the company by working at the lower levels of the sport; for this reason she markets her company as the lowest-priced in the genre. On the advice of the UK royalty collection body, the Performing Right Society (PRS), she obtained a license for the use of 1,000 tracks per year (which she can increase as the company expands); this allows her a lot of flexibility and is accepted by the PRS because the squads perform in established venues that are already licensed for the use of music.[11]

Social media is a vital marketing tool for her company. Normally Chantal sends one tweet a day but in the competition season: 'I just don't stop. Every single minute, every single team that competes, I will tweet. They then respond with: "Oh, Synergy Sounds just said something really nice about us!" or, "Oh look, we can get live updates about the competition that we're not at". So, then people can see what's actually happening at the competition – I'm like the news feed.' Post-competition, this can garner around 3,000 views on the Twitter page and it is an efficient way of drumming up business.

Another initiative that she has developed is a promotion for groups to get a free cheer mix, by entering a prize draw: 'I've been tweeting constantly, every single day, asking people to enter their details on my website to potentially win a free cheer mix; all entrants will get 15 per cent off any orders as an incentive. So even if they don't win, I can email them all in future.'

This is all hard work; competitions sometimes run from 8am to 11pm and Chantal travels all round Britain to sports arenas such as Birmingham NEC, Bournemouth BIC and Telford International Centre.

Chantal's identification (above) of her mother's dentistry practice as a positive inspiration for her own company is interesting; Kariv (2013: 56) cites '. . . a strong body of evidence that links entrepreneurs to parents who are themselves entrepreneurs', and this is borne out here. Chantal, as a female producer, sees her mother as a role model; although she works in an entirely different area the advanced technical experience, networking ability and business skills of her mother's practice would have been very much to the forefront in her upbringing. She also acquired a lot of necessary business knowledge in part from online sources and partly through trial and error. A large bill from HMRC for national insurance taught her to apply for an exemption, for instance; she cites making mistakes as a vital part of her learning process: 'You freak out at first: "Why is *this* happening?" and then you learn the whole process after that. You just have to be willing to do your research, willing to learn, willing to hit dead ends, to make mistakes, to fail. Failing is the biggest learning curve of all; when you hit rock bottom the only way you can go is up, so you've just got to keep positive and go from there.'

Chantal is also able to motivate herself and work completely on her own. During our conversation, she frequently referred to 'we', which led me to wonder if she was working with someone else. Unbidden, she explained later that as a sole trader, she is concerned that people should feel confident about what she is able to deliver. As a matter of professional practice, she hints at a larger operation behind her activities to encourage the confidence of her clients and she does understand that she will have to employ people in the future as orders increase.

Although an unusual facet of music production, Synergy Sounds follows a pattern that is common to the creative industries. The 'cultural cluster' that Chantal finds herself in is unusually widespread physically and is held together and consolidated by the use of social media. The 'independent enterprises acting interdependently in complex and specialised ways' identified by Rae (2007: 56) combine amateur and professional activities that Chantal has been able to capitalize on through her insider's knowledge of cheerleading and the genre of music that accompanies it. This type of entrepreneurship, as Rae puts it, is: 'the intelligent application of skill' (ibid: 57). As well as being facilitated by internet connectivity, Chantal's business has also been facilitated by the growth in home computer technology that has allowed her to participate in 'the creation of new subgenres and musical phenomena' (Anderton, Dubber and James, 2013: 83). There is also no doubt that as a female producer, the access afforded by a laptop has made her professional journey much less difficult (Wolfe, 2012).

For a business such as Synergy Sounds, the integration of original music production into the 'world' of sports competition, itself straddling the fuzzy divide between the amateur and the professional, is both an advantage (the clarity of what is required and the fact that new, more up to date music is likely to be needed at regular intervals to ensure currency and variety) and a disadvantage (the increasing popularity of the sport will lead to more competition, especially from bigger companies that want to add the genre to their portfolio, and who have more robust promotion methods). Her non-mainstream business and its innovative use of the internet illustrate Anderson's observations about the new ways of running a company in the twenty-first century.

Long tail theory depends on two major factors: a feeling of optimism by the supplier, and the solvency of the purchaser. Anderson mentions his surprise at the aisles in the US supermarket that are packed with unusual jams (2007: 170–2); the manager tells him that they are very popular. To follow the analogy: can we then imagine the larder at home packed with the jars of dipped-into exotic jam past its sell-by date, with the simpler and more traditional flavours being regularly consumed and replaced? Niche markets are risky; they are not infinite, often depending as they do on volatile factors and (as Anderson observes), sometimes obscurity. In spite of the advantages of the Internet as a supply and marketing tool, small businesses still face common problems, summarized here by Rae: '... finding and attracting their market to grow the demand for their businesses; attracting able people, financial and technical resources; making strategic choices on how to compete, collaborate and specialize in order to adapt to a changing environment; and, at a personal level, considering whether a long-term career in the creative industries is sustainable, since certain segments of these industries are dominated by fashion, taste and a young demographic' (2007: 59).

To summarize, Chantal combines excellent sound engineering skills, an extensive knowledge of current musical trends, an awareness of the activities of the diaspora of cheerleading activities (from the UK to Europe, Canada, the USA and a growing enthusiasm in Japan), and up-to-date business and marketing skills, to work as a sole trader in music production for a niche market. After the initial idea her financial investment consisted of the purchase and maintenance of a computer and software, plus travel and accommodation; the time investment requires a degree of dedication and energy that is a common factor to entrepreneurs whatever industry they work in.[12]

Case study: Helen Atkinson (Producer/Engineer at RAK Studios)

To demonstrate that entrepreneurial skills and the essential work ethic that supports them have now become part of the role of any contemporary studio practitioner, even within more mainstream studio practice, the subject of my second case study is Helen Atkinson, an engineer at RAK Studios in St John's Wood, London. Helen is in her early thirties and has frequently been self-employed; she has recently become a specialist in recording live broadcasts. Unlike Chantal, she did not go to university but instead entered the recording industry straight after school, and rather than servicing a niche industry on her own, she has entered a mainstream organization, albeit through branding herself as a specialist within that industry. In a different approach to that of creating her own business from scratch to cater for a niche market, Helen has negotiated her way through various roles as a sound engineer. She spent eighteen months working at the residential studio Ridge Farm as a junior engineer (where she was eventually replaced by a more senior engineer when business became more quiet) followed by a period of sending out hundreds of CVs to studios: 'Everybody that was listed in the *Showcase* book that I could get to within an hour or so in my car or by train.' She describes 'luck and good timing' as a factor in her opportunity to work at RAK; there was no identifiable 'big opportunity' that came her way, but an approach to work that she felt helped her: 'Every client that you get on board and that wants to use you, you have to be aware of the opportunities that might come up and be open to giving something a go that's not necessarily within your comfort zone.'

Helen persuaded RAK that they needed her as an in-house engineer at a time when they were exclusively employing freelancers; small things like making sure microphones had clips, screens were cleaned and that pianos were returned to their rightful place were being overlooked: 'I made a role for myself here at RAK and then I made it so they needed me here, and I made it so that they've continued to need me here.'

Retained as a part-timer, she is also able to work freelance for the 'X-Factor', creating mixes for iTunes of the Saturday-night live TV shows that go on sale at midnight the night after; she also records festivals for Abbey Road Live and recorded the sound at the O2 in London for the movie *One Direction: This Is Us* (Directed by Morgan Spurlock for Sony, 2013). One of the most useful skills that she says she has is the ability to read music: 'I was in the school choir and things like that, so, I could read music, which isn't a key aspect of being an engineer, but actually people kind of like it, it's another thing that means that you're more flexible, it means that they can put you on a string session where you might need to follow a score, or they could put you on an orchestral session. As a child, I had learned the Kodaly method for seven years, which I think gave me a great foundation in music.'

Her training in classical music thus adds to the body of knowledge that Helen brings to the job, potentially linking the cultural and subcultural capital aspects of music in a very practical way. 'Unseen' skills like this contribute to the smooth passage of cultural change, whether commercial or purely aesthetic and can pull a niche genre towards the mainstream. Rae cites the importance of cultural diffusion to the development of the creative industries in Britain, because of the '. . . deep-seated discontinuities in British life between "the creative" and "the mainstream" which stem from long-standing differences in cultural, educational, social and economic contexts and which affect interactions between the creative economy and the other constituencies' (2007: 54).

Conclusion

The flexibility of the digital world can facilitate a seamless route between creative activity and the market, repurposing digital information (seen here by Chantal's recycling of hit tracks into tailor-made mash-ups that perfectly match gymnastic routines), and marketing the resulting product through the same computer screen in a series of drags and clicks that can potentially send that product anywhere in the world in an instant. As a micro-entrepreneur, Chantal may find that she is challenged in future by what Leadbeater and Oakley term 'the missing middle' (1999: 12), the bridge between her 'one-[wo]man-band' company and the expansion and development necessary to survive against the inevitable competition. They comment that 'Businesses based on service provision often go through a period of feast, followed by a famine; they have been so busy delivering their current projects that they cannot find the time to sell new ones' (ibid: 27). Will Chantal need to diversify as she expands the business? She plans to employ other people to take on aspects of the work that she does not enjoy so much, but the income needs to be there for her to make this commitment. Capital investment may become an option, but many entrepreneurs feel that this weakens the focus of their business and their direct connection with its products (ibid: 23).

For both practitioners, social capital (another term coined by Pierre Bourdieu) is vital. The producer Richard Burgess summarizes his practice with the wry comment, 'Good connections are essential – you'll never see an ad for a record producer.' He continues: 'Job satisfaction is extremely high. [but] When you finally think you've got it all pinned down, reality intervenes to explain that the only constant is change' (Burgess, 1997: 228). For Helen, the embracing of this change is embedded in a sense of teamwork: 'I think it's probably one of those genuine industries where it really is a meritocracy and people don't come into work because it's regular or because they *have* to turn up every day; they want to turn up every day and work with a team that they like to work with, so, finding that team that you fit well with, personality-wise, skills-wise, that's really important.'

In contrast, Chantal's sense of social context is forged through her embedded-ness in the sport that she provides a service to; for both, proactivity is a vital element in their self-management (Kariv, 2013: 520–2). Part of the charm of Chantal's business is actually the story behind it, which gives her as an entrepreneur a unique selling point; her practice is a logical development from the production methods described by Negus where the '"entrepreneurial mode" meets the "art mode" in a collective-synthetic approach . . .' (1992: 88). The main difference between the two producers described above is the degree of risk that each of them faces; Helen is as good as her last project, but has a strong reputation in the industry as a reliable and talented engineer. Chantal responds to the 'chaos and disorder' that Negus identifies, and which is ordered to a degree by the internet; but even Anderson admits that '. . . for the vast majority of us who live, work or play in the Tail, the cultural shift towards minority taste is already bringing a richer, more vibrant culture. How and when the money will follow is something that the next few decades will reveal' (2007: 254). In other words, it is people's ability to buy niche products that wags the Long Tail.

Negus concludes that 'the music industry is not organized around mechanical inputs or outputs nor the linear transmission of products along a straight line from producer to consumer. The process is far less stable, riddled with fluctuations and bifurcations' (1992: 154). Internet distribution as described by Anderson is in reality a progressively much fuzzier shape than he would have us believe and of the two case studies one could conclude that Chantal's approach is the most risky of the two; but by remaining adaptable and positive, it is highly likely that both Chantal and Helen will continue to thrive as music producers in years to come. In their adaptability, they demonstrate a feature that has always been part of studio practice: willingness to experiment with new ideas and technologies. For instance, the demand for cheer music (especially in the UK) is a relatively new phenomenon; so is the demand for live versions of music from TV talent shows. New genres of music that evolve as a result of continuing developments in music technology and distribution systems are going to present new challenges for those entering the industry (as demonstrated by Synergy Sounds), but new practices and market demands are also evident in the more mainstream side (witness Helen Atkinson's time-pressured production of 'X-Factor' tracks for iTunes). There are also other possible new routes of employment; for instance, the aforementioned need for specially tailored mastering, cutting and manufacturing processes for the growing vinyl market; or the digital archiving of back catalogue analogue material from record labels and existing public music archives, such as the National Sound Archive, which will require engineers not only skilled in shellac, vinyl and tape transfer, but also genre-specific listening and production skills. For stables of labels such as the Beggars Group, this is a commercially viable activity, which will result in increased sales of digital music. Funding for this process for public archives, however, will be at a premium and as such presents a challenge of its own; this could be a further development from the commercial audio activities described above; could an imaginative approach to funding by an entrepreneurial group of audio professionals 'corner the market' of what might prove to be a very long-lasting and potentially lucrative process?[13] There are undoubtedly unimagined future genres of, and purposes for, recorded music both mainstream and subcultural that will take the industry by surprise; in spite of the volatility of music audiences, we depend on the ideas, risk-taking and potential success of entrepreneurs to avoid stasis both culturally and economically. Niche activities provide a vital collective contribution to a differentiated cultural experience. As Anderson explains: '. . . we can now treat culture not as one big blanket, but as the superposition of many different threads, each of which is individually addressable and connects different groups of people simultaneously (2007: 183–4).

Notes

1 This term, coined by the American philosopher Thorstein Veblen who was active in the early twentieth century, is used to describe the concept that technology controls humans, rather than the other way around.

2 Issues discussed at the Art of Record Production Conference, Oslo, 2015.

3 See Finnegan, 2007, for an account of amateur music making that articulates clearly the relaxed interface between amateurism and professionalism in a wide variety of musical activities in Milton Keynes.

4 http://www.soundonsound.com/sos/jan12/articles/biophilia.htm

5 Vinyl mastering needs a particular equalization process that is different to CD or file mastering, because the bass response of vinyl discs is much greater.

6 http://www.stereo-mike.com/

7 http://ukmusic.platinumrye.com/

8 http://www.cuesongs.com/

9 http://www.bbc.co.uk/cbbc/shows/my-team-the-cheerleaders [accessed 4 September 2014].

10 http://www.cheersounds.com/ [accessed 4 September 2014].

11 IP problems can be a major difficulty for creative entrepreneurs, according to Rae. Overcoming these at the outset had, no doubt, a very positive effect on Chantal's ability to get her business off the ground (see Rae, 2007: 202).

12 Time management is a major issue for everyone in the creative (and other!) industries. There is a roaring trade in time management literature: see for instance Forster, M. (2006) *Do It Tomorrow and Other Secrets of Time Management*, London: Hodder and Stoughton.

13 The National Sound Archive's estimate of the duration of this process was originally fifteen years, and has now been revised to forty-two years. Andy Linehan, speaking at 'Keeping Tracks: a one day symposium on music and archives in the digital age', British Library Conference Centre, 21 March 2014.

References

Aggestam, M. (2007), 'Art-entrepreneurship in the Scandinavian music industry', in C. Henry (ed.), *Entrepreneurship in the Creative Industries: An International Perspective*, Cheltenham: Edward Elgar, pp. 30–53

Anderson, C. (2007), *The Long Tail: How Endless Choice is Creating Unlimited Demand*, London: Random House.

Anderton, C., A. Dubber and J. Martin (2013), *Understanding the Music Industries*, Los Angeles, London, New Delhi: Sage.

Benjamin, W. (1999), 'The Work of Art in the Age of Mechanical Reproduction', in *Illuminations*, London: Pimlico.

Bourdieu, P. and J.-C. Passeron (1973), *Cultural Reproduction and Social Reproduction*, London: Sage.

Brown, R.K. (1974), *Knowledge, Education and Cultural Change: Papers in the Sociology of Education*, London: Tavistock.

Burgess, R.J. (1997), *The Art of Record Production*, London: Omnibus.

Finnegan, R. (1989, 2007), *The Hidden Musicians: Music-Making in an English Town*, Middletown, CT: Wesleyan University Press.

Forster, M. (2006), *Do It Tomorrow and Other Secrets of Time Management*, London: Hodder and Stoughton.

Frith, S. (1996), *Performing Rites: On the Value of Popular Music*, Oxford: Oxford University Press.

Henry, C. (ed.) (2007), *Entrepreneurship in the Creative Industries: An International Perspective*, Cheltenham: Edward Elgar.

Hesmondhalgh, D. (2007), *The Cultural Industries*, 2nd ed., London: Sage.

Kariv, D. (2013), *Female Entrepreneurship and the New Venture Creation: An International Overview*, New York: Routledge.

Leadbeater, C. and K. Oakley (1999), *The Independents: Britain's New Cultural Entrepreneurs*, London: Demos.

Leadbeater, C. and K. Oakley (2001), *Surfing the Long Wave: Knowledge Entrepreneurship in Britain*, London: Demo.

Negus, K. (1992), *Producing Pop: Culture and Conflict in the Popular Music Industry*, London: Edward Arnold.

Prior, N. (2009), 'Sampling, Cyborgs and Simulation: Popular Music and the Digital Hypermodern', in *New Formations*, 66: 81–99.

Rae, D. (2007), 'Creative industries in the UK: Cultural diffusion or discontinuity?', in C. Henry (ed.), *Entrepreneurship in the Creative Industries: An International Perspective*, Cheltenham: Edward Elgar, pp. 54–71.

Theberge, P. (1997), *Any Sound You Can Imagine: Making Music/ Consuming Technology*, Hanover and London: Wesleyan University Press.

Thornton, S. (1995), *Club Cultures: Music, Media and Subcultural Capital*, London: Polity.

Wolfe, P. (2012), 'A Studio of One's Own: Music production, technology and gender', *Journal on The Art of Record Production*, http://arpjournal. com/2156/a-studio-of-one's-own-music-production-technology-and-gender/ [accessed 11 November 2014].

Websites

All accessed 11 November 2014.
http://arpjournal.com
http://ukmusic.platinumrye.com/
http://www.bbc.co.uk/cbbc/shows/my-team-the-cheerleaders
http://www.cheersounds.com/
http://www.cuesongs.com
http://www.soundonsound.com/sos/jan12/articles/biophilia.htm
http://www.stereo-mike.com/
http://www.synerygysounds

7

Recorded Music

Jeff Izzo

The traditional recorded music sector – compact discs, vinyl records and cassette tapes – continues to experience, perhaps more so than any other sector of the modern music industry, a seismic transformation. Globally, downloading and streaming recorded music is rapidly closing in on, and by most accounts will likely soon be overtaking, sales of the aforementioned 'old-fashioned' hard media. As a result, record companies are in a state of flux trying to determine and chart these massive changes and keep abreast of them, but all the while clinging desperately to old ways. The question becomes, then: in the wake of changes in how recorded music is delivered to the consumer, will traditional models go the way of the dodo, or will such models and practices morph into new methods and means of doing business in the twenty-first century – the goal of which is twofold: pleasing the consumer and staying in business? This writer firmly believes that the efforts of entrepreneurs – that 'loaded' word that has two very different connotations between the UK and the US – will ensure that those two goals remain alive.

In an effort to bring these issues to the fore, this chapter will examine as case studies the careers of two very different individuals. The first is Jay Frank, an American music industry executive who, in a distinguished music business career that spans nearly twenty years, is now the owner of DigSin Records, a company that offers user-listeners the ability to download music for free – and, more importantly, do so *legally*. The second is Mark Orr, a young British entrepreneur who created a record label, whilst still studying at university, featuring artists with no major label affiliation, thus serving the distribution needs of the *independent artist*. These two individuals were chosen as case studies essentially because each one demonstrates, in his own unique fashion, that it is possible to create and operate new music industry models that co-exist successfully and healthily in the new landscape of the recorded music business. In that light, each has responded to the needs of both artists and consumers whose modes of creating, purchasing, and listening to music are, as indicated in the first paragraph above, undergoing a sea change.

This chapter will begin, however, by taking a step back and examining the recorded music sector as it now stands, including how it has evolved, and indeed is still evolving, and the social and legal challenges it faces. However, such an examination cannot be adequately conducted without at least a cursory discussion of copyright law – limited here, for brevity's sake, to provisions of US copyright law relevant to the recorded music industry. Following this will be the proposition that the industry needs individuals and companies poised to face these challenges – ultimately segueing into the case studies, to demonstrate that each one is up to the task of these challenges, and each is, in every sense of the word, an entrepreneur. The chapter will close with a brief analysis of the case studies, followed by some musings about the future of the industry.

The recorded music sector

Talking pictures. The phonograph. Television. The 45 rpm record. The cassette tape. The 8-track tape. The videotape. The compact disc. Cable television. Each and every one of these now seemingly antediluvian technical formats and devices enjoyed a brief but very visible infamy as the purveyor of a specific entertainment sector's imminent demise. Who on earth will want to watch actors *talk* on screen? Who will travel and pay hard-earned money to watch a film in a movie theatre when comedy, drama, and variety shows are available in the comfort of one's living room at the flick of a dial on a small box? Who will purchase a big, bulky, brittle piece of plastic when consumers can get the same amount of music on a small encased magnetic tape that fits in a car's glove box, and that they can fast forward and pause at will without worrying about how and where to drop a tone arm onto a revolving platter? And who will buy *that* when a small disc that is not prone to scratching and near impossible to break and even more portable is available? What will the film industry do? How will the record companies survive?

To paraphrase Mark Twain's famous quote, 'the reports of the record industry's death have been greatly exaggerated'.[1] Because in reality, while each of these few example 'breakthrough' technologies (there are many, many others) has indeed made at least some measurable market impact on the status quo (Katz, 2010) each also presented its own unique set of technical and sociological limitations. For instance, a cassette tape is indeed portable but does not offer the wide sonic spectrum that vinyl does. A CD, while portable as well as durable, does not have the 'romance' of a 33⅓ LP, with its size allowing more intricate cover art, creative sleeve inserts (remember the moustache kit that was included in The Beatles' Sgt. Pepper album), and of course easier-to-read liner notes. In 2014, CD album sales still outsold album downloads – 140.8m versus 106.5m, with vinyl sales bringing up the rear at 9.2m sold – all but vinyl sales reflected a decrease from 2013.[2] However, in none of these instances have the walls come tumbling down on the film, television, or – most relevantly for this context – the music industry. Destruction was imminent, but the warriors staved it off. They all survived.

But how did they – and do they continue to – survive? The focus of this chapter will not be to precisely dissect and analyze industry sales figures and trends – although naturally that must necessarily comprise a large part of the picture. Instead, what follows is based on the presumption – hardly arguable if one does indeed examine current sales figures noted above – that sales of hard media in the record industry have been, and continue to be, in steep decline. Taking that presumption as the launching pad, the focus will be on how a company – for instance, a record company – can either buckle under and surrender to the threat of the download, or rise to the challenge and redefine itself or, better yet, create a new model within which to operate. Once again, this is where the so-called entrepreneur comes in.

As has been suggested earlier in this book, forging a precise definition of the word 'entrepreneur' can be an elusive enterprise. What has also been pointed out previously is that the connotations and implications attached to the word can vary wildly from country to country, industry to industry within those countries, and sector to sector within those industries. Is this of any consequence?

Regarding the first question – What is an entrepreneur? – I believe that the cornerstone concept is that being an entrepreneur involves a higher element of risk as compared to a manager. Such risk can be monetary, involve one's reputation, or even threaten an industry. To be an entrepreneur is to rock the boat, to challenge the status quo.

As for the second matter, well, whereas the word apparently carries negative connotations in the UK, in the US it conveys near mythical, even spiritual, overtones. Perhaps it's that 'pioneer' spirit that pervades American social and political culture – Horace Greeley's famous 1865 directive of manifest destiny, 'Go west, young man'[3] comes to mind – that plucky American 'can do' attitude and 'rags-to-riches' mentality that perhaps can, to a more reserved set of social standards, come across as presumptuous and even obnoxious. In any case, in the USA the notion of entrepreneurship is canonized along with its many saints – Steve Jobs, Bill Gates, Mark Zuckerberg, Oprah Winfrey and David Geffen (to name a few). Contrast this with the often-negative light in which, for example, Sir Richard Branson, himself a 'rags-to-riches' multi-billionaire, is held by the British media.

So it is with the recording industry. As alluded to above, there is no way of getting around the fact that digital delivery of sound recordings is not merely the wave of the future, but the reality of the present. The new found 'novelty' of vinyl releases – in addition to re-releases, re-masters, and mono recordings of classic recordings such as The Beach Boys' 'Pet Sounds' and The Beatles' entire catalogue, artists as diverse as Jack White and Dr John have released new material in the format – has so far not been much more than a barely suppressed blip that appeals mainly to a small group of audiophiles and/or nostalgia adherents.[4] And while that number continues to grow (Caulfield, 2014), it is difficult to dispute that today, recorded music to the vast majority of consumers means digital delivery.

This is perhaps an appropriate point in the discussion to mention two very significant events that recently occurred in the US music industry, and which are perhaps poised to affect the worldwide music business. In early November 2014, pop superstar Taylor Swift abruptly removed her entire catalogue from music streaming company Spotify, followed approximately a week later by country superstar Jason Aldean removing his most recent album from the service (his previous recordings remain) (Knopper, 2014; Lee, 2014).

Responding to the utter astonishment of fans, music journalists and music industry figures to this announcement – especially in light of the fact that in its first week, 1.287m copies of her latest LP, 1989, sold, becoming the first platinum level record (1 million sales) in the US, and eventually went on to sell 3.66m copies in 2014[5] – Ms Swift and her record label, Big Machine Label Group, have been fairly vocal on the reasons for the catalogue withdrawal. In a recent *Rolling Stone* Op-Ed, Ms Swift commented on online music piracy: 'Music is art, and art is important and rare. Important things are valuable. Valuable things should be paid for. It's my opinion that music should not be free, and my prediction is that individual artists and their labels will someday decide what an album's price point is. I hope they don't underestimate themselves or undervalue their art' (Roberts, 2014).

Although these comments were made, as noted above, in reference to Ms Swift's concerns about music piracy – a practice which Spotify, operating in a zone of complete legality, most certainly does not condone – commentators have suggested that this statement is a clue as to why the pull out occurred (Grow, 2014). However, in a widely circulated blog post, Spotify's founder and CEO, Daniel Ek, agreed with Swift on the issue of piracy but vehemently distinguished Spotify from illegal music streaming: 'Taylor Swift is absolutely right: music is art, art has real value, and artists deserve to be paid for it ... Piracy doesn't pay artists a penny ... Spotify has paid more than two billion dollars to labels, publishers, and collecting societies for distribution to songwriters and recording artists ... that's two billion dollars worth of listening that would have happened with zero or little compensation to artists and songwriters through piracy or practically equivalent services if there was no Spotify' (Peters, 2014).

Notwithstanding Mr Ek's somewhat odd justification for the Spotify business model – which seems to be, 'be thankful at least it's not piracy' – it is the mechanics of that business model itself that Ms Swift, Mr Borchetta, and Mr Aldean appear to have issues with (Ek, 2014). Those issues seem to include: (a) what Spotify actually pays, out of that two billion dollars described earlier to recording artists (and how that company's payouts compare to Pandora's for instance), and (b) whether a Spotify presence takes away from hard album sales of these artists – which generate more income for the artist.[6]

The purpose of this chapter, however, is not to finely dissect and closely scrutinize the specifics of Spotify's business model. That is a subject requiring a far wider scope than is available in this setting. What the Swift/Aldean/Spotify controversy *does* demonstrate – even with the relatively limited analysis – and what *does* make it relevant to the topics considered in this chapter, is what happens when traditional modes of marketing and selling records clash with emerging business models. If Ms Swift and Mr Aldean are indeed pulling out of Spotify in order to boost sales of their hard copies, is that an appropriate response to the marketplace of the twenty-first century and beyond? Another way to pose this question might be: which is more viable today, a *creator*-oriented business model, or a *consumer*-oriented one? Do the needs of the artist take the upper hand, or the needs of the listener, without whom the artist could not make a living?

Figuring this out requires one to look at both industry specific methods as well as techniques that fall outside the realm of the music industry, and to dip deeply into the waters of sales and marketing philosophy and theory – again, a set of topics that to examine in depth is well beyond the confines of this chapter. That said, there is much overlap between the two research areas, and consideration of these concepts – target market identification, demographic and psychographic analysis of potential customers, mission statement formulation, USPs (unique selling propositions), SWOT analyses (strengths, weaknesses, opportunities, threats), marketing plans, business plans, and so on – can be successfully used in guiding one along the path to determining what sort of business model works best in the current music industry environment (Sisario, 2013).

Copyright issues

As indicated earlier, no thorough discussion of the record industry would be complete without at least a brief foray into the world of US copyright law – specifically, in regard to the law's treatment of sound recordings.

Compared with Europe, the US has a curiously 'out-of-step' and admittedly confusing policy regarding sound recordings.

US copyright law has been through two major iterations – the 1909 Copyright Act,[7] which was replaced almost seventy years later with the 1976 Act (actually becoming effective in 1978).[8] Under the 1909 Act, sound recordings enjoyed *no* federal copyright protection – leaving any possible safeguards to the perplexing and often contradictory whims of individual state statutory and common law. That situation was remedied somewhat with the Sound Recording Amendment of 1971,[9] which finally afforded federal protection to sound recordings – but *only* to those fixed on or before the Amendment's effective date of 15 February 1972.

The 1976 Act expressly pre-empted all state statutory and common law that addressed legal and equitable rights that were 'similar' to those rights that were expressed in the copyright law. Regarding sound recordings, what this meant was that because rights in pre-1972 sound recordings were not addressed in the 1976 Act, then any protection for such recordings remained within the boundaries of state law (until 2067, when this right becomes pre-empted, like virtually all other copyright matters, apart from Federal Copyright Law).[10]

To further complicate matters, missing among the specific rights granted by the 1976 Act to the sound recording copyright owner was the right of *public performance* – a right that was clearly attached to the copyright owner of the *underlying composition*. In other words, from a US royalty perspective (the scenario would be very different in Europe), terrestrial radio play of the 1988 Mel Tormé recording of the Donald Fagen (of Steely Dan fame) song The Goodbye Look, would generate public performance income for Fagen (the songwriter), but none for Mel Tormé (the recording artist).

This was modified in 1995 with the passage of the Digital Performance Right in Sound Recordings Act of 1995 (effective date of 1 November of that year). Now, to use the preceding example, Mel Tormé and Donald Fagen would each receive a royalty when The Goodbye Look was played on satellite radio or streamed on Spotify and Pandora – but would still 'shut out' Mel royalty-wise for *terrestrial* radio play. Once again, pre-1972 sound recordings were left out of the federal mix – their sole protections remained within the confines of state law. Which is confusing, to say the least.

Finally, and not that this requires an additional level of confusing complexity, the royalty rates collected on behalf of songwriters and publishers by the US Performance Rights Organizations (PROs) – ASCAP, BMI and SESAC – and the royalty rates collected on behalf of recording artists and labels by SoundExchange, are all set by the Copyright Royalty Board. However, songwriters, publishers, artists, and labels are all free to negotiate *directly* with the relevant outlets of their publicly performed music and sound recordings, thereby 'by-passing' the PROs and SoundExchange. Add to this that in the digital realm, there is a great discrepancy between what songwriters/publishers receive as compared to recording artists/labels. All of the above – how royalty rates are set, what happens with direct negotiation, and the song/sound recording discrepancy – are the subjects of intense controversy at the moment in both US Courts and Congress.

This *very* abbreviated but still bewildering primer in the labyrinthine complexities of US copyright law mercifully serves as an illustration that all of the discussion about emerging business models, creators versus consumers, hard sales versus streaming and downloads, and the like, must be considered within this statutory framework. Recognizing that will hopefully allow the reader to understand why all the 'fuss' for recording artists is generated regarding services such as Spotify and Pandora, and consequently why the potential game changers in the industry – such as the subjects in the two case studies that shortly follow – seem to focus so much on digital delivery of sound recordings.

What this all boils down to is a repeat of the question posed at the beginning: does the modern recorded music industry, in the guise of the twenty-first-century record company, collapse under the weight of technological innovation and customer satisfaction (i.e. consumers who want their product NOW), or do players who wish to have a valuable stake in the game change their business ethos, an ethos that has remained intact for 100 years?

The record company entrepreneur

The first part of any answer to the above question must naturally be – has anyone in fact risen to this challenge? That is a supremely easy one, to be summed up in one (trademarked) word: iTunes. It does not take a scholarly paper or a book to reveal that Apple, thanks in large part to its entrepreneurial leader, the late Steve Jobs, revolutionized the recorded music sector in 2001 with the introduction of iTunes, followed by the various devices that could use the service: iPods, iPhones, iPads, and Apple TV, as well the non-Apple machines that the service is available on. But Jobs' trailblazing in this sector reveals a curious aspect about the concept of entrepreneurship. Apple was not the first to devise a way to deliver recorded music digitally onto a tiny player, as such devices were being conceived as far back as 1979 – British scientist Kane Kramer is credited with inventing the world's first digital media player called the IXI, in that year.[11]

Following Kramer's invention, history becomes littered with various other corporate 'players' attempting to enter the field in the portable digital media game. Among them were: Audible. com's 1997 Mobile Player, the first production-volume portable digital audio player;[12] the 1998 Eiger MPMan from Saehan Information Systems; and the first truly commercially successful device, Diamond Multimedia's Diamond Rio[13].

So why have these names and others been relegated to the 'where are they now' file in the history of portable music players, not merely forgotten and ignored by the vast majority of consumers, but totally unknown to them? Why have 'Apple', 'iTunes' and 'iPod' become virtual synonyms for 'digitally downloaded music'? I would argue that it is because of Jobs' visionary – and *entrepreneurial* – leadership. In addition to constantly refining the iPod's technology and user interface, he

also worked hard at *obtaining* the content for the devices –
forging relationships with record companies to license their
master recordings to Apple to make them available, for a
reasonable price, to customers. Make that *immediately*
available. He essentially turned a still relatively new technology
into a streamlined, elegant experience. With a masterstroke
combination of technological advances, legal negotiations, and
deft marketing, Apple – under the guidance of Jobs – turned
the recorded music industry on its ear, which has forced other
players to re-think how they operate in this new environment.
Jobs and Apple took risks, and they paid off (handsomely, of
course) – with the added element of expanding customer base
and markets. *That* is the mark of a true entrepreneur.

But this chapter is not about Apple or Steve Jobs. It is about
what challenges remain post-iPod revolution, and who, if
anyone, has risen to these challenges, and how they have gone
about doing it.

Case study: Jay Frank (DigSin)

For the first case study I turned to Jay Frank,[14] a Nashville
based music entrepreneur. After graduating from Ithaca
College in 1993 with a Bachelor of Science degree, Jay quickly
began making his mark in the music industry: managing a live
venue, programming radio stations, and creating local music
video shows. A veteran of nearly twenty years in the digital
music business, his credentials include stints at Ignition

Records as Label Manager, Senior Managing Director at The Box Music Network, an executive at both Yahoo Music (Vice-President of Programming and Label Relations) and MTV Networks. For Yahoo and MTV, he cultivated the audience bases of both businesses by using data analysis in order to assist them in finding new opportunities. In late 2011, he formed DigSin, a new model digital label that was founded on the notion of analysing how people actually consume music instead of traditional labels that tend to have *past* consumer behaviour as their guide. Soon after, he formed DigMark as a data-driven marketing company that encouraged other entertainment brands to work with them to help grow their digital presence. Finally, he's also written two books on digital music: *Futurehit.DNA* which was a top-selling music business book on Amazon and *Hack Your Hit*.

So while Mr Frank can be considered a twenty-year 'veteran' of the music industry, he was asked to be the subject of this case study because his latest venture – as owner and CEO of DigSin, a singles-focused music company that allows subscribing fans to obtain music for free – is the culmination of his journey to become an increasingly influential player in the music business. We discussed issues relevant to entrepreneurship via email in September 2014.

In speaking with Mr Frank – as well as Mark Orr, and indeed virtually every musician and music industry figure this writer has spoken to or worked with – it is glaringly evident that what drives these individuals into the industry, and what allows them to excel, is an initial love of the art form: 'I always knew I wanted to be in the music business. I say the day I started was when I was in high school and sold my baseball cards to buy DJ equipment. I had a small handful of non-music jobs like working at a Blockbuster Video and a pizza joint. Truthfully, though, music chose me and I never thought about doing anything else.'

Jay recognized that quality not only in himself, but also in one of his early inspirations: 'in the music business, I've always been inspired by a man named Howie Klein. Howie started an independent label with a lot of cool acts that I admired and eventually ran a major record label. Howie also went on to be a very passionate activist, which has always been a part of him. That ethic of being passionate about great music and great causes would be enough inspiration. Howie also met an unknown nineteen-year-old me at a CBGB showcase for one of his bands and took the time to talk to me and even introduce me to Joey Ramone. To be that great, run a label and take a moment to talk to a young kid who didn't know him? That's a special kind of person. I combined this inspiration with a work ethic I got from my parents, who instilled in me a drive to achieve anything I wanted to as long as I put in the hard work to get there.

'I had an internship at a record label called Big Life straight out of high school. There was an opportunity to go work for them before I even had a day of college. The label president at the time had never finished college. While it was tempting, I ultimately did decide to go to Ithaca College, which was very valuable. Main reason is I got to experience many new ways of thinking about the world, which inevitably led to much of the creative decisions I've done in my music business career.'

The conversation soon turned to talk about some of his specific achievements once he became more ensconced in the industry – the challenges he's faced, opportunities both taken and missed. I found this to be among the more interesting aspects of Jay's career arc, as much of the commentary that followed illustrates many of the points made previously in this chapter – especially regarding the importance of new business models, tapping into new audiences, and, to use an age-old cliché, 'reinventing the wheel' (see the above discussion on the current Spotify issue): 'Before I started DigSin, I kept asking myself one question. Why is the music business model said to be so broken, yet more people are consuming more music than ever before? I pondered that for several years, and every time I identified a problem in that question, I inevitably found a potential solution. At some point, I felt confident enough that it was worth taking the leap into making it a reality. In some ways, it felt like starting the company was a spontaneous decision. However, it was several years of thought to know it was a measured risk to get the company started. I also have used every bit of experience I've had to date to make this work. In that way, every career decision I've ever made has been a key step to make this a valuable opportunity. I wouldn't change a thing. The mistakes I've made have been learning opportunities. The hard struggles have been met with justified rewards.

'Writing a book was one of the biggest challenges I ever gave myself as well as one of the most satisfying.[15] It took enormous discipline to take disjointed ideas in my head and then put it together in a cohesive fashion that could be well understood by musicians. After that, I decided to self-publish the book, which was still a rather bold thing to do at the time. I had to learn every aspect of the distribution process from scratch and trust myself to market the book. The end result was not only a lot of sales, but was speaking about the subject in a dozen countries and continually having musicians tell me how positively the book has influenced them.

'Streaming will overtake ownership as the primary revenue driver for recorded music. This will fundamentally change marketing plans, artist cash flow, and the elements of the songs that become hits. Flash-in-the-pan songs will have a much harder time becoming successful, while long-lasting music will have to grind out its revenue over a greater timespan. Data will become more important in determining marketing efforts for artists as the need to spend time and money wisely will become increasingly more important. As people get used to data informing these decisions, there will be greater gains to be had, creating more wealth for the business as a whole.'

As the conversation drew closer to concluding, Jay shared his thoughts on entrepreneurship and how that might relate to the changing music industry landscape: 'Being an entrepreneur means taking a chance on something that could very well be the future before anyone else sees the opportunity. It means taking a greater risk to reap a greater reward. It means being able to have success or failure ride solely on your shoulders and all that comes with that.

'I would prefer that more people would be open to the new elements in music discovery. Despite the fact that there are now thousands of new ways to gain an audience's attention, many folks are still reliant on the way that business has been done for decades. That has some merits, but it blocks out the greater opportunity of where things are going. If we spent time focused on the positive merits of streaming and digital marketing rather than spending time worrying about the negative merits of perceived royalty inequities and file trading, we'd find our days would be much more profitable across the board.'

Finally, he shared some advice for young folks eager to enter the music business: 'don't get into the music business! If you ignore my advice without hesitation, you have a shot at succeeding in the music business. Seriously, have a stomach of steel. The highs are incredibly high, but the lows are incredibly tough. If you don't have the will to knock it out, you will fail and hurt yourself in the process. Also, allow yourself a lot of time. Most major labels take one to two years to break a new act's first single. If it takes them that long, it will only take music entrepreneurs longer to break their artist, technology, or media outlet. Realize it's a marathon and don't sprint.'

In reading Mr Frank's responses above, one might be left with the impression that success in the music business is in the whimsical and unpredictable hands of fate. One cannot know where an opportunity will lead, or what success a road not taken may have resulted in and that is to some degree true – the entire notion of following the wind whichever way it blows is, as was pointed out above, the very touchstone of a true entrepreneur. Taking risks, imagining new models, *creating* – not just seeking – new opportunities are what an entrepreneur does. For every industry naysayer who gripes and groans about lost revenue, evaporated markets, and abandonment of the 'old ways', there will be a Jay Frank (or a Steve Jobs or David Geffen) to step in and take his or her place.

It is an exciting time to be in the record industry – precisely because of this 'cosmic upset' in the business. As the saying goes, all bets are off – which in turn means that the playing fields are level. It is anyone's game at this point.

Okay, so the above may sound a little fanciful. But should that not be the kind of encouragement given to young people wishing to enter the music business? There is obviously still much to be said for continuing traditional methods and models in a music industry or business curriculum. Certainly, there are theories of marketing, for example, that remain relevant even in this Brave New World. But what must not be forgotten – and what cannot be overstated – is the importance of instilling in students (as well as professionals facing these industry changes) the drive to create new ways of approaching old problems. There are myriad clichés and axioms scattered about the above several pages, but here is one more: *think outside the box*. Ask questions. Figure out what consumers want – perhaps even before they know they want it (a phone that holds 20,000 songs comes to mind).

Jay worked his way up to creating DigSin by first gaining experience in what one might consider more traditional settings – Yahoo Music and Ignition Records, to name two jobs from his CV. This is not a unique path to entrepreneurial success – learning the ropes of the 'old' methods is an excellent foundation for blazing new trails, as it breeds familiarity with novel problems and challenges that established methods are not adequately addressing. Much as a composer, for instance, learns seventeenth century counterpoint before dipping his or her toes into atonality, so grounding oneself in the tools of traditional record company operation is no bad thing. Learn the rules – then learn how to *break* them.

One very important aspect of the record company entrepreneur – indeed, anyone involved in virtually any aspect of the music business – that has yet to be mentioned is the concept of *balance*. Mr Frank's responses are rife with talk about numbers, business models, revenue, and yet he is always very quick to point out the reason why he has arrived at where he is today: his passion for the music. So while he is an astute and accomplished businessman, in reading his responses it becomes abundantly clear not only that he hasn't lost his love of the art form, but also that that passion is bridled by his realization that the music business is just that – a *business*. Recognizing this difference between the tangible and rational aspects of the business of music and its existence as an intangible art form, created by artists often fuelled by irrational motivations, and more importantly balancing these aspects, is often an additional mark of the entrepreneur. Looking to Apple once again, it is not merely the fact that an iPod has x-gigabytes of memory to store y-thousands of songs, it is also the fact that the company makes the process of downloading and listening to music simple, elegant, and beautiful. These are not qualities found on a company balance sheet. They are intangibles that Steve Jobs recognized as being a part of the iPod experience – which in turn have famously led to those excellent numbers that *are* contained on the balance sheet. Jay Frank, in formulating his DigSin model, has taken a similar approach: he recognized that the traditional music business model was broken, and yet more people were listening to music than ever before. His challenge was not only to find a solution to that problem, but a solution that could be *monetized*. Transforming creative solutions, dreams even, into marketable and profitable business models is the true way of the entrepreneur.[16]

Case study: Mark Orr (LAB Records)

My second study consisted of a slightly briefer conversation, completed via email and telephone (in May 2014), with Mark Orr,[17] owner of LAB Records in Manchester, England. Mark

Orr's and Jay Frank's backgrounds, in many, if not most respects, could not be more different. Jay Frank, an American, is a twenty-plus year veteran of the music industry, and founded DigSin after stints at traditional record labels and large corporations. Mark Orr, on the other hand, is a twenty-six-year-old Englishman who started LAB Records, as he states in his interview, in his dorm room at university in 2007. It has since grown into a legitimate label, with a lengthy roster of successful artists in its stable, and has a partnership with Atlantic Records in New York. But if one digs deeper into Mr Orr's experiences, what emerges are many similarities between his entrepreneurial endeavours and Jay Franks'.

Mark began, much like Jay, with an intense love of music. As is often the case, this involved a fair amount of working for little or no money – putting on shows in his hometown of Blackpool, for instance, he does not mention any sort of remuneration. But such is the by-product of passionate undertakings – one hopes that with enough drive and luck, at some point they may begin to pay off – as they did in both Mark and Jay's cases.

Mark cites numerous essential but basic elements that helped guide and shape his entrepreneurial travels. One of those is, again, the music itself: he attributes much of his love of the art form to his Uncle Paul, who schooled him on artists such as The Hollies and The Beatles. So once again, it is the initial pull of the music that draws the likes of a Mark Orr or Jay Frank. And at the risk of being repetitive, it is the entrepreneur's power to recognize new markets, methods, and niches that enables him or her to turn that passion into a marketable commodity.

Mark's claim to entrepreneurial fame is in large part about the type of label LAB Records is. All of its artists enjoy distribution *without major label involvement*. With the constant development of an internet with ever-rising speeds and bandwidth, and the increasingly ubiquitous presence of social networking, self- or non-major-label modes of distribution are more and more becoming the choice of young recording artists trying to make their voices heard in the vast wilderness of digital delivery of recorded music.

Mr Orr's entrepreneur credentials must also include his being a young person who dove head first into starting a label whilst still at university. This speaks volumes about his drive to break from the traditional mould of obtaining gainful employment after graduating with a degree. Turning for a final time to Apple, Mark's story is not at all unlike the almost mythical tale of how Jobs and Wozniak created the first Apple computer in a garage in suburban California.

Summary

Not being averse to risk. Recognizing new opportunities. A strong constitution (or 'a stomach of steel' in the words of Jay Frank). Learning from one's mistakes. Not being afraid of failure. Getting hands on experience. Recognizing your passion and turning it into a career. These are themes that are sung by both of these entrepreneurs, despite them being from opposite sides of the pond. Both took chances. Both responded to a consumer need they identified in the music market place. Both founded, and continue to run, successful businesses that responded to the challenge of meeting these newfound needs.

But the observant reader may remember one of the questions posed very early on in this chapter: what of the difference in how each of these entrepreneurs is perceived in his respective country?

BBC News recognized this palpable disparity in a 2012 report: '[A]s the US continues to produce a wealth of start-up companies that quickly grow to dominate their marketplaces, what are the reasons behind America's continuing entrepreneurial success – and can they be copied?' (Smale, 2012). In that same study, the BBC quoted Californian Eric Ries, a Silicon Valley veteran: 'There are definitely cultural factors in the US's favour, perhaps most importantly a willingness to tolerate failure . . . In Europe if you fail in business you are going to find it very difficult to borrow money the next time around, but in the US it is almost seen as a useful experience to have gone through ... On top of this, some European countries have very high personal liability levels for entrepreneurs, which is a terrible mistake ...' (Smale, 2012). But, as Tom Ryan, founder of the US restaurant chain Smashburger (one of the fastest-growing companies in the States), stated: '[A] little bit of creativity that is not inherent in others ... [the first two key factors to success in business are your product and your business model.] ... The third is work with great people; you need these to make everything come together. Entrepreneurs can't work on their own' (Smale, 2012).

The above seems to align with the Huffington Post found in a 2012 blog post: 'A springtime trip to Washington DC last year revealed a monumental divergence in the attitudes towards entrepreneurship fostered in the US and back here in the UK. When I gave in my notice here in London, friends, family and almost everyone I spoke to bar a precious and vital few were generally pessimistic. The "what ifs" came pouring forth: 'what if you make no money? What if you lose each other? What if you get bored and realize the grass isn't always greener? What about your degree?' My degree isn't going anywhere as far as I am aware. Over in DC, the response was one of wise encouragement. 'Good for you. Have you thought about x, y and z? My son's friend did something similar last year, he would be more than happy to meet you for a drink' and so on. The American Dream may be deferred but it is still very much alive and here in Britain we need one of our own' (Balfour, 2012).

I can say with reasonable certainty that Jay Frank is hailed as the archetypal entrepreneur, albeit one with a fair track record behind him, because of his career arc that has taken him from neophyte to industry bigwig to new-business-model trailblazer.

In Mark Orr's case I am likewise convinced, regardless of the UK's slightly lesser tendency toward lionization of entrepreneurs (compared to the US) that he most certainly deserves to be crowned and celebrated as an entrepreneur. There perhaps is no greater ratification of this than Lab Records' partnership with legendary label Atlantic Records.

Conclusions

In speaking to these individuals, conducting research for this chapter, and indeed in my daily activities teaching copyright, contracts and publishing to university students and practising entertainment law, several aspects, call them trends, are clearly emerging in the recorded music industry:

- Streaming is here to stay. Like it or not, and despite headline news stories about the Taylor Swifts and Jason Aldeans of this world foregoing Spotify audience reach, no one is predicting a return to 'hard format' dominance. Streaming and downloading are not merely the wave of the future; it is the reality of the present. Anyone newly entering or re-adapting to the twenty-first-century music business – on both sides of the pond – will need to recognize and accept this.

- Equitable Remuneration. Chief among the controversies regarding royalty payments to recording artists (and/or labels) is the inequality not only between different types of delivery systems, but also between different companies within a given delivery mode. For instance, there is a difference between the payments an artist receives from Sirius/XM (the US satellite radio provider) and Pandora – but also a difference between Pandora and Spotify.

- Significant Copyright Revision. There is very little disagreement between legal scholars, record industry figures, journalists and other commentators that US copyright law in its current incarnation is not equipped to handle the ever-growing onslaught of digital exploitation of music. Despite numerous attempts at fixes, many of which have been pointed out in this chapter, the law, even on an international level, appears to be playing a constant game of 'catch up'. Part of this may require a re-examination of the essential balance that copyright law is purportedly based on: dissemination of creative works for the good of society against protection of the author of those works. With so much music available so easily in so many forms and formats, perhaps composers, recording artists, writers, painters, filmmakers et al., may have to reassess the monopolized hold on their creations. Stated another way, what lies ahead may be the Age of the Consumer as opposed to that of the Creator. In any event, copyright is an analogue law trying to survive in a digital age – and that is perhaps the most difficult challenge the recording industry entrepreneur faces for the future.

Notes

1   Mark Twain's famous phrase, 'Reports of my death have been greatly exaggerated' is itself a slight misquote of the author's original statement. In an interview contained in the 2 June 1897 issue of the *New York Journal*, Twain was informed by a *Journal* representative that it had been reported Twain was 'dying of poverty in London'. The inimitable author and humourist replied, 'The report of my death was an exaggeration. The report of my poverty is harder to deal with.' Scharnhorst, Gary, ed. *Mark Twain: The Complete Interviews*, Tuscaloosa: University of Alabama Press, 2006, 317–18.

2   See Nielsen (2014), 2014 Nielsen Music US Report, available at: http://www.nielsen.com/content/dam/corporate/us/en/public%20 factsheets/Soundscan/nielsen-2014-year-end-music-report-us.pdf [accessed 15 April 2015].

3   While this phrase is usually attributed to, and supposedly made famous by, Greely, it was very likely first penned in 1851 by an editor of the Terre Haute, Indiana *Express* named John B. Soule.

4   At least by one author's analysis, between 1976 and 1979, for example, US Recorded Music Revenue, adjusted for inflation (shown in 2011 dollars), puts vinyl sales at $47b and cassettes at

$63b. See Degusta, M., (2011), 'The REAL Death of the Music Industry', *Business Insider*, 18 February, available at: http://www.businessinsider.com/these-charts-explain-the-real-death-of-the-music-industry-2011-2 [accessed 13 November 2014].

5   Kang, C. (2014), 'Taylor Swift's "1989" becomes first platinum album of the year', *New York Times*, 5 November, available at: http://www.washingtonpost.com/news/business/wp/2014/11/05/taylor-swifts-1989-becomes-the-first-platinum-album-of-the-year/ [accessed 13 November 2014]. See also Caufield, K. (2014), 'Taylor Swift's "1989" Beats "Frozen" As Top Selling Album of 2014', *Billboard Magazine*, 31 December 2014, available at: http://www.billboard.com/articles/columns/chart-beat/6422411/taylor-swift-1989-beats-frozen-top-selling-album-2014 [accessed April 2015].

6   Jason Aldean: 'The debate the whole music industry is having on streaming is complicated,' he states. 'And while I'm definitely paying attention to the business side of things, I am first and foremost an artist. I'm an artist whose career has been built by the songwriters, publishers, producers and engineers that line Music Row in Nashville. What they do has value, and I want everyone who is involved in making my music to be paid fairly. This is about trying to do what is right for the people who have given me a great life.' Whitaker, S. (2014), 'Jason Aldean Explains Decision to Pull New Album From Spotify', *Taste of Country*, 13 November.

7   Copyright Act of 1909 §1 *et seq.* (1909).

8   Copyright Act of 1976 U.S.C. §101 *et seq.* (1976).

9   Sound Recordings Act, Pub. L. No. 140, 85 Stat. 39 (1971).

10 For an explanation of this, as well as a recent challenge to the law brought by recording artists Flo & Eddie (of the 60s group The Turtles, as well as occasional performers with Frank Zappa), see SoundExchange (2014), pre-1972 copyright background, http://www.soundexchange.com/advocacy/pre-1972-copyright/ [accessed 13 November 13].

11 The tale of Kane Kramer and Apple nearly has the makings of an industrial espionage thriller – lapsed patents, bad blood, personal financial problems . . . In 2007 Apple finally recognized Kramer's pioneering work that contributed to the development of the iPod

and its progeny, even turning to him as a consultant. See: Boffey, D. (2008), 'Apple admit Briton DID invent iPod, but he's still not getting any money', *The Daily Mail Online*, 8 September, available at: http://www.dailymail.co.uk/news/article-1053152/ Apple-admit-Briton-DID-invent-iPod-hes-getting-money.html [accessed 13 November 2014]; Sorrell, C. (2008), 'Briton Invented iPod, DRM and On-Line Music in 1979', *Wired*, 9 September, available at: http://www.wired.com/2008/09/ briton-invented/ [accessed 13 November 2014]; Matyszczyk, C. (2008), 'Apple Admits It Didn't Invent the iPod', *CNET*, 8 September, available at: http://www.cnet.com/news/apple-admits-it-didnt-invent-the-ipod/ [accessed 13 November 2014].

12 See: Audible: an Amazon company (2012), available at: http:// about.audible.com/history/ [accessed 13 November 2014].

13 Smith, T. (2008), 'Ten Years Old: the World's First MP3 Player', *The Register*, 10 March (online), available at: http://www. theregister.co.uk/2008/03/10/ft_first_mp3_player/ [accessed 13 November 2014].

It is worth noting here that the RIAA (Recording Industry Association of America) was the 'power' behind the famous Napster case (the record company plaintiffs in that dispute were all members of the RIAA). Napster was the case that declared peer-to-peer sharing of digital music files to be illegal. See *A&M Records, Inc. v. Napster, Inc.*, 239 F3d 1004 (2001). But the RIAA first got its feet wet in this realm when it sued Diamond Multimedia, alleging that its Rio device was in violation of the Audio Home Recording Act of 1992. See *Recording Indus. Ass'n of Am. v. Diamond Multimedia Sys., Inc.*, 180 F3d 1072 (9th Cir. 1999). The court found that the Rio was not a digital audio recording device subject to the restrictions of the Act, and consequently denied the RIAA's request for a preliminary injunction against the manufacturing and distribution of the device.

14 Smith, T. (2008), 'Ten Years Old: the World's First MP3 Player,' *The Register*, 10 March (online), available at: http://www. theregister.co.uk/2008/03/10/ft_first_mp3_player/ [accessed 13 November 2014].

It's worth noting here that the RIAA (Recording Industry Association of America) was the 'power' behind the famous

Napster case (the record company plaintiffs in that dispute were all members of the RIAA). Napster was the case that declared peer-to-peer sharing of digital music files to be illegal. See *A&M Records, Inc. v. Napster, Inc.*, 239 F3d 1004 (2001) But the RIAA first got its feet wet in this realm when it sued Diamond Multimedia, alleging that its Rio device was in violation of the Audio Home Recording Act of 1992. See *Recording Indus. Ass'n of Am. v. Diamond Multimedia Sys., Inc.*, 180 F3d 1072 (9th Cir. 1999). The Court found that the Rio was not a digital audio recording device subject to the restrictions of the Act, and consequently denied the RIAA's request for a preliminary injunction against the manufacturing and distribution of the device.

15 Jay Frank is the author of *FutureHit.DNA* (2009) and *Hack Your Hit* (2012).

16 Associated web sources for Jay Frank:

http://digsin.com/
http://jayfrank.brandyourself.com/
http://www.futurehitdna.com/
https://www.facebook.com/repojay

17 Associated web sources for Mark Orr:

http://labrecs.com/
https://www.facebook.com/labrecords
http://labexposure.com/

References

Anderson, C. (2008), *The (Longer) Long Tail: Why the Future of Business is Selling Less of More*, 2nd ed., New York: Hyperion, pp. 1–14.

Balfour, X. (2012), 'Why Britain Needs a More American Attitude to Entrepreneurship', *Huffpost Lifestyle*, 9 February, available at: http://www.huffingtonpost.co.uk/shrimpy-balfour/why-britain-needs-a-more-american-attitude_b_1840852.html [accessed 14 November 2014].

Big Machine Label Group, website: http://www.bigmachinelabelgroup.com/

Caulfield, K. (2013), 'Beyonce Breaks U.S. iTunes Sales Record, Sells 617,000 in Three Days', *Billboard*, 16 December.

Department of Culture, Media and Sport (2001), Creative Industries Mapping Document 2001, London, DCMS.

Ek, D. (2014), '2 Billion and Counting', Spotify, 11 November, available at: https://news.spotify.com/sg-en/2014/11/11/2-billion-and-counting/ [accessed 13 November 2014].

Freeman, J., 7 October 2011, available at: http://www.musicrow.com/2011/10/jay-frank-announces-new-venture/ [accessed 22 December 2014].

Gerber, M. (2005), *E-Myth Mastery: The Seven Essential Disciplines for Building a World Class Company*, New York: Collins.

Grow, K. (2014), 'Taylor Swift: "Music is art, and art should be paid for"', *Rolling Stone*, 7 July, available at: http://www.rollingstone.com/music/news/taylor-swift-music-is-art-and-art-should-be-paid-for-20140707 [accessed 13 November 2014].

Hull J., T. Hutchison and R. Strasser (2011), *The Music and Recording Business*, 3rd ed., New York: Routledge.

International Federation of Phonographic Industries (2014), *The Recording Industry in Numbers 2013*, London: IFPI, pp. 1–50.

Kang, C. (2014), 'Taylor Swift's "1989"' becomes first platinum album of the year', *New York Times*, 5 November, available at: http://www.washingtonpost.com/news/business/wp/2014/11/05/taylor-swifts-1989-becomes-the-first-platinum-album-of-the-year/ [accessed 13 November 2014].

Karubian, S. (2009) '360° deals: An industry reaction to the devaluation of recorded music', *Southern California Interdisciplinary Law Journal* 18: 395–462.

Katz, M. (2010), *Capturing Sound: How Technology Has Changed Music*, Berkeley: University of California Press.

Knopper, S. (2014), 'Taylor Swift Abruptly Pulls Entire Catalogue From Spotify', *Rolling Stone*, 3 November, available at: http://www.rollingstone.com/music/news/taylor-swift-abruptly-pulls-entire-catalog-from-spotify-20141103 [accessed 13 November 2014].

Krasilovsky, M. and S. Shemel (2007), *This Business of Music: The Definitive Guide to the Business and Legal Issues of the Music Industry*, 10th ed., New York: Billboard Books.

Lee, E. (2014), 'Jason Aldean Follows Taylor Swift's Lead, Pulls New Music From Spotify', *US Weekly*, 10 November, available at: http://www.usmagazine.com/entertainment/news/jason-aldean-pulls-new-album-from-spotify-just-like-taylor-swift-20141011 [accessed 13 November 2104].

Maeda, M. (2012), *How to Open and Operate a Successful Independent Record Label*, Ocala: Atlantic Publishing Group.

Passman, D. (2009), *All You Need to Know About the Music Business*, 7th ed., New York: Free Press.

Peters, M. (2014), 'Big Machine's Scott Borchetta Explains Why Taylor Swift was Removed From Spotify', *Hollywood Reporter*, 10 November, available at: http://www.hollywoodreporter.com/earshot/big-machines-scott-borchetta-explains-747781 [accessed 13 November 2014].

Roberts, R. (2014), 'Taylor Swift doesn't like Spotify, says her work has "greater value"', *Los Angeles Times*, 13 November, available at: http://www.latimes.com/entertainment/music/posts/la-et-ms-taylor-swift-spotify-battle-20141113-story.html [accessed 13 November 2014].

Schulenberg, R. (2005), *Legal Aspects of the Music Industry: An Insider's View*, New York: Billboard Books, pp. 558–60.

Sisario, B. (2013), 'As Music Streaming Grows, Royalties Slow to a Trickle', *New York Times*, 28 January, available at: http://www.nytimes.com/2013/01/29/business/media/streaming-shakes-up-music-industrys-model-for-royalties.html?pagewanted=all&_r=0 [accessed 13 November 2014].

Smale, W. (2012), 'What drives US entrepreneurship?', BBC News, 29 January, available at: http://www.bbc.co.uk/news/business-16742137 [accessed 14 November 2014].

UK Music (2013), *The Economic Contribution of the Core UK Music Industry*, London, UK Music.

Vogel, H. (2010), *Entertainment Industry Economics: A Guide for Financial Analysis*, 8th ed., Cambridge: Cambridge University Press.

Young, S. and S. Collins (2010), 'A view from the trenches of music 2.0', *Popular Music and Society* 33 (3): 339–55.

8

Digital Music Distribution

Clare K. Duffin and Allan Dumbreck

Digital distribution of music in the last five to seven years has evolved to meet the increasing demand of instant, accessible audio. We are living in an increasingly 'noisy' online world (Vaynerchuk, 2013), meaning digital distribution companies (along with every other digital platform competing for business) must be focused on meeting the needs of listener-consumers, as well as those of artists and record labels. Examining the traditional distribution of physical products to retailers, we may consider the decline of HMV and the growth in popularity of iTunes or Amazon MP3 to be simply the arrival of new mechanisms. However, this is not the complete picture. The apparent paradigm shift of music artists becoming more in control of their audio repertoire from a rights holder perspective (PPL UK, 2014) has arguably presented new opportunities for digital distributors in the facilitation of artists' seemingly entrepreneurial activity.

The International Federation of Phonographic Industries (IFPI) reported another increase in global digital music revenues in 2013, with the upwards trajectory moving steadily since 2008. Sales of digital downloads, however, have been in decline since 2012 – the latest reporting a slight decrease of 2.1 per cent. However, this is being offset by an increase in streaming and subscription services to produce the overall rise in global digital music revenues in the majority of markets across the globe (IFPI, 2014). This surge in streaming and subscription services – such as Deezer, Rdio, Spotify and more recently Tidal – indicates an interesting change in music consumption habits. It suggests consumers are taking another step away from the notion of owning music as an artefact. Instead, consumer needs are satisfied by an apparent 'convenience culture' facilitated by the evolution of integrated applications (apps) and enhanced smartphone functions. Devices (both mobile and desktop) appear to be supporting this surge; and digital distribution services are morphing into digital Swiss army knives to match consumer desires, geared towards producing personalized, enhanced online experiences.

The digital landscape has become a playing field for a variety of new tech businesses, where the focus on enhancing the end-user experience is at the fore. Buying behaviour has shifted; and so the distribution of music to meet evolving consumer needs has progressed to include broader social media options (generally, online sharing). This is changing the nature of music consumption altogether.

Web 3.0 and digital music distribution

In essence, the shift from Web 2.0 to Web 3.0 – 'a global platform based on Tim Berners-Lee's idea of the "semantic web" in which web pages will contain enough metadata about their content to enable software to make informed judgements about their relevance and function' (Naughton, 2010) – has led to more personalized online experiences. Arguably, this is the key component magnetizing end-users to the 'experience culture' versus that of 'ownership culture', or, as Boyle similarly describes in the context of the 'information age': 'a shift from tangible to intangible goods, from things to ideas, from tractors to software' (Boyle, 1997: 1). Consumers are perhaps considered to be more than 'end-users' sometimes now referred to as 'prosumers' (Ritzer and Jurgenson, 2010) – the latter referring to the notion of consumers, who are at the fore of consumption technology and lifestyle; at times co-create content. This behaviour shift highlights internet-based technologies encouraging interest in *processes* over products.

Independent artists as prosumers: Tools for digital distribution

Extending the idea of 'prosumers' (producer-consumers), the empowerment of independent music artists must be considered. The morphing of digital distribution services has not only occurred based on listener-consumer demand, but also that of the producer-consumer: music artists. Independent music artists are given closer consideration here based on the aforementioned entrepreneurial activity that is facilitated via digital dashboards – the online tools providing access for the global distribution of digital music to streaming, subscription and download platforms. Examples include (but are not limited to): BandCamp, Music Glue and ReverbNation, all of which provide tools for artists to distribute their music digitally (and physically) to fans via the recognized web outlets. These particular platforms also allow distribution direct-to-fans (i.e. potentially from the artist themselves, straight to their market). Such tools, as suggested previously, are geared towards supporting artists and (usually smaller) record labels in their efforts to manage their products online. The notion of 'online presence' and 'interaction with fans', however, distinguishes said platforms from other more traditional-physical music distribution forms. Data on consumer/fan habits (such as geographical sales distribution, date and time of sale and consumer demographics) is available at the click of a button on virtual dashboards; feedback on purchases can be instantaneous.

Artists using these platforms have more in-depth consumer insights and therefore a better understanding of who their fanbase really is, in terms of geographical location, gender, age group, purchasing habits and many other factors. Given this increase in interconnectedness across said virtual dashboards with a broad range of social media platforms (via APIs – application programme interfaces – a set of protocols allowing communication of information such as login details from one platform to another; basically, open linking between platforms), direct interaction with fans can be made possible and a more targeted marketing approach using online promotional mechanisms is possible for the business-aware music artist/ producer. What we have now is the embodiment of sensibilities that were previously more monologue-based between company and consumer, giving way to that of a more dialogue-based interaction between artist and marketplace. In plain English – if you are a music producer (e.g. band/songwriter/remixer-DJ/EDM collective) who can understand the digital distribution mechanisms and can operate the software then you can be your own record company, marketing and selling your work globally from your bedroom. This may, of course, require an element of entrepreneurship on your behalf, but it is possible.

In the remainder of this chapter, we will firstly examine the range of digital distribution platforms and services as they stand at present, examining each one separately, then we will analyse two case studies of individuals working within different sectors of the digital music distribution environment. Finally we will draw some conclusions regarding the UK/US dichotomy on the value of the term 'entrepreneur' and whether our case studies' activity in this area can be regarded as entrepreneurial in nature.

The digital distribution landscape

The digital distribution of music has evolved as a result of increasing demand for accessibility, enhancements in mobile technologies and indeed the rise of digital tools available to independent music artists. A broad and diverse group of companies now offer a considerable (and growing) range of services to the prosumer, consumer and each other. Given that this entire field did not exist just fifteen years ago and the rapid rate of its expansion and development in that time, what each of these services and delivery formats actually does can be bewildering to the casual observer. At the time of writing, there are at least five distinct, identifiable types of online service (although in places their functions may overlap), which collectively constitute the current state of digital distribution. Below we offer an overview of this field followed by a categorization of the different types of service and their functions in an attempt to de-mystify some of the jargon of digital music distribution

Sector overview

Digital aggregators distribute MP3 files to a group of digital retailers and streaming services (e.g. iTunes, Spotify). Digital retailers provide purchasing solutions to end-users in exchange for the download and ownership of digital music. Streaming services fundamentally provide access to music (i.e. allowing audio play/listening) without the requirement to purchase/own a copy or to action a download of the music file. Subscription services can also operate without the option of free streaming, where money is paid (usually every month) to gain open access to their catalogue of digital music and avoid viewing unwanted advertising.

What we also have with some platforms is a blurring of services, dependent on platform-type-capability and consumer demand. Crowdfunding platforms, for example, arrived to help solve the independent music artist self-funding problem, where a new array of more personalized fan/consumer choices are presented in a digital interface. Other constraints may be involved here, for example a time-limit applied in correlation with a specified funding target, which, in turn, impacts on both purchasing and access behaviours amongst fans/consumers.

Digital aggregators

Examples: EmuBands, Ditto Music, Tunecore, CD Baby

These companies fundamentally work with (usually smaller or independent) record labels and music artists, offering a means to make their music digitally available across a variety of different online music stores (digital retailers/streaming/ subscription services). They effectively act as an agent to offer a single point inroad for the music producer/artist/ songwriter or small independent record label to a range of web-based sales outlets where the public can listen to and temporarily access or purchase their music. Different financial models exist to suit artist/label requirements but these organizations offer relatively inexpensive access mechanisms. This removes the time-consuming (and expensive) task of the artist or label trying to work directly with all the online stores one at a time to set up the digital distribution of their work. A service, arguably, that facilitates entrepreneurial activity and links back to previously discussed notions of 'prosumerism' as also depicted in a similar fashion by both Vaynerchuck (2013) and Stratten and Kramer (2012), where the means to engage online audiences are focused on a deeper understanding of individual consumer (or in this case 'prosumer') needs.

Digital retailers

Examples: iTunes, HMV Digital, Amazon MP3, BandCamp

These online stores provide transactional opportunities to consumers, where a digital music file (e.g. MP3) can be purchased. Typically, the file is paid for through the website (by typing in credit card or gift voucher details for example) and then digitally downloaded to a laptop, phone or other consumer device where it is stored for effectively infinite use, as and when the consumer wishes to hear it. Most digital retailers of music offer MP3 as the predominant file format. However, BandCamp and SoundCloud offer higher quality file formats such as Wav, or AIFF. In effect, this is the digital equivalent of visiting a record store, buying a CD or vinyl copy of a single or album and taking it home to keep (the physical record purchase model familiar to music consumers of the twentieth century). What is interesting here is the apparent recent shift from the desire to own the artefact (the digital file, such as MP3) to that of access. Essentially, this is where streaming and subscription services enter the landscape as an alternative form of music consumption. Once again we see processes overtaking products – or as previously mentioned 'from tangible to intangible goods' (Boyle, 1997: 1). The process here being accessibility, or ease-of-access; and more generally, to that of complying with convenience.

Streaming services

Examples: Spotify, Deezer, Rdio, YouTube, Beats Music, Tidal

Streaming services offer end-users the means to listen to music via their online facilities without the requirement to download a digital music file. The artist and songwriter are remunerated via advertising on the website. Alternatively, they also offer monthly subscription options (see also subscription-specific services below) to obtain a higher quality experience of such services (e.g. access to more music; no adverts between songs; offline mode). Spotify, for example, offers free access to their entire catalogue if you accept the on-site advertising. If end-users wish to access the music without the adverts, then Spotify's premium will currently provide this for £9.99 per month (spotify.com, December 2014, UK). Ease-of-access and convenience, again, play a major role here. As consumption habits increasingly call for mobile-friendly alignment, the importance to correspond with fast-paced lifestyles is at the fore. The transformation from consumer to prosumer highlights this.

New developments: Tidal

In more recent developments, we have seen the launch of Jay-Z's Tidal service in 2015 – a streaming distribution platform pitching itself as 'the first artist-owned global music and entertainment platform' (Dredge, 2015). While streaming platforms facilitate arguably higher levels of accessibility compared to physical distribution methods, it has become increasingly apparent that, as a consequence, the value placed on music has decreased. Ultimately, this is where Tidal competes for Spotify's share of the market: through the provision of higher sonic quality (lossless format) streaming. With availability in forty-four countries (Tidal, 2015), Tidal operates in similar fashion to that of Spotify. However, with a further nod to enhancing online consumer/prosumer experiences, Tidal does not include any adverts on its platform whatsoever.

Tidal, being artist-owned, presents itself as a slightly different case here, based on new developments in the field of music streaming. Broadly, this refers to the business models adopted by Spotify, Apple-owned Beats Music and Google-owned YouTube that have resulted in relatively unfavourable (or non-existent) revenue streams for (mostly) independent music artists. Since the music industries thirsted for new ideas to propel monetization after a series of dips in music sales, the evolution and impact of new technologies – particularly streaming – has appeared to dilute the value of music. Undoubtedly, streaming as a means to consume and share music is increasingly popular. However, the ability to manage these online behaviours in such a manner that reinstates the value of music has, in some ways, become more difficult based on free streaming and subsequent low royalties as a result. Tidal may well be adding a new dimension to the digital distribution landscape.

Subscription services

Examples: Google Play Music, Qoboz, Sony Music Unlimited

Subscription services usually operate as an extension to streaming services, but with a monthly or annual price tag. The fee usually provides the subscriber with access to a wide range of music to stream across a multitude of devices. Services such as Spotify and Deezer, for example, also operate subscription services. Spotify's premium subscription service, for example, provides end-users with access to a wide range of music available to stream without adverts and with an offline mode. Debate surrounds both streaming and subscription services regarding the lower rate of return to artists and songwriters (compared with physical record sales' royalties) but as previously mentioned, while both streaming and subscription services are in the ascendancy, physical sales and download purchases are currently in decline. Music artists and record labels alike are battling with access versus ownership, where the former (in streaming terms) provides a smaller royalty return. However, streaming services can often act as a promotional shop-window – potentially leading to the sale of a digital music file (e.g. MP3).

Crowdfunding platforms

Examples: Kickstarter, Sponsume, PledgeMusic UK, Bloom VC

An added demand of independent music artists – and indeed of any music entrepreneur – is the means to raise money for project development. Online crowdsourcing platforms such as Kickstarter, PledgeMusic and Sponsume offer campaign creators the option to do so – with a host of dashboard management tools. They take a percentage of the capital raised, leaving the bulk of the funds to the campaign creator (e.g. the music artist or record label) to progress the project (usually to make a new record, music video or fund a tour).

Crowdfunding platforms offer a different pathway for fans to engage with artists through the 'reward' infrastructure; where the end-user/fan will receive personalized or limited edition items upon donation to the crowdfunding campaign. Once again, these online crowdfunding platforms offer dashboard tools (e.g. widgets) that can be integrated across a range of social media sites to digitally distribute content – reiterating the shift to prosumer level online behaviours.

End-users of such crowdfunding platforms essentially act as project managers and thus, we could question the impact of the related online tools on music artists, behaviour – whereby such platforms arguably contribute to a moulding effect on the music artist (or indeed record label) mind-set, to uproot entrepreneurial or managerial skills. Crowdfunding platforms per project usually comprise a monetary target (the cost of recording the album for example). This is usually set upon the launch of the campaign and a series of rewards for contributing fans/investors agreed (e.g. signed copy of the album, limited edition T-shirts, priority tickets to the launch) that are then promised in exchange for monetary donations from fans/end-users on completion of the project. The site tracks the on-going total amount and if/when the required investment is reached, the album (for example) is recorded and released and the investor rewards distributed. If the total amount is not obtained by the deadline then the funds may be returned to the fans (specific terms vary depending on company policy), thus encouraging the music artist or record label project managers to think strategically about the campaign as well as nurture the relationship with the new digital audience (i.e. end-users making donations in return for set rewards).

This model again places project control in the hands of the music producer and/or smaller record label, suggesting beneficial outcomes to those with initiative and drive. Facilitating such control once again caters for the newer, prosumer-level behaviours – now very much the norm for the independent music sector.

Digital content management platforms

Examples: Music Glue, BandCamp, ReverbNation

These platforms provide the means to manage a music artist's online presence via a digital dashboard. A set of tools is provided in the dashboard allowing artists to distribute music and related media content from a central online hub. BandCamp, for example, facilitates merchandise sales, streaming, digital downloads of high quality music files and a range of widgets. This offers a greater range of services than the digital aggregator who primarily works with recorded music only. Essentially, such platforms cater for producer-consumers, whereby the toolkit (i.e. virtual dashboard tool) supports both creator and sales solutions for the artist or record label. In this context, the music artist or record label may again be interchangeably referred to as prosumers. The existence of such platforms recognizes the artist/label desire to connect directly with fans (see also Stratten and Kramer, 2012; Vaynerchuk, 2013) and more generally aspects of (what in some senses can be deemed to be) entrepreneurial activity. Arguably, such platforms operate in a more palatable manner for those with a higher internal locus of control – where it is more likely such individuals view their achievements as a result of their own efforts (see Hay et al., 1990): an entrepreneurial trait, as also presented by Burns (2011: 40). The tools available in such digital content management platforms provide the means to control and analyze online actions in order to measure small successes (e.g. a record sale via BandCamp) in relation to predetermined actions – such as a competition, or a free download – that may have directed the end-user/fan to the purchase webpage. Thus, in some respects, what we appear to have is a combined prosumer-entrepreneur platform as a result of the apparent shift in consumption and creator habits.

Each of these mechanisms offers the artist/manager/record label access to and control over the online presence of the act and associated products. That development, however, obviously requires significant additional innovation (artwork, web design, creative online activity) and management (continuous monitoring and update, communication with online services). There is also a risk factor. Where an established major record label has a global promotions and sales network and significant market and product placement knowledge, the independent artist/manager may not. Selecting the correct image, target market and appropriate promotion mechanisms (and negotiating the best price) could be outwith the abilities of the novice. However, it again opens the door for entrepreneurial activity.

Case study: EmuBands (Ally Gray)

Whilst studying at Liverpool University, Ally Gray developed a parallel early career working in concert promotion and artist management. From the outset he demonstrated initiative: 'my first job in music was working for myself – promoting concerts'. Upon completion of his undergraduate qualification he initially began working for an innovative digital rights management company where he learned the practicalities of music data management. His original intention was to develop his own record company. Discovering that the biggest problem would be setting up digital distribution for his label releases he co-founded EmuBands in 2005, an online aggregation service for independent artists and labels wishing to get access to the larger platforms (notably at that time, iTunes). This was previously expensive and complex. Setting up a 'flat-fee' single cost model which allowed the rights owners to retain 100 per cent of their royalties made the service highly attractive to the independent marketplace and created an opportunity which greatly simplified their promotional and distribution requirements. Having now distributed over 50,000 tracks across over 10,000 releases from over 5,000 users (either artist/label accounts) and employing a full time team of five plus additional freelancers, the company has grown to become a central part of the independent recorded music network.

Certainly, parts of his marketplace continue to see growth, although the overview of digital music sales has recently become quite complex. The broader recorded music industry (including physical sales – CD/vinyl) generated the equivalent of $15bn worldwide in 2012 (IFPI, 2014). While total sales have been in recession for some time (down from over $20bn in 2005), a part of that turnover, revenues from digitally distributed music (downloads, streaming, subscription services), had been increasing steadily over the seven year period. Growth of global digital income by 4.3 per cent in 2013 to $5.9bn (ibid) was the most recent high water mark (up from $4bn in 2008); however, as indicated earlier, UK download sales have seen a slight decline in the last two years (Pakinkis, 2014). On the other hand, streaming and subscription services in 2013 showed very significant growth (a 53 per cent increase on 2012 figures) in both revenues and user numbers. At the start of 2013 there were 28m subscription service users internationally (IFPI, 2014). This has sustained the growth of the digital music markets. Globally, digital now accounts for 39 per cent of total recorded music industry revenues and the medium now generates more than 50 per cent of recorded music sales in three of the world's top ten markets. This is partly due to increased availability: legal digital music service providers were operating in 195 countries in 2013, a rise from fifty-eight in 2010 (ibid).

However, as noted, since 2012 digital download sales in the UK have slowed. While digital sales now account for 99.6 per cent of all UK singles, the inclusion of streaming into the official UK charts in July 2014 could be seen as recognition that the marketplace is moving towards access instead of ownership. Possibly the largest increase in the UK digital music marketplace, however, has been in streaming itself with more than 3.7 billion tracks accessed in 2012 – 140 for every household (IFPI, 2014). In addition, music streaming services rated very highly for satisfaction (93 per cent) and awareness (80 per cent). This leads to the speculation that the British music buyer is tending more towards the access model.

This is supported by the news that revenue for the UK arm of Spotify grew by over 40 per cent in 2013, finally entering profitability. 'According to the company's latest set of financial results, published by Companies House, year-on-year revenues grew from £92.6m ($147m) in 2012 to £131.4m ($210m) in 2013, a rise of almost 42 per cent. Of arguably greater significance, especially to critics of the streaming model and its long term economic viability, was Spotify UK's turnaround of an £11m ($17.6m) net loss in 2012 to a £2.6m ($4.2m) profit, after taxation, the following year' (Smirke, 2014).

In the US, digital sales superseded physical sales (CD, vinyl, cassette) in 2012 and in 2013 constituted 60 per cent of all recorded music revenue. Individual US artists are now regularly breaking digital sales records. In December 2013, Beyonce broke the iTunes album sales record, selling 617,000 worldwide in three days (Caulfield, 2013). On 26 June 2014, the RIAA (US record company representative organization) named Katy Perry as their most certified artist in terms of digital singles sales (RIAA, 2014). They credited the Capitol Records' performer with 72 million downloads and streams for her eighteen recognized single releases.

As part of this fluctuating sector, EmuBands supports artists and labels in uploading their music to download and streaming platforms and so offers access to the broadest range of digital delivery mechanisms. In common with a number of other entrepreneurs Ally Gray was inspired by the success of other driven individuals. He states, 'My initial aims had been to set up a record label that would emulate labels like Creation Records – being a teenager during the Britpop era, Alan McGee was a massive inspiration to me. However, when I did form a record company in 2003/04 I found the usual barriers of distribution to be a problem.' This was exacerbated by a perceived failure within the marketplace to progress historic business models: 'I encountered a complicated licensing structure that was still rooted in the "old world" of physical product licensing and royalty splits. The simple thought of "I would have paid someone £X just to do that job for us" was one of the main drivers of the idea of what eventually became EmuBands.'

Having encountered the problem and identified the business opportunity, he then refined the offer. 'We came up with a flat-fee model which would allow distribution to digital services in return for a one-off payment.' Through EmuBands, by the simple expedient of a single payment to a single company for each track or bundle they release, independent artists and labels can gain access to a near exhaustive range of distribution mechanisms operating globally. 'We are now in a position where we have helped thousands of artists sell their music online', Ally stated.

In terms of previous work experience, Ally credits his non-music employment with pushing him towards an industry he enjoyed and the discovery that 'I wanted to be my own boss!' He accepts that this work did give him 'an insight into working environments and what type of management and leadership styles did and didn't work', admitting that this was 'fairly valuable'. The work he undertook within music led him to the point where the vision to create EmuBands occurred.

Regarding his education, Ally first studied for an HND in Business and Music Industry Management at college, then completed a BA (Hons) in Management, Business and Administration and finally an MBA in Music Industries. This puts him amongst the best educated young entrepreneurs we interviewed. He believes these qualifications gave him 'a good grounding in a variety of subjects that have been important, for example law (specifically music industry related), finance and management'. However, he adds 'but so much of the work I have done in my professional career could just not be taught', highlighting the rapid growth of digital music delivery which didn't exist when he was a student. This again echoes the experience of other interviewees who, while advocating education, stressed the importance of parallel experiential learning.

Ally was one of the first young developers to express a dislike of the term 'entrepreneur', as already discussed in the introductory chapters, associating the word with 'people wanting to make a fast buck, drive flash cars and wear sharp suits'. In common with Richy Muirhead, who features in the final chapter, he does however genuinely value his lifestyle. 'I love being in this position, the freedom of not having to work for someone else, the responsibilities and pressures of building something meaningful, Sometimes a regular "nine-to-five" job does sound appealing, but that feeling quickly wears off. Yes, starting a business is very hard work and can be stressful, but it's also very rewarding. Being involved in a daily basis in the music industry is a great reward in itself – being involved in great new music, in even a small way makes it all worthwhile.'

Looking to the future, Ally suspects that the streaming of music may increase and that the desire to possess a physical or digital copy may decline. He sees the next five years as being crucial in the access versus ownership debate. This clearly is a significant break from the previous mindset: a move from 'buying' to 'renting'. Ally's viewpoint here is that the purchaser will ultimately benefit: 'It'll be interesting to see where the access versus ownership debate goes. With the recent rise of streaming services it's certainly pointing towards the access model. Just now you have ever evolving music services offering more and more music. I think it's a great time to be a music fan. I don't know where we're going to be in terms of technology and connectivity in five years' time but I think that's where any major developments will stem from.'

When asked to identify the attributes required by a prospective music entrepreneur, Ally engaged at some length. 'Determination, discipline and a strong work ethic. Without them, you'll struggle. There are constant demands on your time, and you have to make sure that you're doing what needs to be done.' This is no easy option and able co-workers are vital he advises: 'the pressures can be relentless – financial pressures, the pressure of responsibility – being in charge can be great as you have no one to tell you what to do – but that can also be a burden and it's why building the right team is essential.'

Taking critical decisions, such as that to develop the concept or to become self-employed in the first place, and then acting on those decisions is obviously a key part of becoming an entrepreneur. Ally demonstrates this in several instances in his responses: 'The simple thought of "I would have paid someone £X just to do that job for us" was one of the main drivers'; 'I wanted to work in an industry I enjoyed and I wanted to be my own boss!'; 'We are where we are because of the decisions we've made and actions we've taken, and I'm happy with that.' The will to act, as identified by Litunnen (2000), quoting Tibbets (1979) and Bird (1989), while examining entrepreneurial personality, is seen as an important characteristic for the entrepreneur, cited as 'being in part the product of experience' and 'probably connected with the entrepreneur's training and resources under his/her control' (Litunnen, 2000: 295). The crucial difference here is essentially that where many may see the opportunity, the potential gain, the market gap, the entrepreneur is the one who makes the decision to take action and then does so.

Ally makes it clear that running your own company is taxing, but also that EmuBands is not a one-man operation: 'the pressures can be relentless . . . and it's why building the right team is essential'.

'Your team will be representing your brand, so it's important to pick the right people', he continues, pointing out that it is still the responsibility of the boss to take the reins when under strain. You need to be 'able to shoulder the burden of the workload if things get tough for the team.'

Pointing out (in common with many of our interviewees) that networking is a key skill, particularly in relation to possible funding agencies, Ally states: 'research what support is available to you – at present there are [a series of] enterprise and business agencies ... who can provide support and in some cases, even financial assistance. If you're on the radar of these agencies a good opportunity may come up for you.' Finally, Ally cites longevity as a motivator: 'I think it's important to try to build something long-term, something sustainable ... to build something meaningful, something you can take a step back from now and again and look at with pride.'

Case study: Jessica Carmody (Account Manager at PledgeMusic UK)

PledgeMusic UK is a prime example of a company that, in many ways, has sought to become more than just a digital distributor. Formed in 2009 by Benji Rogers and industry A&R veteran Malcolm Dunbar (responsible for signing Julian Cope, Lloyd Cole and the Commotions, and Liberty X), distribution is only one part of their operation. In terms of its functions, PledgeMusic UK characterizes much more; offering fans greater contact with the artist and a broader range of products and services, arguably to meet new markets of demand and consumption. The full range of its operations extends beyond simple crowdfunding to behaving as a digital record label (they have an A&R team, regional scouts actively seeking new music talent and emerging acts to present to their marketplace). Increasingly, however, PledgeMusic is developing new mechanisms including working with existing traditional record labels. In 2013 it was instrumental in assisting Sony's Search and Destroy label with the band Bring Me The Horizon, raising their album 'Sempiternal' to No. 3 in the UK and No. 1 in Australia by working with the band's most committed fans (Ingham, 2014). It can therefore be evidenced that this company is actively innovating fan/artist interaction. Essentially, we have arrived at a point where digital distribution is not just mirroring that of the traditional-physical, but it is now a counterpart to social media platforms aiming to provide new business opportunities to independent (and increasingly, major label) music artists.

In October 2014, Jessica Carmody of PledgeMusic UK was interviewed to gain insight into PledgeMusic UK as a digital distribution platform and also to ascertain whether Carmody considered herself to be either an entrepreneur or, more generally, entrepreneurial in her career. Jessica has worked at PledgeMusic as a campaign manager for nearly three years, before that she was studying at the British Academy of New Music as an artist. She also has an English Literature degree from Sussex University. She considers her most significant achievement to be 'having met, and worked with, a number of my idols and ran their campaigns at PledgeMusic successfully, which I'm very proud of'. Her inspiration? 'Artists continue to inspire me, especially when their record gets in the charts as a result of the PledgeMusic project. When artists are happy with the experience through PledgeMusic and astounded by how many people have supported them and decided to pledge, it encourages me to continue spreading the word and running prosperous campaigns.'

She had no employment/experience prior to working in music she claims. 'Absolutely none, I was quite pugnacious with my teacher in music school, so much so that he asked me if I wanted to interview for a job at PledgeMusic as he thought I would fit right in! I would say that the music industry is one of the only industries you don't need experience and it's more about being savvy and thinking quickly on your feet.'

What would she like to change within her sector? 'I guess I'd like to see us be able to work with smaller bands who don't have a fan base at all but we just believe whole-heartedly with their music, it would be good to figure out a way that PledgeMusic could support them.' The most valuable attributes for a young entrepreneur wishing to enter the music industries? 'To be intelligent, creative and strong-willed.'

When asked to give an example of her own entrepreneurial behaviour she responded, 'I set up a PledgeMusic open evening in which we invited labels, artists, managers, PR, lawyers, etc. to an evening where they could hear about what PledgeMusic does and how we could work with them. It was, and still is, a successful monthly night that enabled us to be in closer contact to labels and managers that we had never worked with before.' Is this, however, the employee behaving as an entrepreneur or simply a staff member demonstrating initiative? Curiously when asked what being a music entrepreneur means to her, she replied, 'Sadly I don't think I am really . . .'

'I'm not an entrepreneur': A British perspective?

Although Carmody quite clearly does not consider herself to be an entrepreneur, what we must consider is the notion that in the UK, the 'British perspective' may indeed be skewed. The dichotomy in perspectives on entrepreneurs – as discussed elsewhere in this book – between the USA and the UK appears once again in this interview with Carmody as it did with Ally Gray in the previous case study. Oddly, however, Carmody exhibits entrepreneurial tendencies in the networking events she has established for her company as seen in response to the question that requested her to comment on entrepreneurial activity she had undertaken. Hence, she has no difficulty with the adjective but rejects the noun. The difficulty in the UK does seem to relate specifically to the moniker. It would appear that British music project developers are happy to be entrepreneurial, to engage in enterprise, but object to being labelled an entrepreneur. Might this relate to stereotypes or media portrayal? We will examine this in greater detail in the conclusions at the end of the book.

The discomfort with identifying or labelling oneself as an entrepreneur in the UK is addressed elsewhere. Burns (2011) in the book *Entrepreneurship and Small Business: Start-up, Growth and Maturity* presents a range of character traits, antecedent influences and other theorists' definitions of what makes an entrepreneur, most of the latter derived from an economist perspective. Most (if not all) underline the core characteristic to be that of profit-making. We can indeed unpack a broad range of terminology used and consider a multitude of interpretations of, for example, what can be deemed 'economic resources' (Drucker, 2007) to argue who is and is not (based on the criteria) an entrepreneur.

We could, for example, consider eradicating completely the word 'entrepreneur' from studies of business activity in the arts, or we could add further definition or a prefix to the word 'entrepreneur' (such as 'cultural' or 'art') for the enterprising British individual to feel they can relate to the term. What we must also be mindful of is the notion that those such as Carmody may indeed be engaged in a variety of entrepreneurial activities, yet feel nonetheless uncomfortable with the exclusive label of 'entrepreneur' based on negative portrayals of such people in popular culture (Sir Alan Sugar's 'The Apprentice' springs to mind). What we might require is a new term to suit the apparent modesty (or discomfort) of the British.

Finally, as mentioned earlier in this chapter, so-called music entrepreneurs can be grown through the evolution of digital distribution platforms (e.g. Music Glue, EmuBands, BandCamp) in what such technologies offer independent music artists. Indeed, the founders or creators of said platforms can be deemed entrepreneurs. However, it could be said that as a result of such Web 2.0 technologies in this field, we have a new breed of entrepreneur: the independent, curator-creator music artist.

References

Boyle, J. (1997), *Shamans, Software and Spleens: Law and the Construction of the Information Society*, Cambridge, MA: Harvard University Press.

Burns, P. (2011), *Entrepreneurship and Small Business: Start-up, Growth and Maturity*, 3rd ed., Basingstoke: Palgrave Macmillan.

Caulfield, K. (2013), 'Beyonce Breaks U.S. iTunes Sales Record, Sells 617,000 in Three Days', *Billboard*, 16 December 2013.

Dredge, S. (2015), 'Tidal: 10 Things You Need to Know', *The Observer* (online), available at: http://www.theguardian.com/music/2015/apr/05/tidal-10-things-you-need-to-know-jay-z-madonna-music-streaming [accessed 5 May 2015].

Drucker, P.F. (2007), *Innovation and Entrepreneurship*, London: Heinemann.

Hay, R.K., T. Kash and M.J. Carpenter (1990), 'The Role of Locus of Control in Entrepreneurial Development and Success', *Journal of Business and Entrepreneurship* (online), available at: https://www.questia.com/library/journal/1P3-1396398021/the-role-of-locus-of-control-in-entrepreneurial-development [accessed 20 December 2014].

IFPI (2014), *Digital Music Report 2014* (online), available at: http://www.ifpi.org/downloads/Digital-Music-Report-2014.pdf [accessed 1 November 2014].

Ingham, T. (2014), 'Living on the Pledge' (PledgeMusic), *Music Week*, 26 September, pp. 11–13.

Litunnen, H. (2000), 'Entrepreneurship and the characteristics of the entrepreneurial personality', *International Journal of Entrepreneurial Behaviour and Research* 6 (6): 295–309.

Naughton, J. (2010), 'The Internet: Everything you need to know', *The Observer* (online, last updated 20 June 2010), available at: http://www.guardian.co.uk/technology/2010/jun/20/internet-everything-need-to-know [accessed 1 November 2014].

Pakinkis, T. (2014), 'Can streams come true?' (Record Sales analysis, Q3, 2014), *Music Week*, 10 October 2014, pp. 16–19.

Ritzer, G. and N. Jurgenson (2010), 'Production, Consumption, Prosumption: The Nature of Capitalism in the Age of the Digital "Prosumer"', *Journal of Consumer Culture* 10 (1): 13–36.

Smirke, R. (2014), 'Spotify U.K. Sees Big Jump in Revenue', *Billboard*, 8 October 2014.

Stratten, S. and A. Kramer (2012), *Unmarketing: Stop Marketing. Start Engaging.* Oxford: John Wiley & Sons.

Tidal (2015), 'Tidal is Available in These Countries' (online), available at: https://tidalsupport.zendesk.com/hc/en-us/

articles/202453191-TIDAL-is-currently-available-in-these-countries [accessed 5 May 2015].
Vaynerchuk, G. (2013), *Jab, Jab, Jab, Right Hook: How to Tell Your Story in a Noisy Social World*, New York: Harper Collins.

Websites

BPI – http://www.bpi.co.uk/ – accessed 14 November 2014
PPL – http://www.ppluk.com/ – accessed 17 December 2014
RIAA – https://www.riaa.com/news_room – accessed 22 November 2014

9

Music Publishing:

How to Understand and Engage with Copyright in the Digital World

George Howard

Introduction

As entrepreneurs assess a potential market they analyse a number of factors to determine if entering the market has a likelihood of success. Certainly, all entrepreneurs, whether formally or otherwise, conduct, for instance, a SWOT analysis. This analysis scrutinizes their idea with respect to the market from both an internal perspective (the entrepreneurs and their ideas strengths and weaknesses) and from an external perspective (opportunities and threats). While rudimentary, this SWOT analysis provides a prima facie view of the entrepreneur's idea vis-à-vis competition, competitive advantage, growth of the industry, growth of customer demands, etc. In fact, most business plans are simply detailed expansions upon this type of SWOT analysis.

Entrepreneurs in the music space are often initially compelled to act after engaging in this type of prima facie analysis, because there seems to be tremendous need for disruption. That is, a rudimentary SWOT analysis will present the music industry entrepreneurial aspirant with initial indicators that encourage entry because the music industry appears to share similar qualities with other industries that have recently been disrupted. Specifically, technological developments will appear to have merged with customer demand; essentially, Kurzweil's Law of Accelerating Returns (2001).

This prima facie observation is further buoyed by the aspirant's belief that in some ways, as I have stated for years in various forums, the music industry is a canary in the coalmine, and that as goes the music industry, so too will (eventually) go other industries. Thus, as music was the first of the entertainment sectors to offer customers the opportunity to stream virtually any musical recording in an on-demand manner, it simply foretold the path we are now seeing via movie/TV streaming sites. Or, as music was the first to facilitate the entry of aspirants into the market without the requirement of intermediaries, such as labels or distributors, now too virtually every creative industry allows aspirants to create their products and bring them to market without intermediaries.

Entrepreneurs, thus, view the music industry as one with tremendous potential for disruption, both because of their perception (not incorrect) of entrenched institutions (labels, etc.) faltering at the hands of technological innovation, and customer demands (Paschal and Rogers, 2013). This is an enticing combination for any industry, but nearly irresistible when combined with the inherent 'sexiness' of the music industry, which seems to draw entrepreneurs from other industries much in the way the Sirens lured Odysseus.

And, as with many mariners drawn to this irresistible allure, entrepreneurs entering the music space believing that they have found their bliss, too often end up amongst the rocks. For, what a prima facie SWOT analysis, or even a detailed business plan, will not adequately address is the complexities – both legal and institutional – that surround the core and immutable asset of the music business: music publishing.

This chapter explains music publishing and copyright issues that comprise this catch-all term to make transparent that most obtuse of all music industry subjects so that entrepreneurs may make better decisions about whether and how to enter this space. The chapter begins with an overview of the development of music copyright as it relates to music publishing and the dual nature of the copyright in the music business as it relates to music publishing. It then goes on to examine the relationship of the music business generally to publishing and the potential for revenue growth and the dilemma the music business entrepreneur faces. Then I will present a case study on Caroline Gorman, who works with music copyright at Rage Music in the UK and finally I will draw some conclusions relating to entrepreneurial activity in this sector.

The details provided below will serve two purposes. First, I have attempted to distil the history of, and issues surrounding, music publishing down to their most essential elements so that, once and for all, there will be clarity related to both the rules around music publishing and how they relate to the overall music business. Second, that the information provided below will allow for better decision making on the part of entrepreneurs when considering whether or not to enter this evolving space.

I have intentionally avoided specifics around current issues – for instance, interactive versus non-interactive streaming, and the related music publishing issues. I have done this not only because this information is widely available, but dominantly because after twenty-five years in the music business, I know of only one thing for certain: no one knows what the future of music will be (and anyone who says they do is lying). Therefore, I have focused on what I believe to be the constants; the elements least likely to change, and therefore most likely to influence decision making both over the near and long term.

History of music copyright

For the entrepreneur who is not familiar with the music industry perspective, this business can seem to operate by a set of byzantine, if not draconian, rules that appear arbitrary, capricious and malleable. There is also a confusing side.

Since the inception of the era of recorded music, there has been a tremendous information asymmetry. Those on the industry side – labels, publishers, and, frequently, managers and lawyers – have commanded a disproportionate degree of understanding regarding the rules governing the industry as compared to the artists and songwriters.

The artists and songwriters, of course, are not blameless in allowing themselves to be 'out educated'. The information, complex though it is, is and has been available. However, there has been an institutionalized schism between those in the know in the industry and the creatives. This divide began as the industry emerged, and carries forth to the present day. The reasons for this divide are numerous, but ultimately revolve around the rationale for any type of informational arbitrage: financial benefit via the exploitation of imperfect information.

This is exacerbated by the psychological underpinnings endemic to the artist/label relationship, to take one example. That is, artists have historically 'needed' labels as much for emotional validation as for economic/marketing assistance. As such, labels have been able to leverage their positions as 'king makers' to incent artists to subjugate rationality in favour of emotion. To fully understand how this exploitation has historically taken place, as well as to conceptualize the current exploitation, it is crucial to understand the fundamental frameworks and paradigms (both legal and cultural) of the music industry. While technology has clearly impacted the music industry, this has always been true, and, as will be made clear, the music industry has had a fascinating relationship with technology from its inception.

A *brief* history of the recording industry with a specific emphasis on music publishing is instructive, as it displays just how little has changed since the early 1900s in terms of the underlying legal and business structures, vis-à-vis artists and labels, that continue to inform today's music publishing.

Before there were discs containing recorded music, and, of course, long before there were CDs and downloads, there were piano rolls. In many respects the technological advancements that led to piano rolls established the rules that continue to govern much of the music publishing business even today. In *White-Smith Music v. Apollo*, the court found that piano rolls were not – under then-current copyright guidelines – copies of the underlying musical composition, but rather extensions of the player piano itself. This decision compelled Congress to act. The Copyright Act of 1909 was the first major revision to copyright law since the 1790 Act. Before the 1909 Act, as evidenced by the *White-Smith* decision, there was no codification around rights of reproduction and distribution. *It is crucial for the entrepreneur to understand that music publishing is that the entire firmament upon which the record industry was created, and continues to rest upon, issues forth from these rights of reproduction and distribution.* The vast majority of issues in the record industry revolve around these rights, and no technological developments will likely ever diminish their import.

In a statement that, arguably, could be made with the same resonance today, no less authority than then-President Theodore Roosevelt stated in 1905: 'our copyright laws urgently need revision. They are imperfect in definition, confused and inconsistent in expression; they omit provision for many articles which, under modern reproductive processes, are entitled to protection; they impose hardships upon the copyright proprietor which are not essential to the fair protection of the public; they are difficult for the courts to interpret and impossible for the Copyright Office to administer with satisfaction to the public.'

Responding to *White-Smith*, the 1909 Act had a specific agenda. In short, the Act sought the following: 'The main object to be desired in expanding copyright protection accorded to music has been to give the composer an adequate return for the value of his composition, and it has been a serious and difficult task to combine the protection of the composer with the protection of the public, and to so frame an act that it would accomplish the double purpose of securing to the composer an adequate return for all use made of his composition and at the same time prevent the formation of oppressive monopolies, which might be founded upon the very rights granted to the composer for the purpose of protecting his interests.'

This quote should resonate loudly with entrepreneurs. As will be discussed in depth below, it is clear that 'the very rights granted to the composer' are in fact being used and mis-used by certain bad actors, who while not strictly monopolies do, in fact, act and operate in ways in which, from the standpoint of entrepreneurs wishing to enter the market, may as well be monopolistic.

The other salient details of the Act include:

Sec. 5. That the application for registration shall specify to which of the following classes the work in which copyright is claimed belongs:

(e) Musical compositions;

Be it enacted by the Senate and House of Representatives of the United States of America in Congress assembled, that any person entitled thereto, upon complying with the provisions of this Act, shall have the exclusive right:

(a) To print, reprint, publish, copy, and vend the copyrighted work;

(c) To deliver or authorize the delivery of the copyrighted work in public for profit if it be a lecture, sermon, address, or similar production;

The above stipulations with respect to the exclusive right to 'print', 'reprint', 'publish', 'copy', 'vend', 'deliver or authorize the delivery of the copyrighted work in public' will be later more cogently defined as the exclusive rights to: reproduce, distribute, publicly display and publicly perform.

Additionally, it is of interest with respect to historical continuity to note that the 1909 Act essentially prefigured a rule with respect to what has become known as 'sampling' in today's music industry (that is, inserting a segment of a pre-existing sound recording and composition into another work; such as the use of the sound recording of The Police's 'Every Breath You Take' in the Puff Daddy work, 'I'll Be Missing You'). The Act states as follows:

> Sec. 6. That compilations or abridgements, adaptations, arrangements, dramatizations, translations, or other versions of works in the public domain, or of copyrighted works when produced with the consent of the proprietor of the copyright in such work, or works republished with new matter, shall be regarded as new works subject to copyright under the provisions of this Act; but the publication of any such new works shall not affect the force or validity of any subsisting copyright upon the matter employed or any part thereof, or be construed to imply an exclusive right to such use of the original works, or to secure or extend copyright in such original works.

As with the above exclusive rights, which were later more crisply articulated, Section 6 above, eventually became the exclusive rights to create 'derivative works'. While certainly the drafters of the Act could never have anticipated what we now know of as 'sampling', it is important to see how effective and thorough the Act was in terms of covering existing and future uses.

I present these points in such depth in order to show the landscape the entrepreneur enters. While the copyright law has evolved to attempt to continue to strike the right balance between the rights of the individuals and the progress of society, as is shown above, even in 1909 many of the issues that are relevant and applicable in 2014 were addressed.

Crucially, the Act also introduced the compulsory mechanical license.

Section 1(e) of the 1909 Act introduced a compulsory license for which:

> ... would allow any person to make 'similar use' of the musical work upon payment of a royalty of two cents for 'each such part manufactured.'

However, no one could take advantage of the license until the copyright owner had authorized the first mechanical reproduction of the work (Peters, 2001).

This section was clearly an attempt to avoid the inequity that occurred based upon the *White-Smith* decision. The chosen terminology '*mechanical* license' is a specific descriptor in reference to the *mechanical* reproduction of music via piano rolls. This terminology will soon evolve to be classified as 'phonorecords', but the concept *and* nomenclature of 'mechanical' reproduction is pervasive even in today's music business, and must be understood by entrepreneurs.

This becomes increasingly relevant to entrepreneurs due to the fact that in the 1909 Act, 'proprietors of musical compositions were granted initial mechanical recording rights, subject to a compulsory licensing provision' (Peters, 2001). In fact, 'The act, which came into force on July 1, 1909, is with some minor amendments, the basic law in force today.' The amendments to the 1909 law, however 'minor' they may have been, were not insignificant with respect to copyright law attempting to keep pace with technological advancement. One crucial development, for instance is, in hindsight, a relatively glaring omission regarding a specific grant of copyright to the sound recordings. This was not remedied until the 1971 Sound Recording Act, the purpose of which was as follows:

> To amend title 17 of the United States Code to provide for the creation of a limited copyright in sound recordings for the purpose of protecting against unauthorized duplication and piracy of sound recording, and for other purposes.

The nature of the dual copyright in the music business

The music business evolved via the move from piano rolls to other means of reproductions: specifically, acetates, vinyl, CDs and, later, downloads and streams. In so doing, the entrepreneur is able to connect the foundational laws that govern the music industry with the more current landscape.

With the 1971 Act we have clear delineation of the two fundamental copyrights relevant to the music business:

The copyright of the composition; which is denoted by the © symbol.

The copyright of the sound recording; which is denoted by the ℗ symbol.

There are numerous resources available to help you understand the bifurcated copyrights related to the music business. For obvious reasons, I'm partial to the one I wrote (http://www.tunecore.com/guides/sixrights), but other good resources include Donald Passman's *All You Need to Know About the Music Business* (2013) and Brabec and Brabec's *Music, Money, and Success: The Insider's Guide to the Music Industry* (2011).

The very short version of all of this is, if you write a song, you are to be paid each and every time it is reproduced via the statutory rules related to mechanical license. This royalty stands alone and must be paid to the songwriter (and only the songwriter), not the performer. The core underpinnings of the music business, therefore, are related to copyright law, and, specifically, to the two distinct copyrights the © of the composition and the ℗ of the sound recording that are currently, and have been historically, at the root of the entire music business. One of the fundamental premises of copyright law is that when a composition (denoted by the © symbol) is mechanically reproduced or distributed, the party who reproduces and/or distributes the music *must* pay a royalty to the holder of the copyright for the sound recording. This payment is referred to as a mechanical royalty; so called, because it relates back to when songs were first *mechanically* reproduced on piano rolls.

As this particular element of copyright law is so germane to the issue of entrepreneurship in the music industry, it is essential to have a clear understanding of the guidelines of the mechanical license. Specifically, Section 115 of the Copyright Act provides the guidelines for those wishing to avail themselves of a mechanical license. Section 115 provides that under certain specific circumstances, iterated below, the copyright holder to the composition (the ©) *must* grant a license.

Should any of the mechanical license not be adhered to by those using the compulsory mechanical license, upon notice, the licensor may terminate. In so doing, any further making or distribution, or both, of all phonorecords for which the royalty has not been paid, will be viewed as actionable as acts of infringement under section 501 [17 USC 501] and fully subject to the remedies provided by sections 502 through 506 and 509 [17 USC § §502–6 and 509] (Peters, 2001).

It is imperative to note that the licensee must provide notice *prior* to distribution. Additionally, it is crucial to note the 'notice' requirement, which acts as an affirmative authorization, and, as such, precludes, for example, so-called bootlegging. While, as detailed below with respect to methodology for acquiring licenses, there are certain mechanisms and firms (e.g. The Harry Fox Agency) in place to facilitate the licensing process, no such facilitation agency or firm exists for the facilitation of meeting the necessary requirements for importation/exportation of licenses related to digital mechanical reproduction. While admittedly somewhat complicated, this dual copyright structure is not beyond the scope of understanding for the average person engaged in the music business (whether on the artist-side or the business-side) Additionally, as noted, the information *is* available widely; it is not 'hidden' in 'obscure' statutes.

While there *may* have been an argument on behalf of those in the industry that the rules were both overly arcane and difficult to find at some point in time (though, of course this does *not* relieve anyone of their duties), these arguments are simply not viable in an era in which publications such as the one above (and numerous others) are made widely (and freely) available.

The relationship of music publishing to the music business

The easiest way to parse this rather complex maze of participants is via deconstructing a well-known music industry term: A&R. Most everyone has heard the term A&R, and most people assume it relates to the person who signs an artist to a label. While this is largely factually correct, what most people do not know is what A&R stands for, or how it has evolved over the years. A&R stands for artist and repertoire. This was, in the early days of the recording industry, a very accurate description. An A&R person's job at that time was to marry a performer (that is, one who was signed to a record label, and sang the songs on the albums that the labels released; in our example above, 'Whitney Houston') with appropriate songs in order to make recordings that the public would buy.

Prior to artists such as Little Richard, Chuck Berry, Buddy Holly, Smokey Robinson, Bob Dylan, The Beatles and The Rolling Stones, all of whom composed their own material and performed it fantastically, there was an entire industry devoted to composing songs for others to perform. In this era, very few performers actually wrote their own songs. Elvis Presley, for instance, wrote virtually none of the songs that he sung. Similarly, Frank Sinatra did not write his songs. There was an entire industry of people, therefore, who wrote songs to be performed by people like Sinatra (if they were lucky). Some of the better-know songwriters were: Leiber and Stoller, Goffin and King, Doc Pomus, and others.

In this way, there was created the bifurcated system described above. On one side were the performers: people with wonderful, expressive voices, and a specific 'look'. On the other side, at places like Tin Pan Alley (so named because cheap pianos were described as sounding like tin pans), you had a somewhat anonymous group of people who wrote songs (or 'repertoire'), the same way others make shoes: as a craft. The A&R people were responsible for finding material (or 'repertoire') for these great voices (the 'artists'), and they would often go to these songwriters to pair up a song with a singer.

Understanding this process, via the A&R phrase, should bring further clarity to the entrepreneur with respect to the importance of publishing generally, and the mechanical license specifically. In essence, the writers were paid when the artists recorded their repertoire via the mechanical royalty. Labels would sign these artists, and typically fund the recording of the artists' recordings, as well as promote and distribute these recordings. In exchange for this funding and service, the labels would typically be the sole owner of the sound recording (the ℗).

However, and this is a *crucial* distinction, the labels did not (and do not) own the songs that appeared on the recordings they released (and frequently own the copyrights to). The songs remain under the copyright of the songwriter. If the songwriter is also the performer signed to the label, then the songs the label releases are referred to as 'controlled compositions', because the artist controls the rights to the song. The labels frequently contract with the songwriter to reduce the amount of royalties paid to the songwriter signed to the label for these controlled compositions (this is referred to as a 'controlled composition clause' in contracts between labels and artists signed to the label), but, without any contractual arrangement, the label must pay the same rate as defined in Section 115 (Peters, 2001).

Of course, if the songs that the label releases were *not* written by the artists signed to the label (these types of songs are accurately referred to as non-controlled compositions, because the artist does not 'control' the rights to the song, and informally referred to as 'covers'), the label must either negotiate a lower rate with the writer (or publisher) of the songs that the artist who is signed to the label records, and are released by the label, or pay the full mechanical royalty rate.

It should be clear to entrepreneurs from this distinction that the real money to be made in the record business is more often than not via the songwriting side. That is, while an artist who is signed to a label is paid a royalty by the label typically based upon a percentage of the suggested retail list of the sale of the recorded music (the percentages vary, but historically, they range from 8 to 20 per cent of the list price) only upon recouping any advances and, increasingly, also recouping costs associated with marketing, the songwriter is paid from the first reproduction of the copyrighted composition by the label via a mechanical royalty.

The significance of music publishing as a revenue driver

Given the nature of this money flow, it is hardly surprising, therefore, that an entire industry has emerged around exploitation, registration and collection of moneys related to compositions. This industry is known as music publishing.[1] The recorded music industry will always function in a state of flux but one constant will be to publish whether digitally or physically. This is because no matter how music is consumed, whether via physical copies, digital downloads, streams or broadcast, the holder of the copyright to the composition must be accounted to.

A publisher's job, therefore, is, as above, to register, exploit and collect on behalf of a songwriter who has contracted with the publisher. The types of deals between writers and publishers vary. On one end of the extreme, a writer assigns over the copyright to their compositions to a publisher in exchange for 50 per cent of whatever the publisher collects (and, typically, a large advance from the publisher and/or an on-going payment).

On the other extreme, the writer maintains 100 per cent of the rights to their compositions, and the publisher acts solely as an administrator registering and collecting on behalf of the writer, and keeping an administrative fee for their efforts. In all cases, the songwriter is either the owner of the compositions or the beneficial owner of the compositions, with the publisher operating on their behalf. To understand this concept, consider that unless and until a songwriter assigns their work (or a portion of their work) to a publisher, the artists themselves *are* the publisher.

Again, in all cases, even with a full assignment, the writer would maintain the so-called writer's share of the publishing revenue, while the publisher would be entitled to the publisher's share. This separation of writer's share versus publisher's share was created to avoid conflicts in which a writer would be left with nothing. In fact, the performance rights organizations in the US (ASCAP, BMI, SESAC)[2] were created with the intention of making certain that writers were appropriately paid for the exploitation of their works. In fact, these PROs will *not* pay the writer's share of publishing revenue to publishers, they will only pay directly to the writer. Significantly, aside from certain gradations, administrative deals, co-publishing deals, the types of deals between writers and publishers have changed very little over the past nearly 100 years.

The expectation of these deals from a writer's perspective is that, at minimum, the publisher will register and collect. Registration is obviously a key component to copyright generally, for, as we have seen above, registration not only allows for those desiring to use a compulsory mechanical license to provide notice, but also, registration is required for a copyright holder to bring suit against an alleged infringer. Thus the publisher registers the writer's work with the copyright office and also with the writer's performance rights organization. In this manner, the writer authorizes the PRO to both issue licenses to those desiring to publicly perform his/her work (this includes everyone from the corner restaurant/venue, to radio stations (large and small) to television networks, and internet sites) and to collect on their behalf when such public performances occur. Of course, as above, the publisher, beyond honouring their fiduciary duty with respect to registration, is often economically incented to do so as well, as they receive some or all of the publisher's share of these public performances. Not surprisingly, therefore, the enlightened entrepreneur entering the music industry frequently does so in the music publishing field.

As shown above, with respect to the mechanisms in place to register, exploit, and collect on behalf of songwriters, it should be clear that what may appear to be a rather simple industry of delivering music to customers is anything but simple.

Case study: Caroline Gorman (Rage Music)

Caroline Gorman has worked at Rage Music for the past seven years, recently taking over the running of the company. They are essentially a music production and licensing company with offices in Glasgow and London, and now with support from Scottish Development International (part of Scottish Enterprise), Los Angeles. They create and commission music for films, TV, video games and adverts amongst other media and Caroline's work is mostly setting up agreements for the use of the music Rage represents. This is essentially the composition of bespoke music for specific use as Caroline has to match music to media and negotiate agreements between composers and broadcast users.

After completion of her undergraduate qualification in Commercial Music, Caroline joined Rage in 2007 to manage the musical output of Paul Leonard-Morgan, then the only composer at the company, who operated from the Glasgow office as a music composer and producer. Since then, they have grown to a team of eight composers, and two further offices to access markets worldwide. She travels internationally on a regular basis to secure the use of her composers' work. Music publishing and the associated rights and revenue streams are therefore a key part of her remit.

The global music publishing market can be gauged by examining the total revenue of the royalty collection societies around the world. These organizations are collectively represented by CISAC, which tracks income and trends in music publishing. In 2012 the performance/communication royalty revenue of this sector was 7.8bn euros (CISAC, 2014), which equates to £6.2bn or $9.7bn at 2014 exchange rates, representing a considerable marketplace approximately two-thirds the scale of the global recorded music market of 12.1bn euros (£9.6bn/$15bn; IFPI, 2014).

Revenue derived from the use of original compositions in the UK is collected by PRS for music (previously the Performing Right Society and now incorporating MCPS which originally collected for the manufacture of mechanical copies of compositions on behalf of the composer). This revenue is generated from a series of sources including but not limited to radio and television use of compositions, film and video use, live performance at larger venues and the use of music in retail. Given that PRS for music collected £641.8m for its members in 2012 (2014), this is clearly a significant potential income stream for young entrepreneurs. PRS for music then pass royalty payments on to composers and their music publishers. The ranking of music publishers in the UK has not changed significantly with the dissolution of EMI in 2012. The catalogue of the former British record label and publishing house was broken up with Sony/ATV acquiring EMI music publishing. This assisted Sony/ATV in holding and in fact increasing its lead in the UK music publishing market in 2013 to a 31 per cent share of the albums market and a 35 per cent share of singles. Universal Music Publishing held second place with 17.6 per cent (albums) and 18.2 per cent (singles) (*Music Week*, 2014).

Even taking administration costs of PRS for music into account, 90 per cent of all collected revenue is passed on to be divided amongst the composers and lyricists (and their publishers) who wrote the music which was broadcast. Beyond this, UK Music investigated music publishing as a sector in 2012 and attributed a value of £509m to the associated export trade as well as an overall gross value added (GVA) to the UK economy of £402m and around 1,000 direct employees (UK Music, 2013).

Although technically Caroline is employed by Rage Music, she sees herself as an entrepreneur in the sense that she has to identify potential markets for the company's products and then personally engage in the negotiations with TV channels, film producers and video games companies, which in turn generate income for the composers she represents (and a percentage for the company which then pays her). This then is an example of the nature of employment in the music industries that by examination of the work undertaken rather than the job description within the company defines the individual as an entrepreneur rather than an employee.

Caroline herself states: 'Traditionally, an entrepreneur would be someone who has identified a gap in the market, and built a product or company to fill that gap. But in the broader sense (and certainly in this industry) an entrepreneur can be thought of as a self-employed/freelance person – or even someone within a larger company, who works hard at identifying potential further business growth opportunities. To be "switched on" – constantly soaking up information and trends that will inform their choices, to be disciplined and focused and able to see the "bigger picture" – by which I mean able to raise their head from the day-to-day business activities, to take stock of the ever changing landscape of the industry in which they operate – and those that connect with it, to see where they fit in, where their business model fits and how it might be adapted/expanded to provide further business opportunities.' Can an employee be described as an entrepreneur? None of the key entrepreneurial characteristics identified in our opening chapter (innovation, determination, risk-taking) are exclusively the domain of a self-employed person; an employee can also exhibit these traits, *if* they are given leeway to do so.

She considers her greatest achievement to be 'that I am lucky enough to have a job that I absolutely adore (which I put down to a mixture of hard work, happy coincidence and making the most of opportunities that present themselves)'. In common with around half of our interviewees, Caroline identifies positive parental influence as a significant factor in developing her career. Citing her father as well as her original line manager at Rage, a business mentor and her university lecturer as inspiration, Caroline also recognizes that she has clearly benefited from a considerable level of support and guidance. The positive family influence has previously been noted as a factor in entrepreneurial development. Henderson and Robertson, for example, note in their research into the attitudes of young people to entrepreneurship as a career that 'in examining who or what influenced . . . career choices, the dominant factors were cited as the interviewees' own experiences together with family views' (1996). While further or higher education courses (college or university) were often deemed to be significant in their influence by *our* interviewees, teachers and career guidance officers in schools were not in the research of others, mostly as it was felt that they had 'insufficient knowledge' of entrepreneurship by the young people who were interviewed (Henderson and Robertson, 1996). Hence, while some aspects of the education system may be seen as assisting entrepreneurship, others may not.

Caroline rates her education as 'hugely valuable', specifically identifying business projects set up as part of the course as the most valuable aspect: 'It is often these extra-curricular projects and connections that eventually lead to employment.' Further, she believes that 'education should never stop. You don't have to be in a classroom to be continually learning'. In common with other interviewees, she goes on to identify her work experience as equally valid in assisting her professional progression: 'I had completed work experience while still at university for EMI records in London (in their Creative Dept within Parlophone) and also at an indie record label back home in Glasgow. Like many students I had various part-time jobs to help pay my way through university. These included the usual (shop assistant, call centre, receptionist) and the more unusual (debt collector, medical secretary) as well as the many gigs and events that I got involved in through college and university (fashion shows, music gigs, band showcases, etc.) but each and every one of these jobs has helped me gain valuable experience. Even if I didn't realize it at the time, learning how to work in a team, communicating effectively and leading a group – these skills have come through "real life" work situations.' Here the balance between education and experience becomes clearer. Each has an individual value but when combined they can add greatly to career progression.

When asked about the work that she actually undertakes, she gave several examples. First, a successful project where she was asked to identify a track that was clearly a 'band' recording rather than a mood piece produced as backing for visuals that she is often asked for. In this case, she was able to place a track by an emerging Scottish guitar act in a high-profile advertising campaign: 'It is projects like this that gives us the energy to wade through demos from band after band, as every so often you come across one that really excites you and if you get to work with them and help get their music heard (and get paid!), while making a client ecstatic, then it's all worth it.'

However, not all projects end so successfully. 'Recently, there was a certain large chocolate manufacturer for whom we composed music for their new advertising campaign, only to find, after almost a year of work, that the campaign was cancelled as they were instead going to broadcast the version created in a different country – which had music on it that was suspiciously similar to ours. A painful lesson to learn, but our business is better for having learned it – even if it was the "hard way".'

Other interviewees also pointed to bitter experiences being important lessons rather than barriers to progression. Mark

Orr, for example (see Chapter 7), discussed one example from the early days of LAB records. 'One of (the) first big physical records we put out in 2009 was by a rock band in America . . . and the distributor at the time was all over it, absolutely loved it and I think we were in about 85 per cent of shops, we were staggered by it, really happy, and on the first pressing of the CDs we started to get some feedback and started to get some emails through (there were about 2,500 CDs pressed) and it was sounding a bit weird and no one could put their finger on what it was. I started to realize that the running time for the record should have been 49 minutes and every one of our first 2,500 CDs was 52 minutes and so [the whole record] was 8 or 9 per cent slowed down from start to finish. It turns out it was a switch that had been flicked at the manufacturing plant, I don't know why it had been done, afterwards but they took full responsibility . . . it was nightmare, it was probably the most horrible phone call I had to make as the distributor had tried so hard and put everything into it and so to have to call her and say look we're going to have to recall these CDs – [that] was a hard phone call to make but there's not much you can do, you just have to do everything in your power.' These examples highlight the 'failure as education/resilience' philosophy that we will examine in the conclusions section.

Caroline's view on the key skills required by the budding music entrepreneur is that it is vital to possess a 'strong work ethic' (this is also stated by Ally Gray at EmuBands in his interview in the previous chapter), and to 'always be looking for an opportunity to take on extra responsibility'. Specialization in your area of expertise is also identified, 'Aim to make yourself the best at whatever it is you do, become "THE" person at whatever skill, service you are selling. You need to make yourself the number one person in that field, that others are confident to personally recommend, then you will always have work.'

Agreeing with other interviewees, notably Goc O'Callaghan at ArcTanGent and David Riley at Signature Brew, Caroline points to networking as an essential element: 'Make yourself well known and well connected. Always introduce yourself properly to people, ... so that (they) have an informed impression of who you are and what you do. Try to make everyone you work with, in any capacity, your personal promoter. Work, projects, jobs all come via word of mouth.' The often repeated cliché that 'who you know is more important than what you know' was referred to but modified by many of our interviewees. The significant correction being that who you know and what you know were of equal value. Caroline clearly believes this as identified by her comments in the last two paragraphs. Other interviewees reflected this opinion, not always directly but in their references to on-going education and hard work to develop a knowledge base and the focus on communication and interaction to grow a professional network.

Conclusion: The dilemma of the music business entrepreneur

Music publishing, rooted in the historic practices that developed in the early 1900s, and still in full force today, drives the industry. Entrepreneurs desiring to enter the music business today are faced with this historic, legal and institutionalized system that governs all participants.

The entrepreneur thus has several choices. First, the entrepreneur can endeavour to learn and understand the issues and complexities articulated above. Without a law degree and a lifetime in the industry, this is not a reasonable approach. A secondary approach is for the entrepreneur to seek counsel to navigate these dynamics. While on the surface this appears to be the logical approach, this gambit is not without difficulty. Those who understand these rules are either expensive (lawyers) or not talking (those leveraging their information asymmetry for their own benefit). For many entrepreneurs who are bootstrapping, it is simply not financially feasible to hire someone to help them navigate these complexities.

Thus, the entrepreneur who seeks access to the music business landscape (and music publishing specifically) must not only face the complexities as iterated above with respect to publishing, but, frequently, must do so either at an informational or economic disadvantage. Of course, there is a third alternative. That is, the entrepreneur can wilfully or naïvely ignore the rules and regulations regarding publishing. Certainly, it is hard to fathom that certain entrepreneurial ventures did *not* take the approach of 'it's better to beg forgiveness than ask approval' with respect to the rules and regulations surrounding music publishing. In short, the perceived approach is to ignore the above-articulated rules to gain a large enough users' base to become an attractive acquisition target for either a company who is so well capitalized that they can bear the legal assault (this appears to have been YouTube's approach), or a company which is a primary rights holder themselves (this appears to have been Spotify's approach). This is, of course, an incredibly risky gambit, and one that if not successful results in the almost-certain demise of the company.

These are, however, the three approaches currently available to the entrepreneur who wishes to enter the music space. Sooner rather than later, every entrepreneur who enters music is confronted with the complexities surrounding music publishing, and must choose from one of the options described above. None of the options are optimal, and thus many potential market entrants simply avoid the space completely, opting instead for markets with more transparency, less complexity, and less institutional entrenchment.

To foster additional entrepreneurial activity in the space, therefore, certain changes must be considered. First, an attempt could be made to make the laws governing music publishing (that is, copyright, generally) more straightforward. This is unlikely. While the laws are under strain, and certainly are complex, they are arguably sufficient. It is doubtful that legislation to amend current legislation will result in anything more than increased complexity. A second option is for market forces to act as clearing house agencies that address the rights issues. That is, if there is an entrepreneur who desires to create, for instance, a streaming service that sits somewhat outside the current offerings (and if it does not sit outside current offerings, why would one bother?), there must be a more straightforward licensing protocol that is facilitated by either existing clearing house agencies (Harry Fox, PROs, SoundExchange, etc.) or via new entrants. A third option is to cap the risk associated with good faith infringement by entrepreneurs. That is, the risk of litigation would be quantified, and thus made a calculable metric that entrepreneurs could consider as part of their business expense. This too, like the first suggestion above, would require legislative reform, and is thus unlikely. Thus, the second option appears to be the only viable option. Fortunately, this is a more market-driven solution, and therefore the one most likely to occur. Of course, it too will require an entrepreneurial entrant who has overcome the very issues surrounding music publishing that they are attempting to solve for others. Until this Gordian knot is solved, the sad reality is that outside entrepreneurial activity with respect to the music industry will be minimized, and entrenched institutions and thoughts will continue to proliferate. For those who take the time to learn and understand the rules around music publishing, the advantages are myriad, and thus the savvy entrepreneur will do just that.

Caroline Gorman, as one example, began by completing a music business-specific education and has since taken an entrepreneurial approach to sync and licensing negotiations within this field. Her work experience, within and outside music, has collectively contributed to her skillset and with support from family and key contacts she has forged a professional identity. She is, by her own admission, an entrepreneur, and, unusually for the UK is proud of the title. Regardless of the fact that she operates within an organization that existed before her appointment she exhibits entrepreneurial traits (risk-taking, innovation) and perhaps because she represents others is comfortable with the profit-making element of her work. This would place her in the economic definition of entrepreneurship as well as the cultural (Swedburg, 2006).

Clearly, therefore, not all UK music project developers are uncomfortable with the term entrepreneur. Caroline, however, in our experience is amongst the minority.

Notes

1 The phrase originated when songs were printed as sheet music for the public to sing round the piano. Before the advent of radio and the phonograph this was the only way to replicate a song in your home.

2 These royalty collection societies are paid by TV, radio and concert promoters amongst others for the broadcast and performance of the original compositions. They then forward the royalties to the relevant music publisher and composer(s). The US societies (ASCAP, BMI and SESAC) have international equivalents for overseas royalties collection and distribution (e.g. GEMA in Germany and PRS for music in the UK).

References

1909 Copyright Act (USA), H.R. Rep. No. 2222, 60th Cong., 2nd Sess., at 7 (1909).

Brabec, J. and T. Brabec (2011), *Music, Money, and Success: The Insider's Guide to the Music Industry*, 7th ed., London: Schirmer.

Henderson R. and M. Robertson (1996), 'Who wants to be an entrepreneur? – Young adult attitudes to entrepreneurship as a career', *Career Development International* 5 (6): 279–87.

International Federation of Phonographic Industries (2014), *The Recording Industry in Numbers 2013*, London: IFPI.

Pakinkis, T. (2013), 'Music publishing stats', *Music Week*, Q3, 9 May 2014, pp. 14–15.

Paschal, P. and J. Rogers (2013), 'Convergence, crisis and the digital music economy, in S. Diehl and M. Karmasin (eds.), *Media and Convergence Management*, Heidelberg: Springer, pp. 247–60.

Passman, D. (2013). *All You Need to Know About the Music Business*, 8th ed., New York: Simon and Schuster.
Peters, M. (2001), Statement of Marybeth Peters, the Register of Copyright, before the Subcommittee on Courts. The Internet and Intellectual Property of the House Committee on the Judiciary United States House of Representatives 108th Congress, 2nd session, March 11, 2004, Section 115, Compulsory License.
UK Music (2013), *The Economic Contribution of the Core UK Music Industry*, London: UK Music.

Websites

1909 Copyright Act (USA), http://ipmall.info/hosted_resources/lipa/copyrights/The%20House%20Report%201%20on%20the%20Copyright%20Act%20of%201909.pdf
CISAC, Global Collections Report 2014, available at: http://www.cisac.org/CisacPortal/ [accessed 9 December 2014].
Copyright infringement, http://www.copyright.gov/help/faq/faq-general.html
Howard, G. (2010), Psychographics and fan retention, Berklee College of Music, *Music Business Journal*, http://www.thembj.org/2010/07/psychographics-and-fan-retention/ [accessed 9 December 2014].
Kurzweill, R. (2001), Exponential nature of technological change, http://www.kurzweilai.net/the-law-of-accelerating-returns [accessed 9 December 2014].
PRS for music, http://www.prsformusic.com/aboutus/press/Pages/Factsandstats.aspx [accessed 14 November 2014].
Scottish Development International (Rage Music case study), http://www.scottish-enterprise.com/knowledge-hub/articles/case-study/digital-media-creative-industries/rage-music [accessed 20 May 2015].
White-Smith Music V Apollo (1908), http://scholar.google.co.uk/scholar_case?case=12949386652546347561&q=White-Smith+Music+v.+Apollo&hl=en&as_sdt=2006&as_vis=1 [accessed 9 December 2014].

10

The Brand in Music:

Entrepreneurship, Emotion and Engagement

Matt Frew and Gayle McPherson

Introduction

In the twenty-first century, music remains as one of the fundamental universals being found, created and celebrated across all cultures. The power of this cultural art form has seen music become a keystone in the global cultural industries. Music has the power to engage and emotively touch our lives, speaks to our identity and as such fuels consumer capitalism. Interestingly, while this has propelled the music artist to the forefront of success and celebrity, new transformational technologies have produced globally networked 'cultures of co-created convergence' (Frew, 2014: 102) that challenge the traditional trajectory of music, the artist and musical success. This age of acceleration sees the music industry in flux and the route of musical success, from creative individual, entrepreneur to celebrity brand, a dynamic competition between the Leviathans of industry and a global socio-media matrix of digitally empowered consumers. This chapter critically unpacks this phenomenon through an overview of such developments, an analysis of the importance of the 'brand' and brand relationship and the underpinning ideological drivers of the music industry.

The chapter opens with a discussion of the rise of the modern music artist, development of the music industry and the importance of the global circuit of festivity. Following this, the concept of brand, and how the branded music celebrity has become synonymous with the music industry, will be examined before turning to consider the birth of the connected or convergent consumer. Here the emergence of ubiquitous digital and social media technologies is highlighted and the impact of a networked fan/consumer base driven by the visibility, immediacy and engagement of this age of acceleration considered (Dijck, 2013). Framed in this way the chapter turns to practically locate music, brand and the artist through two case studies.

Firstly, Coachella Music Festival is examined as a large-scale festival that openly celebrates its celebrity status and the conspicuous consumption of its fan base. Coachella is positioned as a lifestyle brand where brand associations make it a 'Marketer's paradise' (AP, 2014). The second takes brand association and music focus by highlighting the case of Signature Brew. Here a beer producer and group of musicians work to target the market gap in quality beer at live music venues and gigs. Through the brand partnership of Signature Brew the aim is to capitalize on the music experience and extend the brand by capturing the consciousness of the consumer to make Signature Brew the brand of taste.

Finally, the chapter concludes with a critical discussion that highlights the challenges and future of the music industry and the shift from music entrepreneur to branded artist face in an accelerating age of techno-capitalism. We argue that the creative dynamism that drove the growth of music has rapidly assimilated the rationalization through the managerial practices of modernity. While this approach enabled the establishment of a global music industry of formal production and distribution, live music and festivity, the artist and their music becomes an ideologically contaminated and, increasingly, McDonaldized (Ritzer, 2012) formulaic product.

We argue that modern music and the artist have been framed within the gaze of neo-liberal ideology where music is industrialized with the artist engaged in a production-line process from creative individual to entrepreneurial artist and on to branded celebrity. Ideologically positioned as a mass market, music and the artist have become a managed commodity ripe for modern brand development. However, while such managerialism and McDonaldization drives and develops the music industry, this formulaic process is challenged by the digital democratization of music and the conception of postmodern branding. Today, the underpinning neo-liberalism of the music industry and branded artist clashes with the digital dynamic of modern cultures of convergence (Frew, 2014). The discourse and institutional arrangements of a global music machine now struggle with the pace and personalized emotive engagement demanded of a networked techno-culture (Djick, 2013). The rationalized sameness of McDonaldized music and the de-personalization, distance and detachment of managerialist branding runs counter to digitally convergent fan or prosumer (Ritzer and Jurgenson, 2010). Social commerce is the future of business (Solis, 2014) where digital and social platforms open new spaces to construct music, artist and brand in and through co-create conversations. Importantly, the power and appeal of this accelerating techno-culture is accentuated by lifestyle identities that crave the new mode of cultural capital and digital distinction that the field of music now offers (Bourdieu, 1986).

Interestingly, while the ideological apparatus of the modern music industry, the conception of branding and the branded artist is under siege, techno-culture and the convergent consumer offer a route of reinvention and re-imagination. In networked society music, whether the creative individual, entrepreneur or branded artist, are afforded an omnipresent opportunity to feed a postmodern personalization and this desire for digital distinction. Music is at a new frontier where a new fan, a convergent prosumer, overcomes physical and spatio-temporal barriers to digitally re-connect, release and share personalized emotive experience, which, ironically, lies at the core of music itself.

Music and money:
From creation to consumption

Whether walking down the street, taking a train ride or sitting in a pub, the sound of music surrounds us. Music is a universal cultural form that echoes through the ages to become global given that constantly infiltrates the everyday be it at work, rest or play (Stanley, 2013). It is the nature of music to move us, to transport us, trigger memories and provide us with markers of life, love and loss. It is this emotive, personalized and, yet, mass appeal and power of music that sees it evolve into a global industry. As Owsinski (2014) puts it, 'While people don't need music to live, they need it all the same. It's in our DNA and we're always going to consume it in one form or another.'

From the mid-twentieth century to the present day, music has undergone a revolution in production and consumption. Importantly, the trajectory of music is tied to that of developing consumer capitalism and advancing techno-culture (Katz, 2010). While traced to a concert hall and Tin Pan Alley and sheet music past (Charlton, 2011), the post war period saw a boom in popular music as technologies liberated music directly into the homes and hands of consumers. Throughout the late-1950s, 1960s and 1970s the growth of broadcast radio, TV, mass vinyl production and distribution saw a boom in music.

Artists were now afforded a host of platforms to develop and promote their music as much as create new waves of music (Burgess, 2014).

Importantly, while this period is much lauded for an explosion of creativity, it also produced the infrastructure for development of a now globalized industry (Wikstrom, 2013). The emergence of record labels, with the likes of early developers Columbia Records, Pathe, Decca Records to EMI, PolyGram, CBS to today's leviathan Sony, provided the financial, developmental, promotional and distribution networks that took music from a marginal to a mainstream cultural industry. Running alongside this we witness the trajectory of the music Svengali. From Colonel Tom Parker and Elvis, Brian Epstein and The Beatles, Berry Gordy of Motown, Phil Spector and Joe Meek, Malcolm McLaren and the Sex Pistols, Stock, Aitken and Waterman through to the present day with Simon Cowell and Syco Entertainment, the music industry was and is heavily shaped by the Svengali. However, while these organizational structures and Svengalis drove and developed the early creativity and dynamism of music, they rapidly changed the structure and produced the institutional arrangements of a maturing music industry. Reflecting the trajectory of other industries, music shifted from a broad church position of variety, openness and celebrated experimentalism to one that followed the route, rationalization and management of modernity.

Even in the early days, the likes of The Beatles' Epstein and Gordy of Motown adopted a slick managerial and marketing style to music production and promotion. Again Stock, Aitken and Waterman overly sought a managerial and production line strategy to music through their 'Hit Factory'. However, the systematic application of managerial reason, for the efficient control and calculability of music and, importantly, the artist, their music and image, is exemplified in the corporate endeavour of Cowell and Sony's Syco Entertainment. With Syco Entertainment, music production and promotion is firmly under a managerial gaze of governance.

More interestingly, with techno-culture the music performance is now a captivating media spectacle (Frew, 2013) that sees corporations with little or no affiliation to music jumping on the music bandwagon. Now the likes of H&M, Toyota and Red Bull (Buli, 2014) are keen to work associations and a 'romantic, countercultural cool that differentiates it from an increasingly crowded marketplace' (Flinn and Frew, 2013: 421). Exemplified by Burberry's sponsorship of Josh Record, the artist has become 'a product of an era in British music where image is everything' (BBC, 2014). It is this dominant matrix of powerful individuals, organizations and now parasitic corporations, all underpinned by a neo-liberal mass market ideology, that saw much of popular music shaped into a formulaic production process. Essentially, the popular music industry morphed into a production line; a McDonalidization of music (Ritzer, 2005) where media, image and style were privileged over music, talent and substance. Of course, this trajectory of musical management and manipulation was more a series of contingent circumstance than some grand conspiracy.

However, while music embraced the management of modernity the hand of technology played an ever present shaping role with successive shifts from sheet music to vinyl, CD to mini, MP3 download to now streaming and Cloud. Again, this technological transformation of music was advanced with the emergence of the video and new music channel MTV in the early 1980s. The use of The Buggles' 'Video Killed the Radio Star' to launch MTV not only heralded technological shift but, ironically, the shift from sound to vision where the visual, aestheticized and dramatized performance of music would now dominate. By 2003, the emergent digital revolution produces another seismic shift in music as Apple's iTunes corners the market to 'become the first such digital service to secure agreements with all the major record labels' (Rodgers, 2013: 82). Now, with designated music channels, a plethora of standardized TV shows from 'Pop Idol', 'X Factor', 'The Voice' to new digital download and distribution platforms from iTunes, Spotify streaming to Cloud storage, music finds itself a stylized spectacle where promotion, production and consumption are delivered along an unsurpassed global and digital assembly line. Interestingly, the impact of this industrialized process, or McMusic, produces an interesting paradoxical cycle. On the one hand, it services mass consumption and drives a global music machine; on the other, the conformity of this stylistic mass consumption breeds a creative resistance that looks to the disenchanted, alienated and anti-authoritarian generation music has always spoke to.

Undoubtedly, while the growth of the modern music industry was fuelled by the forces of developing techno-capitalism (Suarez-Villa, 2009) and emergent institutional arrangements, music has always played on the frustrations, dynamism and energy of youth culture (Laughey, 2006).

Music opened an avenue of rebellion and release whilst providing a distinctive feature of youth identity. Interestingly, the expressive demonstration of youth angst, identity and politic through music is typified in the Woodstock festival of 1969, which was mirrored in the UK with the inaugural Glastonbury festival a year later. Here festivity provided a platform where the musical message of countercultural resistance could be mediated to the masses. However, the iconic performances from the likes of Hendrix, Joplin and The Who worked with the cathartic release and exuberance of the audience to provide a magical media mix and future intimation of the power of the global spectacle (Frew, 2014). The spectacle and seduction of this mediated and co-created experiential frenzy was not lost on the corporate and brand elite. Ironically, the very flames of resistance and 'countercultural carnivalesque' (Anderton, 2008) opened a new techno-avenue into homes of consumers and spawned a spectacle that now drives a global industry of festivity and live music (Mintel, 2010).

Today, the festival circuit reflects a music industry that taps notions of extended youth, identity and a postmodern 'nostalgic retro-reinvention' (Flinn and Frew, 2013: 419). Modern festivity exemplifies the welding of money and music as festival experiences are commodified and demonstrates the 'increasing integration and corporatisation of the live music industry' (Bennett, 2004: 13). Glastonbury, heralded as the 'biggest festival in the world' (Henderson, 2009: 12), is the zenith of this process where, importantly, its mediated spectacle is central to Glastonbury the brand. In this era of techno-capitalism, mediation of these music spectaculars is essential as they feed consumer desire for off-world hyper-experiences (Frew and McGillivray, 2008). The carnivalesque emotion, experience and extensions of youth promised by festivity are the stuff that captivates the gaze of a now global consumer. Moreover, techno-capitalism is accelerating and forging new frontiers as we see 'business morphing as music streaming becomes the consumption method of choice' (Owsinski, 2014). In the virtual and visual world online, the emotive and aestheticized experience of music has an almost omnipresent power, which makes it an ideal platform in the warring cycle of brand mediation.

Artists, bands to brands: Celebrity as commodity

Like everything else, music and the music industry cannot resist the dynamic march of progress. As highlighted above, the transformational power of technology has driven a revolution in the proliferation of music, the artist and, importantly, their public profile. Moreover, 'in this techno-dependent, ocularcentric media society' (Frew and McGillivray, 2008: 182) the music artist finds themselves bonded to the constant and critical gaze of celebrity culture (Pringle, 2004). Clearly the emergence of MTV and the proliferation of the music video, now digitally and live streamed into our homes, computers, tablets and smartphones, took the image, performance and impact of the artist and their music to a new level. This visual performative drama and emotive content provides the 'allure, glamour and charisma' that makes the artist and their music and ideal 'mediated spectacle' and so the perfect package for 'celebrity brandhood' (Kerrigan et al., 2011). Of course, a central problem when talking of 'brand' or 'branding' is what it actually means.

According to Kornberger, 'Brands are a fact looking for a theory' (2010: xiii) since they are phenomena that have been narrowly explored or even ignored. Of course, the problem with modern brands and branding is to shake it of simple associations with functionality, practice and consumption (Douglas and Isherwood, 1996). Moreover, brand is not a 'trademark, mission statement, logo or slogan', rather brand is 'engineered, alive (get their identity from meanings), logic and emotion' (Mootee, 2013: 8). Brand, and the modern conception of branding, is now a mechanism of semiotic warfare, loaded with symbolic meaning and a running socio-politic of lifestyle distinction we embody in the everyday (Bourdieu, 1986; Klein, 2000). In the white noise of consumer society, brands constantly try to break through seeking to 'say and do more . . . to be personal, to speak to us, touching us at our core' (Flinn and Frew, 2013: 426). Clearly the 'personal' and emotive 'touching us' resonates well with music. Interestingly, while the modern musical entrepreneur looks to channel, manage or manipulate our emotions, this is not new as it is a running theme from the past. Berry Gordy of Motown, like many others, was famous for the 'development of artists' in a strategically managed and promoted manner, seeing the large venues such as 'Vegas' as cash cows 'where careers and cash would hold up the longest' (Stanley, 2013: 136). Today, a plethora of venues from the traditional Royal Albert Hall to the modern O2 Arena and a global circuit of festivity (Mintel, 2010) provide ideal platforms for artists to build their brand (UK Music Tourism Report, 2012).

The musical artists now shift along a trajectory moving from creative individuals to entrepreneurs whereupon success adopts a managerial and market approach that treads a well-worn path of brand development. Music artists follow that of the sporting superstars (Milligan, 2009). The music artist is constantly managed and manicured into a packaged product that is seen from Beckham to Beyoncé to Beiber. With musical success, the artist rapidly becomes 'part modern pop star part brand' (BBC, 2014). For the music industry, the quest is to uncover, if not shape, the musical enthusiast, to market a centred entrepreneur and, hopefully, a global brand. Moreover, brand association is not only about the branded artist, their management and label. Brand association is all and, while sponsoring brands seek to bask in the positive 'logo' cool music and the artist promises, they are just as keen to avoid negative brand guilt associations artists can also bring (Klein, 2001). This branded artist is often central to their fandom and fits perfectly with the 'prosumer' generation (Kotler, 1986; Ritzer and Jurgenson, 2010) that seeks co-created value and to build their distinction off their idols (Bourdieu, 1986). It is this modern fan base of co-creating prosumers, keen to build and bask in the capital and distinction they can work off the branded artist, that is central to the longevity of artist and their music.

Interestingly, while the relationship and identity of the prosumer fan and branded artist appears reciprocal, it is problematized by the power of a globally networked and convergent conversation (Paschal and Rodgers, 2013). The old and privileged position of brand, its managed and mediated spectacle over that of the prosumer is now challenged as the brand is held to account (Frew, 2014). Brand society is a postmodern inversion of organization where the brand, as much as the organization, is shaped from the outside in (Kornberger, 2010). No longer can traditional notions of brand and branding be simply related to the market share and exploitation of prosumer fan or wider consumer. Rather, postmodern brand understands the need for openness, trust and emotional connection (Gobe, 2009) as brand is sustained by the dynamic interactions between brand and consumer. In the shifting sands of postmodern branding, the modernist and managerialist approach to music, as much as the entrepreneur and branded artist, find themselves in a digital dilemma.

Music branding, social media and cultures of convergence

Throughout this chapter, the role and impact of technology has been a constant if surreptitious presence. Undoubtedly, the trajectory and development of the music industry, entrepreneurial and now branded artist is intrinsically bound to technology and the evolution of modern techno-capitalism. However, it is often difficult, if not controversial, to pinpoint innovations or moments of technological transformation that were of game changing impact. Rather, it is more a series or matrix of innovations that drives change. As highlighted earlier, the music industry and the emergence of the branded artist provided us with precedents as evidenced with the explosion of TV, video, birth of MTV, iTunes downloads, streaming to Cloud storage and sync. Nevertheless, while MTV represented a seismic change in music the evolution of the web, social media and smart technologies reflect an unprecedented paradigm shift for life, let alone music (Dijck, 2013).

Interestingly, while the development of the world wide web – or web – accelerated global connectivity (being distinct from the Internet or the infrastructural computer networks of networks upon which the web runs), it was preceded by the early forms of social media. This goes back to the like of 70s email and Bulletin Board System, 80s Internet Relay Chat, 1990s AOl instant messenger to Napster's file-sharing. However, modern social media refers to advanced Web 2.0 and 'a group of Internet-based applications . . . that allow the creation and exchange for user-generated content (Kaplan and Haenlein, 2010: 61). Now as the 'Facebook era' (Shih, 2010) hits over a billion users, the social media landscape is populated by hundreds of platforms that are open routes of digital democracy as much as dark disruption (Fuchs, 2013). Nevertheless, it is important to recognize that the impact of these transformational platforms of connectivity were accelerated with the smartphone and, in particular, the arrival of the iPhone in 2007.

With the iPhone advances in Web 2.0 and social media merged to produce an unprecedented level of mobile immediacy and interactivity. The aesthetic and deliberately tactile touchscreen technology of the iPhone saw Apple advance a new and personalized piece of technology, which exploded a now burgeoning global market. Strangely, the term 'smartphone' is now a bit of a misnomer as the phone functionality of modern smartphones is secondary to the multi-media and connectivity capabilities of these technologies. Most importantly, and crucially for the music industry, the technological matrix of Web 2.0, social media and smartphones placed the power in the pocket of the consumer. This is techno-capitalism's 'Generation C' where consumers are empowered and look to the '5 Cs of engagement: Create, Connect, Consume, Communicate and Contribute' (Solis, 2012).

No longer can managers and experiential marketeers appeal to an outmoded experience economy (Pine and Gilmore, 1999) and puppeteer the gaze of consumers. With predictions that by 'end of this year, there could be more smartphones on the planet than humans' (Mashable, 2014) and social media platforms, such as Facebook, Google+, YouTube, Twitter and Pinterest, sharing billions of posts, Tweets, images, views and videos daily, global business is indeed social (Solis, 2013). Consumers are engaged in and through a series of convergent conversations that are digitally dynamic as they constantly shift, layer and share with others. Moreover, these digitally savvy and social consumers increasingly look to capture, distil and circulate the content of their techno-lifestyles of which music plays a central role (Frew and McGillivray, 2008).

The modern screenager, as Rushkoff (2006) referred to them, is no longer confined to youth. A casual perusal of gigs, concerts or festivals and you will witness a tsunami of technologies working a four-fold digital process. There is the capture of the live artist, then the co-created experience of the audience, next and, most importantly, the capture of the self in situ and, finally, the uploading and often distilled display online. Music and the artist are now caught in a globalized 'media matrix ... where consumers are now intrinsically bound to the production, consumption and re-production of the events spectacular' (Frew, 2014: 106). Conspicuous consumption is digital and music, the artist, gig, festival or event are to be digitized and discussed in social networks that, interestingly, enable and enhance emotive engagement. Of course, in this vortex the music industry, entrepreneur or branded artist is compelled to cede control, which has not gone unnoticed.

Resistance to the techno-culture of capture has been growing within the live music and festival industry. This has seen an attempt to 'placate broadcasters' and 'high profile events including Glastonbury' who are 'upset that members of the public are posting footage of events on websites including YouTube' (*Daily Mail*, 2011); smartphone companies such as Apple are developing software that will block live music capture. Again, artists voiced concerns over such technologies. For example, Kate Bush argues she wants to 'make contact with you as an audience, not with iPhones, iPads or cameras', whilst Rodger Daltrey of The Who asserts 'I feel sorry for them. Looking at life through a screen and not being in the moment totally – if you're doing that, you're 50% there, right?' (*The Guardian*, 2014). Interestingly, these artists frame their concerns around the desire to connect, engage and be immersed with the fan or consumer. Regardless of the sincerity of the sentiment, it is ironic that this is how techno-culture's Generation C connects and engages. The question remains whether the music industry, entrepreneur and branded artist fully grasp the implication of this phenomenon and need to future proof their industry. The case studies below provide practical contexts that will facilitate future conclusions on how the embodied socio-political and digital dynamic of techno-capitalism impacts upon the creative individual, entrepreneur, branded artist and music itself.

(Credit: Christopher Polk/Getty Images)

Case study: Coachella Music Festival

Coachella Music Festival first started in 1999. It was founded by Paul Tollett, ran over one weekend and it was all about the music. Like many within the now global circuit of festivity, Coachella has moved beyond the basic package camping out to see the latest bands. Rather, Coachella reflects a shift towards an experience economy (Pine and Gilmore, 1999) where its globalized spectacle feeds the desire for the accumulation and display of experiences that generate distinction (Bourdieu, 1986).

In an age when global music festivity is highly competitive, Coachella has been able to grow into a two-week extravaganza due to its management and the marketing of its distinctive brand. Managerially, it accentuates flexibility and responds to the economic pressures of consumers, which is exemplified by a ticket payment plan that spreads cost into eight monthly payments. On the marketing front, Coachella actively promotes a more exclusive, sophisticated, even luxurious, vibe that mingles well with the sun and celebrity of California. Today, the Coachella festival-goer can enjoy the sights, sounds and experiences alongside the A-list celebrities such as Brad Pitt, Angelina Jolie, Gwyneth Paltrow and Jennifer Lawrence (Surtees, 2014). Coachella extends this celebrity cutting-edge cool into its connectivity. Over the years, Coachella has embraced the acceleration of techno-culture (Djick, 2013) by tapping into the digital and social revolution to globally mediate its experiential escapism, a spectacle that appeals to consumers and commerce alike (Frew, 2014). Clearly, the digital and social media strategy, and now with the Coachella app, has been to respond to the digital lifestyles of consumers in a 360-degree process of enjoyment. With its sunshine location and celebrity following, the aesthetic as much as promised hyper-experiences (Frew and McGillivray, 2008). This allows Coachella to tap the visual and dynamic energy of its market base. However, the Coachella brand is technologically astute and has positioned itself as a future-facing festival brand of techno-culture. Nowhere was this more exemplified than with the holographic performance of Snoop Dogg and the late Tupac Shakur in 2012. This was a globally seismic event for Coachella (McPherson, 2012) and cemented its celebrity and cutting-edge cool within the field of festivity.

Given this, it is unsurprising that Coachella has evolved into a festival that aligns itself with those with a more discerning cultural taste. Coachella is a festival that taps a 'rough comfort' (Foley, Frew and McGillivray, 2005) vibe where the gregarious energy and wild side of festivity sits comfortably with an 'all mod cons' rationalized site this is compartmentalized into the now classic VIP areas, upmarket food, array of merchandizing stalls, branded shops, chill-out areas and funfair entertainments. Moreover, this juxtaposition of mud and mod-cons demands techno-facilitation with mobile charging stations and free wifi essential to maximize onsite engagement, online offers and feed external social networks where distinction can be digitally displayed (Frew and McGillivray, 2008). Coachella is a festival that openly celebrates its celebrity-endorsed brandscape and demands of digitally networked lifestyles. However, while revelling in the decadence of consumerism, Coachella makes much of its environmental sensitivity and sustainability. Echoing the Glastonbury environmental ethic (Flinn and Frew, 2013), Coachella promotes its green credentials through the likes of its Global Inheritance 10/1 programme (ten empty plastic bottles and get one free in return), car pooling scheme and clothing recycling programme, which claimed a worldwide resell total of £7.7m for 2013 (Havas report, 2014).

Again the celebrity connection is deployed in conjunction with a social media strategy that sees Coachella and H&M maximize their environmental partnership. Clearly, Coachella has welded the fantasy of festivity and celebrity with techno-cultural frenzy to create a matrix of brand association that works for celebrities, bands, brand partners and, of course, Coachella. Such is the centrality of brand matrix engagement and endorsement that Coachella strategically adopts co-operation rather than resistance competition.

Interestingly, in an age where the gap between poverty and plenty is ever present, Coachella appears to have bridged ideological gaps. Of course, the fantasy of festivity, with its off-world escapist allure, demands a suspension of belief and reality. Only in festivity can brand conscious and digitally networked millennials, celebrity and environmental ethics sit side by side. Again, as contained, compartmentalized and controlled spaces, festivals such as Coachella reflect as cathedrals of consumption where hyper-experiences represent new vehicles ripe for commodification. Coachella, as with most festivals, sees the co-created emotive experience of prosumers as a viral platform for brand partners. With the aesthetics of celebrity, musical performance and self-digitizing of personal experience, all layered with an environmental ethic, Coachella has a sugar-coated story that sees its brand matrix invited into prosumer networks.

BREWING WITH MUSIC SINCE 2011

Case study: Signature Brew

Signature Brew was devised by three young entrepreneurs who were fed up going to music gigs, enjoying great music and bands but drinking horrible lager. They decided to work with musicians to create a branded beer that they could sell and the act would promote. Starting with just 1,000 bottles of beer and teaming up with The Rifles and Craig Finn, the beers sold in no time; they went on to work with others and expanded quickly. A turning point was working with Professor Green on a branded beer 'Remedy' and the rest, as they say, is history. By 2013, they were exporting to the USA and in 2014 started brewing their own Signature Brew; although that goes against how they became successful, they still work with artists to brew some inspiring beers. Their ability to produce great beers and their credibility with the music industry means they can now produce their own branded beers with success. We got the chance to interview David Riley about the process and his role as an entrepreneur in the music industry. What follows is some discussion of that.

As you might imagine, Riley started off with his roots and dreams in the music industry ending up producing the marketing campaign for the highly successful 'Invaders must die', the multi-platinum-selling album by The Prodigy. After this, he and his friend set up their own company, Good Lizard Media, and started doing the digital marketing for various labels and management companies who were keen to get more interaction with their fan base. It was that understanding of the fan base and what people wanted that sparked the idea to match up beers to music and get a better customer satisfaction at concerts and gigs. Thereafter, Signature Brew was born. Most recently the company completed a funding round of £165,000 using CrowdCube (crowdfunding platform) and are now building a new brewery in Leyton. David remains a shareholder and director in Signature Brew.

What is their biggest achievement? Who knows? They are still in their infancy as a company and the opportunities of creating branded beer with artists is exciting. That said, they have to move to that next level and the company has gone on to secure a deal with Morrison's supermarket that has meant they have turned their company. This is significant as they have gone from having a specialist niche market of branded music beer to creating their own Signature Brew and selling that all over the country. More importantly, though, it gave them a stronger pitch to make to artists that they were selling UK wide.

David credits good mentors in the industry, and good partners as key to their success. Going through difficult times is hard but having someone to share that burden and who has the same vision can help. It all came down to the first trial with the Rifles. They had to strike a deal with the band on profit share as all the beer was bought on credit which meant they had minimum risk. They managed to use their knowledge of digital marketing and social media to introduce pre-ordering online to a young audience that was geared for online sales. They tapped into the band's fan base and following as their first target market for the beers, and this of course meant they didn't have new marketing costs. They were then able to expand accordingly. However, as with all young businesses, especially for product-based businesses, cash flow was difficult. They quickly moved to branding ethical beers, again focusing on the young audience which is environmentally aware and seek more than just the music at a gig. Did they see themselves as entrepreneurial? Hmm, not sure they would use that word to describe themselves. They approached every bank in London with the business plan and although the figures looked good, no one would finance them. It took someone they knew in the music industry who was an accountant, who performed the dual role of investing in them and looking after their accounts and his own interests.

We asked David what the most valuable experience was for him in launching the company and he says it was being in a band, making the decisions and working hard. Interestingly, many of those we spoke to talk of this. The bright idea is great but it's the fight of not giving up, even when facing failure or problems, but to find solutions, to keep going and learn by each mistake you make. Again, we ask is this what makes an entrepreneur? David said he wouldn't describe himself as an entrepreneur as 'this brings with it negative connotations of men in suits making huge companies with millions of pounds of investment, especially in the tech world'. He stressed that he was driven by other things, not just making money. For example, he wants to run a business that has a point to it; to make bands more money, to make beer better at music venues. He says that 'if the main goal is to just make money, then it's not worth doing'. We finished off the interview by asking him about the next five years. He highlighted that the pressure on merchandise and brand associations will be key, especially if revenue from recorded music continues to drop. That, coupled with an increase in live music festivals and independent venues they see good opportunities for them to grow in that area. Lastly, he stresses that one of most important skills for the entrepreneur or young person in this business is still networking and having the confidence to speak to people about your business. So, networking, resilience and resourcefulness are the key traits you need to keep you going, and asking yourself 'what's the worst that can happen'. Once you write that down and think it's not that bad, you can stop being scared and try to put everything into what you are doing.

A little further research can reveal that Signature Brew has teamed up with TwentysomethingLondon, an online city guide to independent London and the summer party season of

Rooftop Brewing, to be part of the craft brews on offer at the party that caters to young twenty-somethings (as its name suggests) but who also want good music, good food and good beer. This seems every bit targeted to the prosumers that Ritzer and others have highlighted above. The young people are culturally astute, environmentally friendly, and have disposable cash, which makes them a marketer's and brewer's dream come true. Signature Brew is showing they are every bit a part of that young branded prosumer experience that is for sale.

Conclusion: Selling our soul in the age of social commerce?

Within this chapter we have argued that throughout the twentieth to twenty-first centuries music, as a universal cultural form, has undergone global transformation. Regardless of form, field or individual taste, be it classical to country, prog-rock to pop, trance to techno or rock to rap, music speaks to us; triggers and touches our emotional core. Of course, in the age of accelerating techno-capitalism it is unsurprising that the universality and personalization of music has morphed into mass market.

Modern music evidences a trajectory where the passions and creativity of the artist constantly meet, and often clash, with the managerial development and promotion of the free market. We now witness the trend to shaping and guiding the artist, individual or band, from creative individualism, to entrepreneur and global brand. The rise to techno-capitalism has spawned a global music machine that, underpinned by a neo-liberal ideology, sees music and the artist as a free market commodity. Music is no longer about simple songs, it is an integrated industry that is embedded in the very fabric of personal life and the cultural economies of nations states and cityscapes. The halcyon days of measuring popularity and success through the simple quantifiable competition of 'chart sales' are long gone.

Now music is an industrialized process where artists and bands are brands. In the conveyer belt of a globalized music industry, digital downloads merely touch the commercial power of music. Now DVDs, merchandising, media appearances, fashion lines, endorsements, toys and tours are part of the branded artists' entourage. When layered with the global circuit and tourist draw of festivity, as exemplified by Coachella above, the branded artist is a celebrity welded to commerce. With its mediated spectacle, brand associations, celebrity promotion and merchandising, Coachella demonstrates why major record labels covet their stable of artists and fiercely protect their intellectual property and image rights. In the hands of the record label modernist, management leaves nothing to chance as the branded artist is orchestrated, arranged and manoeuvred for maximum exposure and commercial return. However, even though such neo-liberal managerialism has been highly effective in developing and rationalizing the modern music industry, the reach and power of music and the artist has seen a shift in branding relations that points to a growing resistance.

Now brands with no affiliation or connection to music, effect artist-development strategies, moving them along the entrepreneurial and branded route. In contrast to the case of Signature Brew, where a quality product (beer) was developed to fill a gap with music festivity, other brands have targeted the emotive functionality of music. Currently, brand strategy sees the likes of Red Bull, Mountain Dew, Toyota Scion and even the Hard Rock hotel and restaurant chain, 'with no obvious and long-standing association to music', look to music as a way to add 'cool factor' to their 'brand profile' (Buli, 2014). Again, others deliberately work brand association and placement with artists as 'the brands we choose to work with are those that understand the power of popular culture and believe in our ability to set trends' (Kluger Agency).

Although the grass seeding, sponsoring and support of these brands bring and their help to break new artists, we are now witnessing a new mode of musical 'coolhunting' (Klein, 2001) where brands see music as a springboard of association. Music and the artist are a means to a rather dark end. The emotive content of music becomes a 'Trojan horse ... aesthetically pleasing, experientially dizzying and distracting but always parasitically loaded with the brand militia of consumer capitalism' (Frew, 2014: 114). Interestingly, the use of music and the entrepreneurial artist in this way touches on postmodern branding (Gobe, 2009) as non-music brands subtly link with consumers to strategically build brand from the back. However, regardless of the functionality of such dark branding, the neo-liberal managerialism of the music industry and its production of the branded artist challenged by the rise of digital and social media.

The sophistication and acceleration techno-capitalism is reflected in the growth of digital and social media. Armed with smart technologies where social media platforms enable mobile, immediate and convergent conversations the power of managerial manipulation is not so much ineffective but held to account. Through these technologies the creative individual, entrepreneur or branded artist is brought under a digital and global gaze and is subject to the critique of online networks or cultures of convergence (Frew, 2014). Interestingly, the accessibility and immediacy of these technologies have enabled the more unconventional or anti-authoritarian artists to resist or circumnavigate the institutional mechanisms of the traditional music industry. The very symbiotic technologies that brought the rise and development of the music industry, Svengalis and dominant record labels is now in the hands of the masses. In networked society, technologies of convergence (Dijck, 2013) sees the digital democratization and disruption of music.

Of course, while routes of resistance, the likes of Facebook, Google+, Twitter, YouTube or Pinterest also offer alternatives through which the music industry can further capitalize, clone and commodify their brand artists (Olenski, 2014). Nevertheless, the modern music industry cannot hide from the impact of a sophisticated prosumer market, increasingly armed with digitally disruptive technologies (Flinn and Frew,

2013). No longer can the music industry or branded artist comfortably orchestrate scripted media-mixed performativity for commercial gain. With digital and social media, fandom and wider consumer culture is engaged in an open and, importantly, convergent debate about the brand bodies of artists, their music and motives.

Undoubtedly, modern music finds itself swamped by a technological tsunami where consumers are convergent (Solis, 2013) and desire experiential distinction that is, increasingly, digital. In this globally visual and verbal techno-culture, be they an anti-authoritarian creative romantic, entrepreneur or branded artist, modern music and the artist need to engage and constantly interact in a personal and emotive manner. The neo-liberal managerialist approaches that produce a manicured, branded performativity and formulaic McMusic are creaking under networks of convergent consumers that now seek personal connection, understanding respect and trust through emotive engagement. The aestheticization of music may well persist in a postmodern era dominated by visual hyper-experiences (Frew and McGillivray, 2008). However, the time of 'music where image became everything' is unsustainable. In this age of digital disruption, where 'sync [synchronization] rights' on the plethora of digital and social media platforms represent billion dollar revenue streams, the prosumer fan or convergent consumer has entered the 'battleground between artifice and authenticity' (BBC, 2014). Superficial stylized McMusic must be replaced by personalized, emotive meaning if the digital seams, or sync rights, of gold are to be mined.

Music production and consumption now follows postmodern branding built from the outside in through a digital dynamic. The digital strategy of the likes of the artist Bernhoft, where fans get 'depth and access' to 'immersive and 360 ... emotive and engaging experiences' of the artist, illustrate entrepreneurial engagement of postmodern brand building (Bernhoft, 2014). Today, whether creative individual, entrepreneur, branded artist or emergent industry, the route to musical success is no longer the romanticized dream of youth, blind faith of endeavour or processed, packaged and plastic celebrity of the industrialized music machine. There is no Lego-like click-n-snap to success. No longer is success under the direction or the prerogative of music producers, Svengalis or the artist. Now the design, colour, shape, size and click-n-snap of success is a co-created and convergent conversation; a brand built with and through digitally empowered prosumers. Interesting, that in an age of accelerating of disconnection we find ourselves, ironically, reconnected with the emotion and personalized passion of music through a convergent and cold power found in our pockets.

References

Anderton C. (2008), 'Commercializing the Carnivalesque: The V Festival and image/risk management', *Event Management* 12: 39–51.

AP (2014), http://losangeles.cbslocal.com/2014/04/19/coachellas-young-audience-a-marketers-paradise/

BBC (2014). 'Oh, You Pretty Things: The Story of Music and Fashion,' documentary, 2 October 2014.

Bennett, A. (2000), *Popular Music and Youth Culture: Music, Identity and Place*, London: Palgrave.

Bennett, A. (ed.) (2004), *Remembering Woodstock*, Aldershot: Ashgate.

Bernhoft, J. (2014), 'Islander', available at: http://bernhoft.org [accessed 15 October 2014].

Bourdieu, P. (1986), 'The forms of capital,' in J.G. Richardson (ed.), *Handbook of Theory and Research for the Sociology of Education*, New York, NY: Greenwood Press, pp. 241–58.

Buli, L. (2014), 'No Strings Attached: Why big brands are getting into the music business', *Forbes*, http://www.forbes.com/sites/livbuli/2013/09/05/no-strings-attached-why-big-brands-are-getting-in-to-the-music-business/ [accessed 20 April 2014].

Burgess, R. J. (2014), *The History of Music Production*, New York: Oxford University Press.

Charlton, K (2011), *Rock Music Style: A History*, New York: McGraw Hill.

Daily Mail (2011), 'Now Apple wants to block iPhone users from filming live events with their smartphone' (online), http://www. dailymail.co.uk/sciencetech/article-2004233/Apple-files-patent-block-iPhone-users-filming-live-events-smartphone.html [accessed 25 August 2012].

Dijck, J.V. (2013), *The Culture of Connectivity: A critical history of social media*, Oxford: Oxford University Press.

Douglas, M. and B. Isherwood (1996 [1979]), *The World of Goods: Towards an anthropology of consumption*, London: Routledge.

Flinn, J. and M. Frew (2013), 'Glastonbury: managing the mystification of festivity', *Leisure Studies* 33 (4): 418–33.

Foley, M., M. Frew and D. McGillivray (2005), 'Rough Comfort: Adventure consumption on the "Edge"', in B. Humberstone, H. Brown and K. Richards (eds.), *Whose Journeys: The Outdoors and Adventure as Social and Cultural Phenomena*, Penrith: The Institute for Outdoor Learning, pp. 149–60.

Frew, M. (2014), 'Events and Media Spectacle', in R. Finkel, M. McGillivray, G. McPherson and P. Robinson (eds), *Research Themes for Events*, London: CABI, pp. 101–17.

Frew, M. and D. McGillivray (2008), 'Exploring Hyper- experiences: Performing the Fan at Germany 2006', *Journal of Sport and Tourism* 13 (4): 181–98.

Fuchs, C. (2013), *Social Media: A Critical Introduction*, London: Sage.

Fuse's Teen Advertising Study (2009), in partnership with the University of Massachusetts Amherst.

Gobe, M. (2009), *Emotional Branding: The new paradigm for connecting brands to people*, New York: Allworth Press.

The Guardian (2014), 'Kate Bush asks fans not to use phones or tablets at London comeback gigs', http://www.theguardian.com/music/2014/aug/19/kate-bush-asks-fans-no-phones-tablets-london-gigs [accessed 19 August 2014].

Havas Worldwide (2014), Prosumer Report: The New Consumer and Sharing Economy, 18, May 2014.

Henderson, D. (2009), 'It's Party Time', in P. Rees (ed.), *Q: The Official Glastonbury Programme*, St Ives: Bauer Media.

Kaplan, A.M. and M. Haenlein, (2010), 'Users of the World, Unite! The challenges and opportunities of Social Meida', *Business Horizons* 53: 59–68.

Katz, M. (2010), *Capturing Sound: How Technology Has Changed Music*, London: California University Press.

Kerrigan, F., D. Brownlie, P. Hewer and C. Daza-LeTouze (2011), '"Spinning" Warhol: Celebrity brand theoretics and the logic of the celebrity brand', *Journal of Marketing Management* 27 (13–14): 1504–24.

Klein, N. (2001), *No Logo*, London: Flamingo.

Kornberger, M. (2010), *How Brands Transform Management and Lifestyle*, Cambridge: Cambridge University Press.

Laughey, D. (2006), *Music and Youth Culture*, Edinburgh: Edinburgh University Press.

Mashable (2014), 'There will be more Smartphones than humans on the planet by year end', http://mashable.com/2012/02/14/more-smartphones-than-humans/ [accessed 12 May 2014].

McPherson, A. (2012), 'Tupac's hologram reflects another milestone in his mythology', in *The Guardian*, http://www.theguardian.com/commentisfree/2012/apr/17/tupac-hologram-coachella-festival [accessed 7 July 2014].

Milligan, A. (2009), 'Building a sports brand', *Journal of Sponsorship* 2 (3): 231–40.

Mintel (2010), *Music Concerts and Festivals*, London: Mintel International Group.

Mootee, I. (2013), *60-Minute Brand Strategist: The Essential Brand Book for Marketing Professionals*, Hoboken, New York: John Wiley and Sons, Inc.

Owsinski, B. (2014) 'The numbers are in: Should the music industry be worried?', *Forbes*, http://www.forbes.com/sites/bobbyowsinski/2014/01/07/the-numbers-are-in-should-the-music-industry-be-worried/

Paschal, P. and J. Rogers (2013), 'Convergence, Crisis and the Digital Music Economy', in *Media and Convergence Management*, Berlin and Heidelberg: Springer, pp. 247–60.

Pine, J. and J. Gilmore (1999), *The Experience Economy: Work is Theatre and Every Business is a Stage*, New York, NY: Harvard Business Press.

Pringle, H. (2004), *Celebrity Sells*, Chichester: John Wiley & Sons.

Qualman, E. (2010), *Socialnomics: How Social Media Transforms the Way We Live and Do Business*, New York, NY: Wiley.

Ritzer, G. (1993), *The MacDonaldization of Society*, London: Sage.

Ritzer, G. (2012), *The McDonaldization of Society: 20th Anniversary Edition*, London: Sage.

Ritzer G. and N. Jurgenson (2010), 'Production, Consumption, Prosumption: The nature of capitalism in the age of the digital "prosumer"', *Journal of Consumer Culture* 10 (1): 13–36.

Rodgers, J. (2013), *The Death and Life of the Music Industry in the Digital Age*, London: Bloomsbury Publishing.

Rushkoff, D. (2006), *Screenagers: Lessons in Chaos from Digital Kids*, New York: Hampton Press.

UK Music Tourism Report (2012), VisitBritain.

Shih, C. (2010), *The Facebook Era: Tapping online social networks to market, sell and innovate*, Boston, MA: Pearson Education.

Solis, B. (2012), 'Meet Generation C: The Connected Customer', available at: http://pandodaily.com/2012/03/06/meet-generation-c-the-connected-customer/ [accessed 7 March 2012].

Solis, B. (2013), *What's the Future of Business: Changing the Way Businesses Create Experiences*, New Jersey: John Wiley & Sons.

Stanley, B. (2013), *Yeah! Yeah! Yeah!: The Story of Pop Music from Bill Haley to Beyoncé*, London: W.W. Norton & Company Ltd.

Suarez-Villa, L. (2009), *Technocapitalism: A Critical Perspective on Technological Innovation and Corporatism*, Philadelphia: Temple University Press.

Surtees, J. (2014), 'Coachella music festival and Palm Springs: the sound of California', http://www.theguardian.com/travel/2014/apr/04/coachella-festival-palm-springs-california [accessed 29 April 2014].

Wikstrom, P. (2013), *The Music Industry*, Cambridge: Polity Press.

Website

http://www.fusemarketing.com/

11

Additional Opportunities

Allan Dumbreck

In this chapter we will examine businesses in the music industries other than those core areas already addressed: the peripheral goods, services and events which do not fall naturally into pre-defined categories and yet are a cornerstone to the functioning of music as a complete set of interacting industries.

This chapter investigates the nature of these areas and examines the motivations and strategies of some of the individuals developing businesses within them. Part one will address the scope of these businesses. This is followed by an examination of the role of the entrepreneur within them and an attempt, at least collectively, to define them in order to draw a distinction between these music-focused businesses and the more peripheral, generic enterprises. Part two will analyse case studies of businesses which operate within this area. Given the scale and diversity and the inherent difficulty in categorizing these enterprises we will examine three case studies, each representing a different inroad to music. In this way we hope to offer a better understanding of the entrepreneurs involved and the development of their initiatives. Finally, conclusions to advise the entrepreneur will be drawn from what has been found.

Mapping additional music activity

As we have seen from the previous chapters, a clearer view of the business of music can be obtained when considering the component industries as a series of distinct sectors (for example, artist management, music publishing, live events). Defining these component sectors is a matter of considerable conjecture as Williamson and Cloonan identified (2007). Representative organizations within music itself and many media sources continue to refer to a seemingly unified music industry (singular). As identified in the chapter on artist management, early academic texts on the subject (Negus, 1992, 1998; Shuker, 1994; Longhurst, 1996) tended to focus on the recorded music industry to the exclusion of others perhaps because this sector is the most visible, a view which the recording industry apparently did little to rectify, possibly because this definition placed it centre-stage. Later texts attempting to map and investigate the breadth of the music industries identified several clear sectors of activity (Hesmondhalgh in 2002 identifies recorded music, publishing and live events). Texts written by those actively working in music have often drawn a broader panorama (Passman and Harrison, both music lawyers, each identify more than five sectors), however there does not appear to be any particular consensus on this matter, regardless of whether a business, journalistic or academic perspective is being considered.

This is perhaps not so surprising. Given that we are attempting to study a series of related industries that are in near-constant evolution, the tasks of examination and definition may be close to impossible. One is effectively trying to dissect a living, moving animal; the subject will not remain static long enough to allow definition. In this text we have already broken down music into seven key functions but these do not take every possible element into account. Hence, the authors believe, that to address the rich diversity of emerging enterprises which surround and interconnect the core business activities, a final chapter is required to gather and examine that which is not included elsewhere but which remains essentially music business. But how do we define these remaining enterprises?

Towards a definition of additional music activities

As we have seen, the larger, more easily grouped and identifiable theatres that comprise the music industries might at first appear to collectively constitute the complete picture. These sectors, which may be segregated in different ways, address the key functions of the industries: how to record music (music production), how to deliver music to audiences (digital distribution, live events), how to remunerate writers and performers (music publishing, royalties). There are, however, a large number of support and interconnecting businesses that work alongside the key theatres that are essential in allowing them to operate which do not necessarily fall automatically into any of the previously defined groupings. Disparate and less easily grouped, they nonetheless constitute a significant part of the broader picture and provide gainful employment for thousands of individuals and entrepreneurs. It would be impossible to stage live music events, for example, without rehearsal rooms, equipment hire and security services. Equally, the sale of recorded music is dependent upon photographic, video and artistic services as well as the manufacturing of physical products such as CDs (still a significant part of the marketplace). Additionally, many goods and services stand by themselves, distinct from the key theatres and yet remain a necessary interconnecting cog.

Given that the focus of these areas can be viewed as perhaps unmapped territory, outwith the more recognizable facets of music, it could also be argued that they are even more fertile ground for the pioneering spirit of the young entrepreneur. Here, the emerging project developer must already have some awareness of the more visible commercial music activities and then identify an opportunity which has not yet been made manifest within them or lies in the ground between them. In essence, they are often creating an entirely new product or service, potentially a new sector of operation, one perhaps which has not previously existed in order to fulfil a demand that was not previously identified. This might be viewed as at least one (the introduction of a new product) of the five types of innovation defined by the entrepreneurial theorist Schumpeter (as represented in Casson, 2003) and would appear to at least partially support his theory of the entrepreneur as the prime mover in economic development.

What begins as a perceived market gap can become a sector in its own right. Education, for example, falls outwith the already defined sectors (it is one of the sectors excluded from the UK Music survey of 2013) and so may be considered here. My own experience, as a practitioner, and that of many other music professionals who became educators, was that we found traditional music education delivered mostly instrumental and compositional abilities. Being aware that the contemporary musician increasingly required additional skills (in business and production, for example) led to the creation of a series of music programmes which provided these necessary competencies. The on-going development of contemporary industry-orientated courses of this nature over the last thirty years, increasing recognition by employers and subsequent demand for places has grown this sub-sector to a field encompassing several hundred modern music programmes across the UK alone as tracked by the *Music Education Directory* (UK Music, 2013).

Taking the broader perspective, some of these opportunities may not currently be defined as being within music at all. This concern for the correct scaling of the contribution of the music industries to the UK economy has already been identified by UK Music whose recent report indicates that due to the imprecise international SIC (Standard Industrial Classification) coding of businesses used by the Office of National Statistics (ONS), the scale of these industries may be being under-estimated (UK

Music, 2013). Recognition of the genuine value added by any group of industries to the economic strength of a nation clearly depends inherently on those industries being correctly defined and gauged. This is currently a subject of some debate within the UK music industries. While it could be argued that many of these activities fall naturally outside the music industries altogether and are in fact part of other, separate industries, the overlap does exist and those who work there often define themselves as working within music. In the UK, for example, DCMS (Department of Culture, Media and Sport) has identified several creative industries which clearly overlap with music including TV and radio, film and video, interactive software and performing arts (DCMS, 2001). There will be entrepreneurs who work in these industries who are primarily working on music focused projects, yet they are categorized as operating within a different industry and as such their contribution to UK productivity is counted elsewhere. It can therefore be argued that within this mechanism as it currently stands the contribution made by music to the UK could be significantly undervalued.

The role of the entrepreneur within these areas

The entrepreneur, looking outside of the more identifiable sectors of music, may actually see more clearly the gaps in existing provision and the attendant opportunities. At ground level, these opportunities may, for example, be located in the gaps within the existing business models of supporting or peripheral services, possibly occurring simply by being overlooked at a time when the potential marketplace was perhaps thought to be significantly smaller.

Publications for musicians (for example, *Total Guitar*, *Drum! Magazine*, *Keyboard Player*) have historically catered for predominantly male consumers. This is evident when regarding their covers and reading their articles that almost always feature male performers. This may have occurred as a result of the common perception that most (rock and pop) instrumental players were male. A substantial and arguably increasing percentage of instrumental players are now female; the Musicians Union currently identifies 30 per cent of their membership as female, up from 28 per cent in 2012, a figure which has been increasing incrementally for some time (Ames, 2014; Nicholls, 2012). This demographic could potentially feel that this sector of the media ignores them. Hence, a magazine or website which reports on and targets female performers could be seen to have an automatic marketplace (see interview with Mindy Abovitz later in this chapter). Obvious as it seems in hindsight, this opportunity was under-exploited for several decades. This example highlights what Edward De Bono calls 'sur-petition' (De Bono, 1995). Here, contrary to competition, the entrepreneur develops a product or service that creates a 'new value monopoly' by offering something to a potential client base which other businesses do not or cannot offer.

In the second part of this chapter we will examine three case studies which fall into the areas of print media, health and safety products and a competitive awards event, each of which could be categorized elsewhere, but in each case the entrepreneurs concerned clearly consider themselves to be part of the music industries. This then perhaps leads us to a collective definition of these additional businesses.

In the instance where the proprietor of a business which falls outside the defined categories can demonstrate that the largest part of her/his income is derived from music-orientated interaction and that she/he defines themselves (and their work) as being music-based, the business could potentially be classified as being part of the music industries. Without being able to interact with other sectors of music, the business would cease to exist. Music is therefore inherent to the identity, strategy and existence of the business. The business is dependent on the music industries. The word music is very possibly in the title of the company. It is these entrepreneurs, these undertakings, that fall into the category that this chapter seeks to address.

On the other hand, there are clearly businesses which interact with music but which do *not* derive their primary source of income from music. The security company that is present at music festivals may also be seen at football matches and other sports events, and will perhaps operate through the week outside shopping centres or industrial estates, for example. Music may account for perhaps 10 per cent to 20 per cent of the annual income of this enterprise but you could not say that it was a music-based business.

Therefore, we can arguably state for the purposes of this chapter that an additional music activity is one which operates outwith the more clearly identifiable sectors of music but which makes the largest part (more than 50 per cent) of its income from music and which defines itself (in its promotion or title or in the entrepreneur's definition) as being music-based. Each of the following case studies can thus be categorized in this way as being a music business.

TOM TOM MAGAZINE / A MAGAZINE ABOUT FEMALE DRUMMERS

Case study: Mindy Abovitz
(*Tom Tom Magazine*)

Born in Ohio, Mindy Abovitz began drumming in her early twenties. Branching out into drum programming, live sound and post-production work she sessioned on albums by New York based groups and drummed in a series of videos. After completing an undergraduate programme in performance and a Masters in media she worked for a time in her father's property business (real estate) before founding *Tom Tom Magazine*, a printed journal for female drummers. Currently seventy-six pages long, published quarterly and based in North America but with an expanding global readership, back issues of the magazine appear free on the web as soon as the new edition is printed. The online site and associated social media platforms offer women a vibrant information base and communication network. Mindy is also engaged in staging community events that host and promote female drummers.

As a woman working in music, she recognized that the available media was largely marketing to a male audience and she spotted an opportunity: 'I recognized a segment of the drumming market that went completely underserved and that was the female drummer market'. *Tom Tom Magazine* was therefore founded in 2009. Not exclusively targeted at women, she cites her greatest achievement as 'publishing the magazine every time it comes out' alongside 'daily emails and fan mail . . . when a girl or a guy writes to us and say that they just love what we're doing, it feels like everything'. Having been invited to host performances by female drummers in public spaces such as art galleries and museums has also been a significant achievement. She is clearly fuelled by the continuing development of the project.

When asked about who inspires her she identifies predominantly female role models, the writer Gloria Steinem for example, adding, 'I reference her writing when I'm referring to marketing or media, often'. Further, she points to 'any brazen women who have lead the way, Karla Schickele who started rock camp for girls in New York city, L7, Bikini Kill, the Riot Girl Movement. All of those women were part of the subconscious threat that made up the platform for me to stand on and have given me the possibility to do what I do.'

Mindy herself agrees that the gender issue in music is a focus for her. In response to the question 'what does being an entrepreneur mean to you?' she replied, 'It means being a radical, political feminist who fights for equality for all people in music media'. This perceived lack of balance in media (mis)representation is recognized by many researchers including Marion Leonard, who, specifically in relation to music performers observes, 'all too often journalistic articles and populist books focusing on "women in rock" serve to differentiate female musicians from "regular" male rock performers and thus . . . ghettoise their work' (Leonard, 2007). Mindy takes this a step further. Her perception is that the difficulties facing women attempting to enter music haven't been resolved, in some respects she feels that they have become worse: 'There are so many barriers in this industry and that is partly the reason I do *Tom Tom* . . . I never . . . would have envisioned . . . the music industry regressing in terms of feminism the way it did.' This resonates with existing research, 'problems faced by women in challenging the systems of patriarchy inherent in the music industry . . . [which] . . . continue to marginalise women' as identified by Sheila Whitely summarizing Sara Cohen (Whiteley, 1997).

This issue is echoed in other case study interviews. Goc O'Gallaghan, for example, discussing being a female professional working in the predominantly male environment of live events: 'With production staff in particular there's an assumption that you're male. I've experienced all sorts [of responses] . . . I walked into a production office and introduced myself to the stage manager who said "Goc (pronounced "Jock") O'Callaghan? And you're a girl . . . AND THAT'S COOL!" (swiftly correcting himself). There's a worry that you can't deliver . . . I climb the rigs/scaffolding and get on with it . . . it's not a problem.'

Goc herself brings female trainees into her business on placement and encourages them to take control: 'We work with volunteers and students who are female . . . we had a female stage manager who had to tell an (established) American band to cut their set to avoid over-running (noise/time restrictions) . . . no problem. It depends more on the level of empowerment . . . we had an 11pm curfew, there were significant consequences.'

Figures for female participation in different sectors of music indicate that there is still an imbalance. Statistics come from a series of sources. Thirty-four per cent of those working across all music sectors are identified as female (Creative Choices, 2009, quoted in Nicholls, 2012). In the MU's own listings, women represented 37 per cent of teachers but just 19 per cent of session players (Nicholls, 2012). However, in terms of membership of the Performing Right Society, an organization that administers songwriter royalties and therefore effectively tracks songwriters, a ratio of 13 per cent female to 87 per cent male shows a greater discrepancy, a figure that remains pretty constant among both new and existing members. Sarah Rodgers, Chairman of the British Academy of Songwriters, Composers and Authors (BASCA), says that her society's membership is 20 per cent female to 80 per cent male. Meanwhile, the Music Producers' Guild (MPG) is even less balanced, with women making up less than four per cent of its members (*M magazine*, 2013).

Mindy recognizes that beyond engaging in performance, business development can also be more difficult for certain groups: 'I feel like it is very hard for women and people of colour to be entrepreneurs ... woman are not taught to be confident.' This is part of what drives her to develop the magazine: 'I realized if I wanted to see that change I would have to be part of that change.' Ultimately, however, Mindy is optimistic for the future. In the next five years she expects to see 'a lot more women and girls drumming and a lot more female drummers being represented in the drumming media and the music media'.

Returning to influences and inspiration, Mindy greatly valued her time working with her father: 'I would have to say that one of the most valuable job experiences that has informed me ... was working with my dad's real estate [property] company, I learned a lot about management, people, commission based programmes, incentivised marketing and basically entrepreneurship.' The parental influence, as identified by Kariv (2013) and already referenced by Helen Reddington earlier in this book, whether simply on-going encouragement or taking an active role in training or education is a recurrent theme in our research as we will see in the next case study. Mindy also identified her brother as an entrepreneur, again reinforcing the value of family involvement in business in terms of experience and support.

Finally, Mindy disagreed with the statement that everyone who works in music is in some way an entrepreneur: 'I don't agree. Being an entrepreneur means starting your own business and running it and I do know that some musicians are their own business and some bands are their own business, but often they will hire a manager, a PR team and these people would take on some of the roles that they would otherwise have to as an entrepreneur.' While not alone in this viewpoint not all of our interviewees were found to agree with her.

Case study: Steve Broadfoot (LugPlugs)

Over two decades, Steve Broadfoot worked in a series of related music sectors including stage management, tour management, band transportation and artist management, working with acts such as Biffy Clyro, Link Wray and The View, as well as major UK festivals such as Glastonbury and T in the Park. Leaving higher education without completing a degree in Quantity Surveying, he returned to university as a mature student to graduate with a BA in Commercial Music. Extensive experience in festivals and live performance demonstrated the need for hearing protection for all those exposed to music at high volume over longer periods of time (including the audience). Sensing that serious damage to the ears could be sustained and that events promoters could be held responsible, Steve researched the available hearing protection only to discover that it was mostly sound-preventing (effectively blocking the sound) rather than level-reducing (allowing the listener to hear the sound at a comfortable volume). Further, he also found that the marketed products were small, unattached objects that were easily dropped, damaged and/or lost.

Developing and marketing LugPlugs, he modified existing protective devices to allow lower volumes of sound to enter the ear while simultaneously attaching them to a wristband or neck-lanyard which prevented them from being separated or misplaced. The resulting product was both functionally effective and fashionable, thus appealing to the younger target market that attend, and perform at, live events. The primary difficulty, then, would be persuading the live events industry that they should invest in a health and safety product that by its very existence drew attention to a significant problem in their sector that many were aware of but had not yet been properly addressed.

Steve first became aware of the possibility of marketing a hearing protection product when he developed a device to protect his own hearing on the road as a tour manager: 'it became apparent that hearing damage is becoming more and more of an issue, yet few wear hearing protection, as it's inconvenient, and tends to get lost. Having created my own solution on the road, I thought I might be able to apply it as a business, I sought advice, did the research, and created LugPlugs™, cool, convenient, hearing protection that you're less liable to lose.'

His greatest achievement? 'Before creating LugPlugs it was being the sole person in charge of taking Biffy Clyro and then The View on whirlwind one week trips to New York, San Francisco and Los Angeles. However, now it is LugPlugs. It's my own creation, I'm on a percentage and there are worldwide markets/territories. The fact that there appears to be a need/

demand from those in the industry is my own personal significant achievement, and I hope a beneficial contribution towards an industry I love.' Clearly there exists an altruistic, 'greater good' motivation here but equally the potential income stream is also a driver.

On the subject of motivation and more pointedly inspiration, Steve, in common with other entrepreneurs named his parents: 'I've always followed my heart (encouraged by my mother), and ever since I can remember I've always been interested in music, it's a physical, emotional, thing. This was primarily down to my parents being into music as listeners.' This, however, didn't prevent him from diverting from their advice later in life, 'My dad always fell out with me because I'd ask his advice, and he'd get annoyed when I didn't follow it . . . I'll ask ten people their advice then make up my own mind based on all that advice, taking bits from each perhaps. If you follow someone else's advice, and it fails, you'll blame them. If you make your own decision, and you fail, you only blame yourself.'

This parental influence is identified by several writers on the entrepreneur including Casson in his conclusions to his work on the subject, 'the nature and extent of . . . family . . . connections influence the opportunities that are available to the entrepreneur' (Casson, 2003). This theme was also present in other case studies. 'My biggest inspiration has to be my mum . . . she has a belief in me that encourages me to continue my journey . . . although my biggest critic she is my biggest supporter in following my dreams. There was never an activity I wanted to do when I was growing up she wouldn't let me try' (Nyah, 2014). Equally, 'my father who has been (and continues to be) my number one cheerleader. His pride in my achievements, and the unreserved way in which it is freely expressed, spurs me on to greater things' (Gorman, 2013).

Regarding the most valuable attributes for a young entrepreneur, Steve stated: 'Be open to change, you can always rely on it, things will always change. The only thing you can rely on is unreliability, so get comfortable with it, and move with it.' This parallels Drucker's assertion that entrepreneurs see change as the norm (Drucker, 2007). Steve continues, 'How can you make things better? Where is the market going to go? Where are you going to take it?' pointing to the necessity for developers to make the running rather than wait for others to dictate direction. Again this echoes Casson, 'the essence of entrepreneurship is being different' and 'the entrepreneur believes he is right while everyone else is wrong' (Casson, 2013). In this capacity the entrepreneur has to have the courage to lead the change.

Asked about the value of education, Steve could see both sides. Eventually completing a degree himself had modified his perspective. His first reaction was 'having a strong education is not always needed. Look for opportunities, places that you can "walk into" (bars, venues, companies), and work your way up.' However, he could also see that 'the benefit of a music education is that you'll get access to a lot of specific information in a short period of time, and know which information to trust (that backed by good research), which can give you a competitive advantage . . . education can help you be a better informed person.'

Other interviewees were more positive about their education. Julie Barnes, for example, states (as we have already seen): 'I have an NC in Music and Promotions . . . and a BA (Hons) Degree in Commercial Music . . . Both these courses were hugely valuable and the fact they were recognized within the music industry meant that I was given work experience opportunities which may have been harder to get if I had just tried to get a job in . . . music . . . straight from school.'

When asked to select which job description (ideas man, project manager or entrepreneur) he felt most comfortable with Steve responded, 'I feel comfortable in all three'. He therefore accepted the term 'entrepreneur', stating that it meant 'doing something I love and getting a fair return for the work you put in'. His advice to young entrepreneurs was 'you need to passionately believe in the good of music, and its contribution to the world' and 'don't accept the norm, or people saying "no"'.

Addressing the difficulties UK society appears to experience in embracing the word 'entrepreneur' he saw the potential downside: 'the fundamental problem is entrepreneurship should be celebrated in all areas of society and that is including . . . music', adding 'we are all entrepreneurs at some level, it's just that we don't all realize it.'

Case study: Richy Muirhead (Scottish Alternative Music Awards)

Richy Muirhead began working for a local record label when he was sixteen. He studied for a college qualification in music before completing a BA in Commercial Music and a Masters in Music Entrepreneurship. After winning a place on the MTV fanwalk (he was one of 100 young people selected to walk together for ten days across Europe to attend the MTV electronic music awards in Berlin) he returned home and decided to set up his own music awards ceremony. Six years later the Scottish Alternative Music Awards now benefits from considerable brand sponsorship and hosts performances from emerging acts chosen by public vote on the SAMAs official website which attracts over a million visits each year. The voting takes place over a four-week period before the awards and the show itself sells out a major Scottish venue and is supported by press and radio.

Similar to other case study responses, Richy identifies an altruistic element within his motivation. 'I wanted to incorporate bringing people together to celebrate music into my business . . . for me it's about the prospect of making someone's day that bit more special or that band's moment when they win after all of their fans voting for them around the UK or Scotland, that's really important.'

Richy worked in various hospitality roles, where a good deal of his time involved public interaction, before moving into music; he points to personal interaction as a key skill. 'Communication ... dramatically increases when you work, [you need to] talk to guests everyday and you can bring that into your business in terms of emails, phone calls, confidence if you are meeting people or presenting an idea. But certainly from working in different jobs communication has become critical.' This agrees with research conducted at UWS for the National Music Council (Dumbreck et al., 2003) that surveyed the music industries to establish the key skills they required; personal communication ability (written/spoken) was cited as the singular most important attribute across all sectors.

Education has been a cornerstone in Richy's development, 'without that I honestly probably wouldn't have started the Scottish Alternative Music Awards. It was the fact that we had to do a really strong project and I guess I didn't want to waste anyone's time, I just wanted to get on with mine. That really helped and gave me a good understanding of how to get it off the ground and then I did a Master's degree which let me learn a lot more about the bigger spectrum and the scale you can push things, the innovation side of an idea, like bringing in technology, like app development and really monitoring a social media campaign.'

Entrepreneurship carries an opportunity of personal freedom for Richy. 'It means I can listen to music 99 per cent of the day without having to adjust to someone else's rules. I can have my own rules and my own identity.' He accepts the term as an appropriate description of his work, it was after all the title of his Masters programme, and he would generally agree with the hypothesis that everyone in music is in some respect an entrepreneur. 'I would agree with that. I think there are a lot of times where you could be in any job in this type of industry where you need to make a kind of emergency decision or you need to think outside the box due to someone phoning in ill or a PA breaks down on the motorway, you're going to have to think on your feet fast and professionally otherwise more things are going to start to go wrong.'

When asked if there was anything he would change (to have avoided failure/embarrassment) if he could start again, Richy tapped into a key theme running through many of our interviews. 'No, not at all. I think how it has happened is the way that it should have.' This is familiar from many of the case studies. Ally Gray at EmuBands, for example, stated, 'I'm happy with the direction in which the business is heading. So it's difficult to say if I'd want to change anything in particular from the past, as that would have knock-on effects that take you down different paths. We are where we are because of the decisions we've made and actions we've taken, and I'm happy with that' (Gray, 2013).

Sumit Bothra went even further stating, 'I embrace failure as a guiding path to success because it tells me where not to go and that is just as valuable as only having success, so yeah, I would say, don't be afraid of failure. Failure is great, success by the way of luck doesn't tell you anything.' This vision of failure being the gateway to further success is paralleled in Drucker, for example, who writes: 'Yet if something fails despite being carefully planned, carefully designed and conscientiously executed, that failure often bespeaks underlying change and with it, opportunity' (Drucker, 2007).

Finally, when asked how he would advise emerging entrepreneurs, Richy stated: 'If it is in the live sector, go to a lot of events, invest in earplugs and don't be scared to talk to people and think about what it is you want to do . . . have a bit of confidence, you need to give it a go but you need to consider it to be a hell of a lot of work and it's not going to happen overnight, it might not even happen over two or three years, for most people that is realistic unless you're just a spark of genius . . . know your industry and really have the guts to go ahead with it and believe in it and inspire the next level of people.'

Conclusions

All three case studies presented here clearly represent entrepreneurial activity and all three entrepreneurs were comfortable to define their businesses as being music-based. While *Tom Tom Magazine* could be (loosely?) categorized as being a form of promotion/media, LugPlugs *could* be associated with the live music industry (although they can also be used in recording studios and rehearsals); the SAMAs are potentially either or both. Current business classification (in the UK at least) however often excludes these types of enterprise from the category of music or creative industries. The authors, it should be stated, feel that these areas require to be included in music business research and that a separate category should perhaps be identified to do so if necessary. Without the inclusion of businesses of these natures the scope of the music industries is not fully recognized or gauged, leading to any findings being underestimated and misleading and the position of music within the economy potentially undervalued.

All three entrepreneurs benefited from relevant education at university level. While our research doesn't preclude the success of those who don't possess this level of qualification (many entrepreneurs we spoke with did not have degrees), it does seem, in these three examples at least, to have assisted their progress. All three identified elements of their programmes that were of direct value to their development, in some cases specific to the projects they are managing now. This was replicated in our broader research across the different sectors of music. Whether music, arts or humanities orientated, business specific or in a different sphere, all of those we spoke with who had a higher level education found take-away value which they had been able to use and continued to use in the development of their respective projects.

This is balanced by the experience gained by previously working in music or in other fields. Whether that be wholly within music (live performance in the case of Steve Broadfoot), partially related (hospitality in the case of Richy Muirhead) or quite distinct (property in the case of Mindy Abovitz), the knowledge and understanding gained by being a functional part of a working environment appears to generate an awareness and comprehension of how to do business in a general sense, along with learning skills which are transferrable to the music industries. Where this is backed up with family or peer support the personal confidence gained does (perhaps unsurprisingly) appear to propel the young entrepreneur forward.

Finally, it may be that one critical element here is their response to failure. However obvious it may seem when stated, the simple difference between a successful entrepreneur who sees a significant problem as a learning process and possible gateway to opportunity as opposed to another who retires from the field in the face of difficulties, could be a cornerstone of progress. Is it possible that by drawing more attention to the value of examining our own failure and what it teaches us as part of entrepreneurial education, that a more robust response when this occurs could generate a fundamental change and potentially a greater chance of eventual success? Given that creative industries entrepreneurs can graduate from almost any type of degree programme and that these key skills are of value regardless of eventual professional direction, the first step might be to make entrepreneurship intrinsic to all higher education. This is recognized in the QAA Scotland report 'Creating entrepreneurial campuses' (QAA, 2014), which states: 'For many commentators, the answer is the creation of entrepreneurial campuses, an extension of the concept of the entrepreneurial university, which stimulates the entrepreneurial aspirations of students and provides them with the opportunity to develop relevant skills, knowledge and experience, and offers relevant support and resources to enable them to start their own business. This is achieved through both curricular and extra-curricular activities that create a supportive eco-system that raises entrepreneurial awareness, develops entrepreneurial skills and supports entrepreneurial endeavours.'

This development might better prepare graduates for employment in an environment where they may be inspired to develop project ideas in music or the arts (where working for an employer is less likely and being an entrepreneur is more often the case). Recent research has confirmed the small to medium enterprise (SME) nature of the music businesses: 'the vast majority of music businesses are very small or micro companies, and the music industry has a higher proportion of sole traders and freelance workers than the average sector' (UK Music, 2013). It may also deliver a better understanding of business development generally to all degree level students, which may not necessarily be a bad thing if they ever intend to run the companies they begin working for when they graduate.

References

Ames, R. (email to authors), 16 September 2014.

Casson, M. (2003), *The Entrepreneur: An Economic Theory*, Cheltenham: Edward Elgar.

De Bono, E. (1995), *Serious Creativity*, London: HarperCollins.

Department of Culture, Media and Sport (2001), *Creative Industries Mapping Document 2001*, London: DCMS.

Drucker, P.F. (2007), *Innovation and Entrepreneurship*, Oxford: Elsevier, p. 25.

Harrison, A. (2010), *Music: The Business*, London: Virgin.

Hesmondhalgh, D. (2002), *The Cultural Industries*, London: Sage.

Kariv, D. (2013), *Female Entrepreneurship and the New Venture Creation: An International Overview*, New York: Routledge.

Leonard, M. (2007), *Gender in the Music Industry*, Aldershot: Ashgate.

Longhurst, B. (1995), *Popular Music and Society*, London: Polity.

Negus, K. (1992), *Producing Pop*, London: Edward Arnold.

Negus, K. (1999), *Music Genres and Corporate Cultures*, London: Routledge.

Nicholls, K. (2012), 'A Man's World?', *The Musician*, summer 2012.

Passman, D. (2013), *All You Need to Know About the Music Business*, 8th ed., New York: Simon and Schuster, p. 63.

Shuker, R. (1994), *Understanding Popular Music*, London: Routledge.

UK Music (2013), *The Economic Contribution of the Core UK Music Industry*, London: UK Music.

Whiteley, S. (1997), *Sexing the Groove*, London: Routledge, p. xix.

Williamson, J. and M. Cloonan (2007), 'Rethinking the Music Industry', *Popular Music* 26: 305–22.

Websites

Dumbreck, A., K. Hermanns, K. McBain (2003), 'Sounding out the Future', available at: http://www.musiced.org.uk/news/sotf_report_nav.pdf [accessed 30 October 2014].

LugPlugs: http://www.lugplugs.com/

M, PRS for Music Online Magazine, Issue M48, http://www.m-magazine.co.uk/features/women-in-music [accessed 14 July 2013].

QAA Scotland (2014), 'Creating Entreprencurial Campuses', available at: http://www.enhancementthemes.ac.uk/docs/report/creating-entrepreneurial-campuses.pdf?sfvrsn=14 [accessed 30 October 2014].

Scottish Alternative Music Awards: https://www.facebook.com/OfficialSAMA/ officialsama.tumblr.com/; https://twitter.com/OfficialSAMA

Tom Tom Magazine: http://tomtommag.com/

UK Music (2013), *Music Education Directory 2013*, available at: http://www.ukmusic.org/skills-academy/music-education-directory/ [accessed 22 June 2014].

12

Conclusions

Allan Dumbreck and Gayle McPherson

The journey of bringing this book together has brought out an interesting body of discussion with both academics and industry professionals at home and aboard. It has been subject to many late-night discussions regarding what constitutes entrepreneurship within the changing environment of the digitalization, production and consumption of music in the twenty-first century. Clear differences have emerged as to what constitutes an entrepreneur in the UK and the USA and elsewhere across the globe. We have tried, where possible, to draw out those differences in case study examples, showing potential for one or other to embrace the shifting definitions of entrepreneurship, cultural entrepreneur, art entrepreneur and prosumers as we learn to map our way across each of the sectors that make up the music industries. What follows is a short summary of the key issues that remain at the fore of entrepreneurial activity within the music industries and a discussion of what we think will help shape the future trends in the sector.

The value of entrepreneurship in professional music

We proposed the statement 'Everyone who works in music is, in some way, shape or form, an entrepreneur' to all our interviewees and to a series of more senior music personnel.[1] Nine of our young entrepreneurs (50 per cent) agreed, seven (39 per cent) were undecided and only two (11 per cent) disagreed. While we are aware that this represents a very small group in terms of overall employment in music we did find these views were backed by the responses from those we interviewed who had worked professionally in the music industries for some time (four agreed, while the other two were ambivalent). We are not trying to generalize from this information but rather to point to a trend which would appear to indicate that those who are actively constructing a music business or project do tend to believe that an entrepreneurial mindset has significant value. Reactions varied but the majority agreed, some were quite outspoken: 'I think it [entrepreneurship] is essential' (Malcolm Buckland).

Notably, while a minority of responses were luke-warm, no single interviewee dismissed the premise altogether. Mick Glossop (one of the senior 'maybes') recognized that most professionals in music were entrepreneurial in nature. Replying to the suggestion that based on what he had already expressed, there is a large group of people (in professional music) who are entrepreneurs, he stated, 'Oh, absolutely, and completely significant'. As we have already seen, terms such as 'art entrepreneur' (Aggestam, 2007) and 'cultural entrepreneur' (Swedburg, 2006; Scott, 2012) take account of this and recognize the modifications in behaviour from the more established standard model 'economic entrepreneur'. Across the board all our emerging professionals and industry veterans agreed that most areas of music required an entrepreneurial mindset. Hence, to paraphrase Churchill, some of those we spoke with agreed that everyone in music is required to be entrepreneurial, and all of those we spoke with agreed that many professionals in music are required to be entrepreneurial.

While this was not particularly surprising in itself, some of the more granular detail is worth highlighting. The response from some of those who were effectively employed by others, that they considered themselves not only to be entrepreneurial in outlook but perhaps to be entrepreneurs themselves (and were generally happy with that label) was not expected. Caroline Gorman, for example, who is effectively an employee of Rage Music, accepted the title, stating, 'I am an entrepreneur working within a company'. The idea that all songwriters essentially have to be entrepreneurial foregrounded by Vick Bain (BASCA) at the start of the book: 'we represent 2,000 entrepreneurs', was equally fresh information. These views of course are countered by others, Sumit Bothra for example: 'I can point to ... accountants ... who I don't think are entrepreneurial ... there are lawyers that I know that are not entrepreneurial ... there are people in pressing plants that are not entrepreneurial'. He did, however, qualify this, 'I'm not saying *all* these guys are not entrepreneurial, I'm just saying that there are entrepreneurs within these kind of communities but not all of them are'.

To attempt to draw a conclusion from this data, it would appear that while there are some examples of personnel in professional music (in a certain number of identifiable roles) who do not demonstrate entrepreneurial traits, the prevailing opinion does err towards agreement that entrepreneurship is advantageous to career development in professional music. Hence the research we have undertaken would appear to imply that entrepreneurial engagement will assist progression into many sectors of the music industries. The editors believe this particular issue would benefit from further, more detailed study.

The value of education (including, specifically, entrepreneurial education) in professional music

This conclusion has three separate factors. Firstly, the generic value of a post-school education; secondly, the value of a music-specific post-school education and, finally, the value of being taught entrepreneurship within that experience. We will examine all three in this section.

It is obviously possible that as a result of our own professional orientation (all chapter contributors work at UK or US universities) that we were more likely to locate and interview those emerging entrepreneurs who also had higher level formal qualifications, however, many of the case study personnel were not initially known to us but were identified because they were key examples in the correct sector who were known to our immediate contacts (graduates and our own industry networks). That said, it is also possible that those with a college or university degree may be more inclined to work with equivalently educated individuals who would then proliferate the bias. Even taking this into account, we did notice that a higher level education was noted by most of our interviewees as being of significant value in their career progression.

Fifteen of our eighteen interviewees (83 per cent) have degree level qualifications or above (one further interviewee is currently completing a BA). Within that group the split is almost 50/50 between music-specific qualifications and broader arts subjects, however, almost all of those with post-school qualifications (87 per cent) had BA (arts) qualifications rather than BSc (science). The added value of a college or university education was noted by many of our respondents. Examples begin with the purely practical, day-to-day value. Mark Orr building his record label in the UK told us, 'I have ... a degree in Journalism and English Literature: this is certainly most useful when it comes to the PR side of the business.' More definitively, Julie Barnes stated, 'these courses were hugely valuable'; Caroline Gorman, 'I most certainly would not be where I am now without having studied this way' and Jay Frank in the US, 'I . . . did decide to go to Ithaca College, which was very valuable. I got to experience . . . new ways of thinking about the world, which inevitably led to . . . the creative decisions . . . in my music business career.'

More senior voices in music also identified the progression towards higher-level qualifications in professional life (regardless of sector/employment type) as being advantageous and agreed with our third point regarding entrepreneurship-specific teaching within that education. Vick Bain from BASCA: 'I think . . . education is improving, I saw a student yesterday and . . . she's done a bit of accounting and she's . . . so much better prepared than I was. I am seeing really savvy, younger graduates . . . and their understanding of the business is so much more advanced than . . . twenty years ago.' Jon Webster (MMF): 'I think [entrepreneurship teaching] should certainly be encouraged . . . in education . . . people need to be shown the way of doing things differently . . . that is teaching people entrepreneurship, isn't it?' Mick Glossop (MPG): 'there certainly doesn't seem to be as much [entrepreneurship education] as there should be'.

These perspectives echo the QAA report quoted in Chapter 11: 'For many commentators, the answer is the creation of entrepreneurial campuses, an extension of . . . the entrepreneurial university, which . . . offers relevant support and resources to enable [students] to start their own business.' It is clear to us as researchers that entrepreneurship within advanced education is advantageous. We therefore assert that university level music education (and possibly the broader field of arts generally) should further develop, deliver and nurture entrepreneurial skills as a core part of the curriculum, whether business, performance or technology orientated. In this way we can better prepare our graduates for an uncertain professional career path in a changing workplace.

The UK/US divide: Acceptance/ appropriateness of the term 'entrepreneur'

Most striking in our interviews was the dichotomy between the UK and US responses to the term 'entrepreneur' in general terms but also in direct relation to the interviewees themselves. The US contributors (George Howard, Jeff Izzo), and those interviewees who had lived or worked in the US (Jay Frank, Sumit Bothra, Mindy Abovitz), noted that the term was readily embraced by most individuals there (including themselves), regardless of background or sector. The response from those who were UK based was practically the polar opposite: 'I wouldn't in any way describe myself as an entrepreneur' (Riley). Almost all UK project developers were comfortable with terms such as 'ideas person', 'project developer' or 'project manager'. Some did entertain the 'E' word but mostly it was grudgingly accepted at best, 'I don't really like the term "music entrepreneur" . . . but we did start a music business . . . so I guess it's accurate' (Gray). Some rejected the term outright. The predominant view (echoed by undergraduate students at the University of the West of Scotland) was that the term generally conjured up ideas of sharp, ruthless, profit-orientated city businessmen or incompetent and possibly illegally operating barrow-boys, neither of which resonate with prospective music pioneers.

These negative, stereotyped images are often reinforced by popular media. Those we interviewed regularly identified the contestants on 'The Apprentice' or near-comedy characters in other TV programmes such as 'Only Fools and Horses' as defining examples of an entrepreneur. Ally Gray at EmuBands, for example, stated: 'I . . . always think of the word entrepreneur as being associated with people wanting to make a fast buck, drive flash cars and wear sharp suits.' This contrasts completely with the US vision of the entrepreneur enshrined within the American dream as a key driver of economic development and growth as identified in our research by, amongst others, Jeff

Izzo: 'It is indeed a venerated term here in the States – it represents independence, drive, initiative', and Sumit Bothra: 'being an entrepreneur in the States is . . . highly competitive . . . because everyone's an entrepreneur, even the cab drivers are entrepreneurs, everyone believes they are no matter what they're doing.'

It is possible that this schism has its origins in the art versus commerce debate. Many we spoke with in the UK were keen to stress their love of music, their altruistic drivers, their passion for what they did ahead of any consideration of financial gain: '[you need a] genuine passion for music' (Barnes); '[I am] ideologically driven. Local young people should be able to access music and arts' (Denny); 'make sure you love the music – because it's probably the only thing that'll push you to go further when you're working twelve-hour-plus days' (Orr).

When pushed, those we interviewed in the UK were able to identify individuals they had worked with as entrepreneurs and within the broader mainstream music industries. Interviewees reluctantly named high-profile individuals such as Richard Branson or Simon Cowell as entrepreneurs working in music. The general reaction, however, was that those in the early stages of development saw these highly successful figureheads as distinct or separated from themselves and their immediate environment in terms of psychology and income levels. Hence the term 'entrepreneur' was also attached to that higher, seemingly unattainable (possibly undesirable) level of achievement.

It is not the focus of this work to investigate the idea any further but this dichotomy does lead us to consider whether these different world views could be fundamentally detrimental to the UK economy. If young creatives are dissuaded from pursuing their vision or if they feel they may be shunned by their peer group for the crime of making a profit, then it is possible that they may not develop the more fruitful aspects of their business or indeed begin the venture at all. Our fear is that this emulates the British approach of being modestly successful, rather than celebrating our young entrepreneurs; taking the Beckhams as an example, very successful British exports and entrepreneurs in music, fashion and football but for a long time the press were sceptical at best.

For whatever reason, the 'E' word is a thing of wonder in the US and a thing of deep suspicion in the UK. Does this affect UK business development or is it part of a more refined filtering system so that only better planned business ideas progress to fruition? Statistics appear to be inconclusive. The OECD (Organization for Economic Co-operation and Development), for example, reports the US demonstrating a sustained engagement in venture capital support of entrepreneurship since the start of the recession (over 0.15 per cent of GDP versus less than 0.05 per cent in the UK). However, the same report identifies UK new business start-up rising to 50 per cent above the global average while the US practically flatlines. Unfortunately, these questions are beyond the realms of this book but they do raise further issues for future debate.

Passion as a prime motivator/an alternative definition?

Entrepreneurial characteristics have already been discussed in Chapter 2. What we found in our research did not deviate significantly from previous work in this area. However, one personality trait above all others was referenced consistently. It became clear that our young entrepreneurs genuinely believed in what they were doing and felt passion was a vital part of their work. Equally, that passion was used to drive them to excel in their projects.

The work ethic was the critical second part of this equation. 'To possess a strong work ethic, to build a reputation as a hard worker, a solid, trustworthy team member who can be relied on to work hard, complete tasks, use their initiative, conduct themselves well and always be looking for an opportunity to take on extra responsibility and further their own learning, experience and areas of expertise' (Gorman,

2013). 'Determination, discipline and a strong work ethic, without them, you'll struggle. There are constant demands on your time and you have to make sure you're doing what needs to be done' (Gray, 2014). These key elements, then, were clearly felt to be central to the success of the entrepreneur. This has already been recognized by researchers as identified by Kenny Forbes in Chapter 5, notably Leek and Canning (2011) and in particular Darmer (2008): 'They cannot stop being passionate without stopping being entrepreneurs and humans as well.'

It would appear, however, that the spirit or passion that drives the ambition of those working in music in the UK might be out of sync with the desire to make money. 'Passion. Whatever aspect of the music industry you wish to work in, passion will give you the drive and determination to achieve your dreams. A raw passion combined with talent will fuel learning ... along the way. The music industry can be cut throat, and often unglamorous so without a genuine passion, it's easy to be left behind' (O'Callaghan). The art versus commerce argument may have led young UK project developers away from acceptance of the term 'entrepreneur' but for whatever reason, they are not entirely comfortable in accepting it. There is currently no term that music project developers in the UK are entirely prepared to agree upon which describes what they actually do. 'Project manager', 'self-employed' and 'ideas person' were all examined and found to be inadequate in one way, shape or form in the introduction. Aggestam's (2007) suggestion of the term 'art entrepreneur', Swedburg (2006) and Scott (2012) both using the term 'cultural entrepreneurs', Darker (Chapter 3) calling himself a 'musicpreneur'; all fall short because they use part or all of the original term which many of those we spoke to (at least partially) rejected.

To define the young music project developer who is achievement, self-worth or altruism driven (all clear human motivators as examined by McLelland, 1987), we may need a different term altogether. The key element for all of those we spoke with was 'passion' – almost every interviewee spoke of passion being at the heart of success. These emerging professionals then, these 'passioneers', for want of a better phrase, are not driven by profit or even necessarily by future personal gain. They are primarily motivated by their love of what they do, of what they might create, of what can be done for others (musicians and audiences). Whether it becomes profitable, or even self-sustaining, now or in the future, appears to be less of an issue than what can be realistically (or unrealistically) achieved in the moment. Their pioneering spirit, their determination and above all their love for what they do arguably drives them forward, eventually, for many of those we met, to success and perhaps later to paid employment or financial return for their investment of time and labour in their extended (and largely unpaid) apprenticeship. Potentially, then, this is ultimately the key to profitability. If you care about something enough, you will perfect your métier until you are professional, at which point you get paid. Passion is where you begin, profit is where you arrive. In the UK at least, this appears to be a distinct career path.

Access versus ownership

Something of a by-product to our research, as it at first appears to have no direct bearing on entrepreneurship, the debate surrounding delivery mechanisms is however vital to potential business start-ups in music considering which sector and/or format to invest in. For this reason we will examine the issue.

The emergence of streaming and subscription models as the rising stars of music consumption while physical and digital sales decline points to a sea change in global consumer habits. If this trend continues (as many of our interviewees suggest it might) we may see the death of the record collection in favour of temporary or cloud access preferences. Given that the younger music fan operates predominantly through virtual 'windows' on tablet, mobile phone or laptop where traditionally music buyers owned physical hi-fi systems and in-car entertainment equipment, this could indeed be seen as an extension of an existing way of life, a future norm. On-screen existence is their reality. Why would a person wish to collect and store bulky but limited collections of hard copy when they could temporarily access whatever they want from a near infinite store whenever (and wherever) it is required?

Debate continues over the fairness (in terms of artist and songwriter remuneration) of services such as Spotify with, notably, Taylor Swift withdrawing her entire catalogue from the online provider (as already identified by Jeff Izzo) amid accusations of poor financial returns: 'It's my opinion that music should not be free, and my prediction is that individual artists and their labels will someday decide what an album's price point is. I hope they don't underestimate themselves or undervalue their art' (Ellis-Peterson, 2014).

Meanwhile, witness for the defence, Ed Sheeran (Savage, 2014) has the opposite opinion: 'My music has been streamed 860 million times, which means that it's getting out to people,' he said backstage at the BBC Music Awards. 'I'm playing sold-out gigs in South America, I've sold out arenas in Korea and southeast Asia. I don't think I'd be able to do that without Spotify.'

Whether artists view streaming as a promotional tool with some direct financial return or something closer to unacceptably free access it could become the most significant part of recorded music delivery if the slide in purchasing continues. When considering a direction in professional life, the turnover and consumer behaviour of a sector (live music, artist management or recorded music sales) is a critical factor. It is vital to reflect on whether that sector is likely to grow or diminish. Is the marketplace getting larger or smaller? Recorded music is currently running through a series of crossroads. The digital domain could turn out to be its saviour or its nemesis. Either way it could still be fertile ground for the innovative entrepreneur, if they are prudent in identifying the rising wave.

The digitally literate consumer

The days of mass production and the McDonalized approach to music is gone. We now have digitally convergent consumers or 'prosumers' as you have heard throughout this book. The digital landscape meets social platforms and creates what Solis (2013) terms social commerce. Digital platforms are allowing new spaces in which to construct music, to communicate with artists and are leading to the co-creation of new ideas and output in music. The flurry of activity of both brands and musicians to match up in the early 2000s has shifted to artists and their management understanding that prosumers are seeking a much more open and emotional connection to the artists. The D2F engagement that Tessler and Flynn refer to in Chapter 3 is on the ascendancy, in turn requiring the core skills of the artist to be expanded beyond the entrepreneurial, engaging the digital, marketing, promotion and finance all rolled into one. The future independent musician needs to embrace all of these if they are to continue to be successful or else get on board with the big labels and companies.

Those who are successful now and in the future are embracing that, especially those who understand the link between themselves and the fans who have moved to digital streaming, like Ed Sheeran, who clearly sees that if people are listening to his music, free or otherwise, this has led to sell-out concerts and global recognition. We highlighted the prediction that 'by the end of 2014 there could be more smartphones on the planet than humans' (Mashable, 2014). The reproduction of an artist's music either digitally or from live festivals, ensures that the artist, the brand and the music are featuring on a variety of social media sites and extending the reach of that artist and their work. Interestingly, although some artists are railing against the use of mobile technology at festivals and Apple are developing software that will block live music capture, this just may be a mistake. It is this type of extended conversation that young people are able to share about the spectacle and experience that will ensure the name of the artist, festival or brand continues in the digital limelight. Interestingly, it is the older artist that is objecting the loudest. Kenny Forbes points out in this book (Chapter 5) that live music is in the most privileged position; it is open to that unique relationship between the artist and the fan. Live music has an exclusive position that allows artists and festival producers to create an experience, one that goes beyond the immediacy of a digital download; it is right there with the audience, the food, the culture, the music is all part of the extended consumption that will stay with the fan long after the live experience is over. Musicians need to understand how music is consumed and as live music and festivals grow at a rate greater than ever before and spending at festivals rises (worth £1.3bn in the UK in 2012 (UK Music, 2013), including cashless spending), the scope exists for more entrepreneurial approaches to festival management.

Future trends/further issues

Undoubtedly, the rise of the cashless festival offers a myriad of opportunities for production companies; armed with data on spending patterns, consumption choices, lifestyle preferences; this data is a gold mine for those selling in the live music market. Added to that the increasing engagement with digital downloads, streaming and now synchronization rights represent billion dollar revenue streams, and the consumer is seeking an authentic experience in full knowledge of how much their engagement is worth to the industry.

The definition of exactly which types of enterprise constitute a 'music business' needs to be investigated and definitively categorised. It is possible, even likely, that music industries in all nations are significantly undervalued because many sub-sectors are classified outside the area of examination. This in turn reduces the level of recognition which government and funding bodies will ascribe and potentially unfairly limits financial (and broader) support. In this matter the editors of this book agree with UK Music (2013) and advise those in decision-making positions to urgently review and revise the definitions in order to correctly scale the music industries in a logical way. Only when this is done will we gain a true understanding of the economic value of music.

Gender is another issue that was discussed by those we interviewed and in some of the chapters of this book. Dumbreck, Reddington and Forbes all argue that this is an on-going debate in the sector but Forbes is optimistic mentioning that in the UK, at least, there are a higher proportion of women (51.2 per cent) employed in music, performing and visual arts as a grouping, than men (Ingham, 2014) but the worry is that this is only in certain roles. This would certainly be an improvement on the 2009 Creative Choices survey that 'showed that just 34 per cent of those working in the UK music industry are women' (Nicholls, 2012). Obviously each survey covers a different marketplace but they would appear to indicate that generally, we could be moving towards a more gender balanced workplace.

The final area we would like to draw attention to is the geographical expansion of the music industries globally and to previously untapped markets. As streaming and subscription models overtake the sale of CDs and downloads in Europe and North America, other territories will likely follow suit. As Izzo refers to in his chapter, the walls (of Western record labels) haven't come tumbling down, they are all surviving but the direction of travel is definitely more towards subscription and streaming than buying and owning. This also extends to emerging nations. We mentioned that Africa, Brazil, India and others are fast developing in digital technology leaving the opportunity for digital downloads, subscription and streaming ripe for the taking. The main barriers and challenges in these geographical zones are the security of data and finance and issues such as copyright law, which until now has been uniformly analogue-orientated, if it previously existed at all.

Synchronization rights is another area where entertainment law would benefit from catching up with the opportunities in film, TV, video games and websites with music. There needs to be more specialists in these areas to update the digital variations in copyright law. Whilst consumers may have the technology in their pockets, the risk to the consumer and producer is still a real issue at present, but one thing is sure the consumer is omnipotent in the equation. Music industry entrepreneurs will need to engage with those well versed in global markets and economic exchange in order to tap into this highly lucrative global expansion that is both in demand and within reach.

To finish, it is worth re-iterating Izzo's analysis from his chapter that the business environment in the USA is more willing to tolerate failure than in the UK and that is perhaps why they (the Americans) have more success and more young entrepreneurs. Learning from mistakes and previous failures is certainly something echoed by those we interviewed and all of them valued the experience. Many of our interviewees (Frank, Gray, Muirhead, Gorman, Bothra) identified this founding principle, 'I wouldn't change a thing. The mistakes I've made have been learning opportunities. The hard struggles have been met with justified rewards' (Jay Frank). 'None. As every mistake/balls up/embarrassing incident is crucial learning' (Caroline Gorman). As already stated, we believe that entrepreneurship within post-school education should be standard. Learning to accept and make sense of failure as an essential part of our entrepreneurial development should perhaps become a future trend that we strive towards on this side of the Atlantic. As indicated earlier, this could also become a key element of entrepreneurial arts education.

Note

1 While some of our interviewees were operating in senior positions, the definition of a young emerging professional was someone who was, at time of interview, actively engaged in developing a music project where a senior professional was engaged as a senior member of a representative organization or collection society.

References

Aggestam, M. (2007), 'Art-entrepreneurship in the Scandinavian music industry', in *Entrepreneurship in the Creative Industries*, C. Henry (ed.), Cheltenham: Edward Elgar, pp. 30–53.

Darmer, P. (2008), 'Entrepreneurs in music: the passion of experience creation', in J. Sundbo and P. Darmer (eds.), *Creating Experiences in the Experience Economy*, Cheltenham: Edward Elgar, pp. 111–33.

Ellis-Peterson, H. (2014), 'Taylor Swift takes a stand over Spotifymusic royalties', *The Guardian*, 5 November 2014, http://www.theguardian.com/music/2014/nov/04/taylor-swift-spotify-streaming-album-sales-snub [accessed 18 December 2014].

Ingham, T. (2014), 'Women outnumber men across UK jobs in music and arts', *Music Week*, 27 June (online), available at: http://www.musicweek.com/news/read/women-outnumber-men-across-uk-jobs-in-music-and-arts/058870 [accessed 1 September 2014].

Leek, S. and L. Canning (2011), 'The Role of Networking and Social Capital in Initiation of Relationships in Passion Based Service Networks', paper submitted to the IMP Conference 2011, available at: http://www.impgroup.org/uploads/papers/7695.pdf [accessed 1 September 2014].

Mashable (2014), 'There will be more Smartphones than humans on the planet by year end', http://mashable.com/2012/02/14/more-smartphones-than-humans/ [accessed 12 May 2014].

McLelland, D. (1987), *Human Motivation*, Cambridge: Cambridge University Press, pp. 223–372.

Nicholls, K. (2012), 'A man's world?', *The Musician*, summer 2012.

OECD (2014), *Entrepreneurship at a Glance 2014*, OECD Publishing. http://dx.doi.org/10.1787/entrepreneur_aag-2014-en

QAA Scotland (2014), 'Creating Entrepreneurial Campuses', available at: http://www.enhancementthemes.ac.uk/docs/report/creating-entrepreneurial-campuses.pdf?sfvrsn=14 [accessed 30 October 2014].

Savage, M. (2014), 'Ed Sheeran "owes career to Spotify"', BBC website, available at: http://www.bbc.co.uk/news/entertainment-arts-30436855 [accessed 18 December 2014].

Scott, M. (2012), 'Cultural entrepreneurs, cultural entrepreneurship: Music producers mobilising and converting Bourdieu's alternative capitals', *Poetics* 40: 237–55.

Solis, B. (2013), *What's the Future of Business: Changing the Way Businesses Create Experiences*. New York: John Wiley & Sons.

Swedberg, R. (2006), 'The cultural entrepreneur and the creative industries: beginning', *Journal of Cultural Economics* 30 (4): 243–61.

UK Music (2013), *The Economic Contribution of the Core UK Music Industry*, London: UK Music.

INDEX